Antiques and Art

Care & Restoration

EDWARD J. STANEK, Ph.D.

WALLACE-HOMESTEAD BOOK CO.
1912 GRAND AVE.
DES MOINES, IOWA 50305

COPYRIGHT © 1978
EDWARD J. STANEK

ISBN 0-87069-245-3
LIBRARY OF CONGRESS CATALOG
CARD 77-94662

PUBLISHED BY

WALLACE-HOMESTEAD BOOK CO.
1912 GRAND AVENUE
DES MOINES, IOWA 50305

DEDICATION

To my father, Edward J. Stanek, Sr., who although not yet an antique, has undergone major restoration.

ACKNOWLEDGMENT

I am indebted to my wife, Jackie, for her patience with me and perseverance in following my restoration prescriptions, to Carl W. Youngquist for making my poor photographs look good, to Marjorie Heles for typing herself sick, and to Chet and Betty Klucas for their longtime friendship and upholstering consultations.

I would also like to thank Susan Nicholson for stimulating my first interests in antiques and to Dr. Boyd Nordmark for the use of his surgical facilities for the photograph that appears on the following page.

ABOUT THE AUTHOR

Dr. Stanek is a published historian with a Ph.D. in Physics. His book *Iowa's Magnificent County Courthouses* was written to attract attention to the need for preserving public buildings with historical and architectural significance. He has been a dealer and appraiser of antiques. During the past 10 years, he has combined his scientific training in physics and chemistry with knowledge of the arts to specialize in the care and restoration of valued artifacts.

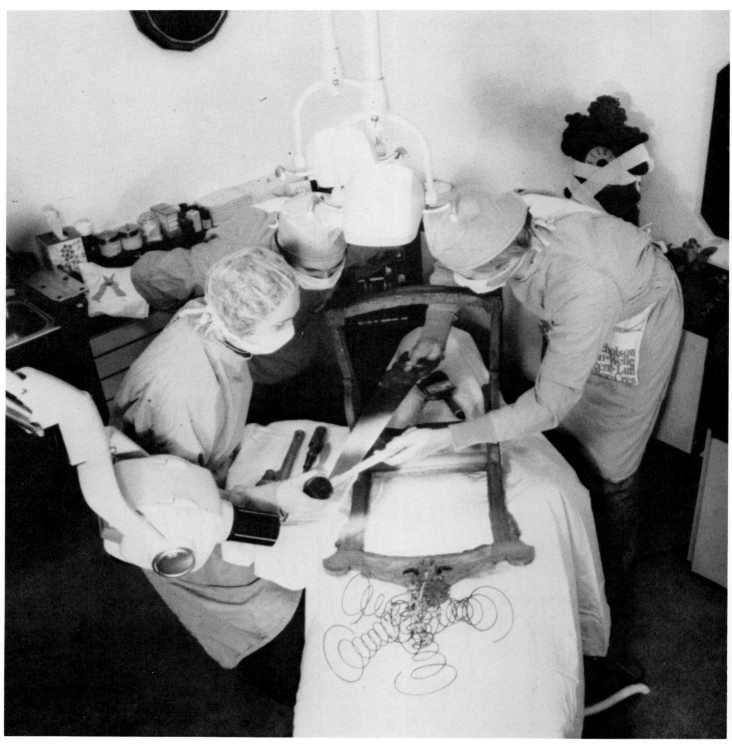

Dr. Stanek (center) with assistant Jacqueline Stanek and Dr. Boyd Nordmark performs surgery on a Victorian chair.

TABLE OF CONTENTS

CHAPTER I

INTRODUCTION

This book deals primarily with the restoration of 19th century artifacts, but many of the techniques employed are also applicable to antiques of other periods. There is really only one rule that applies to the restoration of arts and antiques—never do anything that is irreversible. The materials and techniques that are employed should always be of such a nature that the work can be undone by a future generation that has access to improved materials and better techniques. Some problems will require many hours of perspiration to solve, while others will require patience, diligence and study. In either case, the conservator needs to develop a skill parallel to that of a surgeon. A 100-year-old object is indeed a patient in need of a cure. One careless movement of the hand could permanently maim or even terminate the life of the patient.

I have attempted in this book to document the procedures that have proved successful for me over the past 10 years. I have also tried to point out many of the easy mistakes that could be made without the foreknowledge of someone with experience. I do not guarantee that the techniques will be successful for you in all cases, because so many situations have some unique element that requires additional consideration. However, using this book with its many photographs will provide the basis to develop the skills necessary to deal with almost any situation involving the restoration of 19th century artifacts.

The basic talent required to do a good job is the use of common sense. Do not do something that will perma-nently alter an artifact unless there is absolutely no alternative. And in that case, consideration should be given to doing nothing in the hope that someone will eventually develop a technique or the materials required to do an appropriate job. Because common sense is the basic skill required, every owner of an antique can develop an expertise in restoration right in his or her own home. Where possible, I have avoided descriptions involving the use of equipment or material that would not normally be available to anyone who wanted them. Occasionally, the name of a chemical may seem complicated, but the only way to obtain it is to know what it is and how to spell it.

The major caution I would like to bestow upon you before you proceed with this book is "don't be too cautious". Unfortunately, many of us when working in an unknown area tend to follow directions like a robot without any additional thought. Overcaution and fear of the unknown causes us to put common sense aside and follow a recipe step-by-step, regardless of any consequences. Any work done in this manner is certainly not very rewarding. It presumes that there is only one problem to be overcome, and ignores the possibility that other problems may surface which must be dealt with before the first problem can really be solved. Following textbook-type recipes also precludes the user from using his own creativity to develop improved restoration methods. That stroke of genius will come only if you can be immersed in the challenge and not be shackled by past procedures.

Nothing should ever be attempted blindly in the "hope" that it will work. But understanding a problem and the relative success of available alternatives can allow someone to try a new technique in the "promise" that it will work.

For the most part, this book is written casually so as not to condition the reader into recipe following. However, when an orderly progression is required, especially in more complicated projects, step-by-step instructions are given. Sequences of photographs often help the reader develop a mental image of what needs to be done and the expected results. But in many cases, only reading the text will supply enough background to do an appropriate job, and using common sense is the only insurance that it will be done properly.

Restoring antiques brings us into intimate contact with past generations. The materials, the skills and the time required to originally fabricate the antique is what has made it worth keeping. But it is our actions that make it possible for our descendants to enjoy a similar privilege. If it is true that a picture is worth a thousand words, then being able to touch and see the real antique must be worth millions of pictures. Our preservation of the past is the only way that antiques can become part of the future.

The conservator's role is a romantic one. He must be able to see through the grime and the imperfections. He must be able to see the character and personality of an object as it once was, so that it can be so again. Beauty is in the eyes of the beholder and in the hands of the conservator.

CHAPTER II

CLEAN SHEETS (PAPER)

Just think what it would have been like had paper not been invented. A man with a hernia might have to carry his truss prescription to the pharmacy written on a 200-pound stone tablet. Your Encyclopaedia Brittanica, which admittedly weighs a ton, would literally weigh tens of thousands of tons. And worst of all, people would be so tired from carrying written materials from place to place, they would have very little time to read, and you probably would not have the opportunity to page through this book.

The word paper comes from the Egyptian word, "papyrus". Papyrus was actually a plant that the ancient Egyptians beat into a writing material. At various times throughout history, animal skins have also been used as writing materials after being cleaned, pounded and dried into what we presently call parchment. Paper as we know it today, however, was developed by the Chinese sometime between the 2nd century B.C. and the 1st century A.D. Bark was stripped from mulberry trees and its fiber pounded into thin sheets. For the most part, the secret of paper making remained with the Chinese and was not known to the rest of the world until about the 8th century. The Chinese had attacked the Arab stronghold at Samarkand in 751 A.D. The Arabs repelled the attack and captured some of the fleeing Chinese. After being subjected to some form of Arabian persuasion, the Chinese prisoners taught the Arabs all they knew. The Arabs immediately recognized what to do with paper, as exemplified by the large

number of 9th century Arabic manuscripts which are still preserved.

At first, the Arab paper was made of flax, thereby producing a linen paper. Rags were also used to supplement the pounded flax, and as the demand for writing materials grew, other vegetable fibers were used to supplement the supplies.

Paper-making did not make its way into Europe until sometime in the 12th century. The art of paper-making has changed throughout history from a handcraft, where sheets of paper were produced individually by a skilled craftsman, to mass production through the use of gigantic machines. Handmade papers from the 9th century have been preserved in a state not too different from their original manufacture. Most modern mass-produced papers will not survive more than a few years.

Almost all papers are made from cellulosic fibers. The Chinese used bamboo and rags as the source of fibers. Others used mulberry bark, grasses and straw. After serving as cloth, fiber from flax, cotton, jute and hemp can be used in paper-making.

Originally, fibers were beated into a flat sheet and the spaces between them filled with a form of sizing made either from vegetables or clay. The need for great volumes of paper today, however, requires mass-production techniques that employ either alkaline or acid processes and that usually result in chemical residues remaining in the paper after production. Although the best quality papers are still made from rags, much of the paper used today is made from wood pulp. The wood is cooked to remove the cellulose from the non-cellulose materials. The paper is pressed into sheets and extremely heavy weights are used to remove as much moisture as possible. The method of using sulfuric acid for fiber separation that is extensively employed today was established in 1882. The method of grinding logs into a fibrous pulp was invented in 1840.

Paradoxy

The use of paper as a medium for historical artifacts poses an unusual paradox for the conservator of antiquities. Letters, manuscripts, etchings, lithographs and watercolors are examples which potentially can require restoration. In general, paper made from rags by hand will outlast most other artist's mediums if properly cared for. Prints made centuries ago on good quality paper exist today in nearly their original state, while wooden artifacts made by the same artists or their contemporaries are more likely than not to be in a sorry state of disrepair. Canvases made at that time probably had deteriorated ages ago. Therefore, we see good quality paper as being one of the sturdiest materials used by man that is capable of being preserved for hundreds of years in nearly its original state. On the other hand, paper being a thin material is easily subject to tearing. It can be folded and creased so as to ruin the aesthetic beauty of any work of art placed upon it. It can be attacked by fungi and bacteria, as well as be affected by chemicals in our environment. Some

restoration processes involving paper require immersing it in liquids, which greatly decreases the strength of the paper and makes it one of the most delicate of all conservation practices. Therefore, paper can be both one of the sturdiest and one of the most delicate materials requiring restoration.

The Examination

A paper artifact requiring restoration should be examined carefully with a light shining beneath it. First with the naked eye and then with a magnifying glass, the paper should be checked for tears or holes. It should then be checked for thin spots where improper handling will likely result in one of these conditions. The size in the paper is made from clay, starch, gelatin or other similar material, and may not have been deposited uniformly when the paper was made. Furthermore, abrasion and wear on the paper over the years may have caused properly constructed paper to develop thin areas.

Size is almost always hygroscopic; that is, it attracts moisture. This moisture harbors microorganisms that can attack the paper. Light brown spots are usually the result of a mildew acting on residues of iron salts in the paper. This condition is known as foxing.

If the paper was mass-produced or if it was improperly made by hand, it is only a matter of time before the chemicals residing within it will destroy it. An appropriate chemical treatment to neutralize the deterioration would require a sufficient knowledge of the process used to manufacture the paper.

About the only thing that can be done to increase such paper's longevity is to store it in a moisture-controlled environment in a cool temperature.

True Grit

Hopefully, the only restoration process required for your paper artifact will be surface cleaning. Over the years, dust and grime from the air will settle on the surface of the paper and become embedded in the microscopic valleys of that paper. Simple rubbing of this dirt will abrade the paper, because a lot of the dust may have sharp corners and truly act as a grit to scrape away the size between the cellulose fibers.

The best way to clean surface dirt is to use crumbled art gum, purchased either loose or in a cloth bag from an art or drafting supply store. This material is simply the soft rubber of an art gum eraser that has not been compressed and bound into a solid block. Put the crumbled art gum on the portion of the paper to be cleaned and use a soft cloth to rub it gently over the surface in a circular motion. The examination performed earlier will have alerted the conservator to any tears or thin spots in the paper that must be handled very carefully so as not to make existing damage worse and create new damage. This type of surface cleaning

Surface dirt can be cleaned with loose art gum or a paper dry cleaning bag.

The stained area is placed over a blotter face down and a bleaching solution is applied from the back.

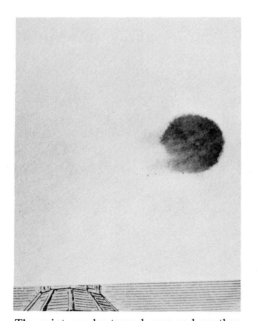

The print can be turned over and another blotter placed underneath. The blotters will absorb some of the stain while the bleaching agent does its work.

cannot be used for unfixed pencil or chalk drawings. But it is wholly adequate for most watercolors and inks on paper. Be sure to use that old common sense and test an unimportant portion of the art work or letter before proceeding to work on the entire artifact.

When There Is A Fungus Among Us

Fungus or mildew as a cause of spotty discoloration on the paper often can be removed by bleaching. Such discoloration does not rest on the surface of the paper, but rather goes into the paper and most likely entirely through its thickness. Different chemicals can be applied on the back of the paper to kill the mildew and remove the foxing. Blotting paper placed under the face of the paper to be bleached will insure that the bleach does not go wandering across the front surface of the paper should it happen to penetrate. The bleaching chemical should be brushed on the back of the paper only on the area that has discolored. This area is then covered with a blotter and a piece of glass placed over the top of the blotter to insure that the blotter is making complete contact with the paper.

Before: A stain appears in the upper right-hand corner of this print.

A number of bleaching agents can be used. Hydrogen peroxide in a two-percent solution as purchased from a drugstore is suitable in many cases. Oxalic acid crystals dissolved in water will sometimes be appropriate, and its strength can be controlled by the amount of water (distilled water, of course) that is used to dilute the acid solution. For watercolors, chalk and carbon ink on paper, one tablespoon chloramine-T crystals dissolved in one quart of water may do the job. For very stubborn stains, a solution of sodium hypochlorite can be used. Regular Clorox bleach is about a five-percent solution of hypochlorite, with the balance made up of inactive or inert ingredients. However, the bleach should be further diluted with distilled water, adding two quarts of water to each cup of bleach used. Of course, the strength of the bleach can be altered by controlling the amount of dilution water, but extreme care should be used because overbleaching can ruin some art works. Carbon ink is relatively insoluble and holds up well to most bleaching processes. However, most other inks, lead pencil and pigment will suffer from bleaching. Judgment must be used to determine whether the art work will be enhanced or hurt by bleaching, and the advantages versus the disadvantages must be weighed carefully. Never immerse watercolors, pastels, chalk or ink washes in a bleach.

After: The print with the stain removed.

Before: Spilled ink mars the sail of the yacht in this otherwise perfect print.

Before: A close-up of the stain.

Never overbleach. Overbleaching turns paper chalky.

In some cases, the entire sheet of paper can be immersed in a tray filled with the sodium hypochlorite solution described above. A sheet of glass or polyethylene should be used to support and hold the paper so that it does not tear when being put into or taken out of the solution. It should be allowed to bathe in the bleach only until the last trace of discoloration is gone. It should then be immediately removed and rinsed in a bath of distilled water. Depending upon how much residual bleach remains, another water bath might be necessary. The last rinse should allow about one-half hour at a minimum for soaking.

After: The same print after the stain has been removed.

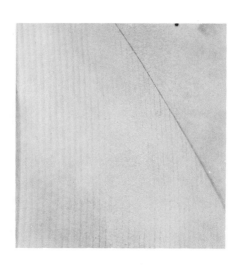

After: The same area after bleaching.

14

An entire print can be bleached, using a wide brush to apply the solution uniformly over the front or back surface.

Before: The stain on the right-hand side of this print will require immersion to get out.

15

The print is placed on a sheet of glass which is put into a tray.

The bleaching solution is poured into the tray.

The solution is poured out of the tray. Don't worry about water marks that may appear on the wet print (like the stripes in the print shown above).

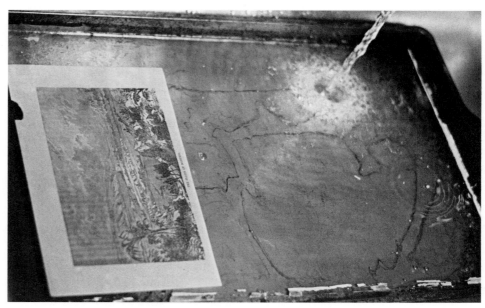

Distilled water is used to rinse the print one or more times to remove any residual chemical.

The glass plate is lifted to remove the wet print from the tray.

When the print is strong enough to be removed from the glass, it is placed between large sheets of blotting paper on a flat surface. Weights are placed over the blotter and the print is allowed to dry.

After: The print with the stain removed.

Bugs

Bugs can cause a number of problems with art work on paper. Unless the flies in your house have been toilet trained, they will leave the remnants of earlier meals on the surface of your art work. These spots are on the surface, and so are easily detected using a magnifying class. Although it may sound gross, these spots can also be felt with the finger. A fingernail or knife blade used carefully will remove fly specks.

Silverfish and other bugs spend their lives eating their way through your library and sometimes paper art works. Fumigation is the only sure way to be rid of these pests. To fumigate the work, place a solution of 40-percent formaldehyde in a bowl at the bottom of a container that can be sealed. Suspend the paper to be fumigated in this container about a foot away from the solution. Then seal the paper artifact in this container for about 24 hours.

Before: This print has a heavy grease stain in the right-hand margin and a lighter grease stain in the upper right-hand corner.

19

Blotting paper is placed under the stain and a solvent brushed over it.

Unsightly Fats

Through some manner of locomotion, bacon grease and other fatty materials sometimes find their way onto pieces of paper where they do not belong. Grease spots can be removed by soaking them with either carbon tetrachloride or benzine and placing the paper between two sheets of white blotting paper. Use a warm iron on the area to help dissolve the grease which, hopefully, will be absorbed by the blotters. Two major cautions are in order: carbon tetrachloride fumes are poisonous and benzine is flammable.

Another blotter is placed on top of the stain and an iron with medium heat is applied over the blotter.

The process may have to be repeated several times.

Sometimes a residual stain will remain. It can be removed by brushing or immersion in acetone.

After: The print with the grease stains removed.

If wax is causing the stain, first use a razor blade to remove built-up deposits, then turpentine applied as described above will remove the wax through the paper. Don't be afraid if the paper turns translucent. It will clear up again when dry. If a slight wax residue remains, immersion in acetone for a few seconds will wash the residue away.

The paper will also dry in a few seconds after being removed from the bath.

Before: Wax has accidentally been dripped on this print in a book. (A)

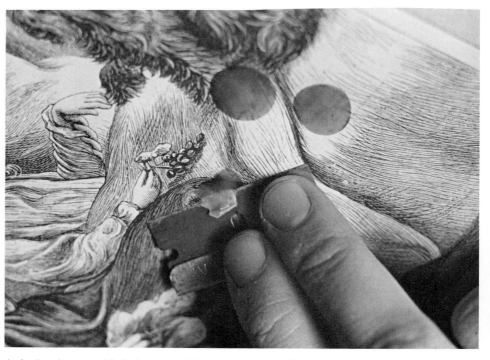

A single-edge razor blade is used to slice away as much of the wax as possible without scraping the paper. (B)

The wax has penetrated the paper and some of the lettering from the reverse side can be seen. (C)

The print is placed face down on a blotter and pressure from an iron with moderate heat is applied to a blotter on the reverse side. (E)

Turpentine is brushed over the wax. A blotter underneath the print is absorbing the dissolved wax. Note that the printing from the reverse side of the paper becomes visible wherever the turpentine has been brushed—it will disappear upon drying. (D)

The area of the wax stains after drying. (F)

After: The print with wax stains removed. (G)

Before: A crease across the middle of this print is highly visible.

Removing Creases

Although sometimes damage can be done to a print when attempting to remove creases from it, the operation is often successful if done carefully. Two methods can be used with reasonable success. One way is to dampen the paper along the crease, cover it with a cloth or blotter to protect it and then iron it with a warm clothes iron.

Or, you can dampen the crease, place blotting paper above and below it, stack weights on top of the blotters while the moisture is allowed to be soaked up, and allow the paper to dry over a period of several hours.

The paper is dampened along the crease and covered with a cloth or blotter to protect it. The "sandwich" is ironed.

After: The crease has been removed.

A Sticky Situation

It was popular during the 19th century to glue lithographs or other prints to canvas before framing. Damage to the paper in such cases sometimes requires removing the paper from the canvas. The print should be placed face down on white blotting paper. Lukewarm water containing some lissapol is sponged through the canvas. Allow some time for the water to penetrate and loosen the adhesive. The print can be separated from one corner of the canvas carefully and pulled off with relative ease. If it does not pull easily or if resistance is found, it should not be forced because of the danger of tearing the print. Additional water should be placed on the adhesive and allowed to soak longer. When the process has been completed, the print should be rinsed in distilled water for about one-half hour to remove any residual adhesive and then appropriate restoration of the paper can commence.

Making Your Own Glue

It is necessary to use some form of adhesive in repairing tears or affixing hinges to prints when making them ready for framing. The adhesive must not have any chemicals that would eventually bring about the deterioration of the paper. In addition, the adhesive must be strong enough to last over the years. Many commercial glues pose the problem of not being strong enough, or when they are they will cause discoloration or deterioration of the paper.

In order to be sure that the glue will be absolutely free of staining material and other harmful substances, the following recipe is recommended. Add four heaping teaspoons of rice starch to one pint of cold water in an aluminum or enamel pan. First, add just enough water to make a thick cream. Bring the balance of the water to a full boil in another pan, then add it to the paste over moderate heat while continuously stirring. This process is similar to making gravy, except that water is used instead of meat juices. The paste is ready when it becomes thick and has a glassy appearance. Allow the mixture to cool and then add a teaspoon of formaldehyde as a preservative to guard against microorganisms. The mixture is good to use for about two days. Always prepare a fresh batch if the job runs longer than that.

Repairing Hernias

If the paper artifact has ruptured sometime during its lifetime, it is often advisable to repair the tear to prevent further damage upon handling. Repairing the tear, if done expertly, also will improve the appearance of a print. Never handle the edges of a tear. If the tear could otherwise have been repaired invisibly, any dirt deposited by the fingers will now make the tear obvious. Even if the hands are thoroughly clean, oils left by touching it can attract dirt before the reparation is complete and the tear will be visible. A piece of mulberry paper can be torn to take the shape of the tear, with about one-half inch overlapping on either side of it.

Then apply the paste mentioned above very thinly to the mulberry paper and press it into place on the back of the item needing reparation. If there are many tears, it is probably advisable not to make multiple repairs, but make one simple repair by pasting a sheet of mulberry paper over the entire back of the paper object. Extreme care should be used in attempting this technique on Japanese prints. Most of these prints were made on mulberry paper, which gets soft when it is wet. Furthermore, Japanese prints usually are made with colors that may run when wet. Be careful not to attempt this technique if the artifact is made from parchment. As with woolen goods, parchment will shrink to a fraction of its original size if wetted and allowed to dry.

Framing

A print or other paper object that is to be framed must first be hinged on a mat. Make the hinges from mulberry paper which is lighter weight and weaker than the paper object to be framed. If, for some unforeseen reason, the object in the frame is jostled or falls, it then is more likely that the hinges will tear rather than the art object. A chain is only as strong as its weakest link, and in this case we purposely use a weak link to avoid damage to the expensive part of the chain.

Use the paste described above on the hinges to attach them both to the mat and to the paper object. Ordinarily, the hinges are bent in half with glue applied along one side. Half the hinge is glued to the mat behind the paper object, and the other half of the hinge folded directly over it is pasted to the object itself. If the object is a print and it will hang on a wall, the hinges should

be placed at the top only. If the print is to be kept in a collection and stored horizontally, the hinges should be placed at the left side. For very heavy prints or those that are large compared to the size of the hinges, a special hinge is fabricated by first pasting strips of mulberry paper to the back of the print at the top and overlapping an inch or two. Then the back side of the top of these strips is pasted to mat board. Then additional strips of paper are pasted across the exposed part of the paper strips for additional support. Do not use so much paste that the liquid will penetrate the mulberry paper and cause the folded hinges to stick together. If possible, it is also advisable to apply the paste only near the middle of the hinge and not to allow it to spread near the edges. This will allow hinges to be removed more easily in the future if it should become necessary. Never paste the print directly to the mat board beneath it.

The mat should be made of 100 percent rag paper. It is composed of two pieces, the frame board and the back board. The back board is a solid sheet of matting material to which the print is hinged. The frame board is cut with a window in it so that the print can be seen through it when it is placed over the top of the print. The purpose of the frame board is to separate the print itself from the glass that is used in the frame to protect the print. The glass keeps unnecessary dirt and grime from making contact with the print. A print or watercolor in contact with the back side of the glass can result in mold and mildew problems. Moisture can collect

For heavy prints, a hinge is made by using two criss-crossed sheets of paper.

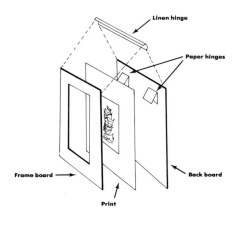

The construction of a properly matted print.

at the print-glass interface, setting up the perfect environment for attack by microorganisms. The mat prevents this condition from occurring. The frame board is connected to the back board by means of a linen tape hinge. Paste a linen strip to the back side of the frame board and back board along their seams so that one can be folded over the other in book fashion. Leave enough space between the two mat boards so that undue tension will not be placed on the binding when the print is secured between them.

A sheet of paper should be pasted or taped across the back of the frame to prevent dirt from getting into it. However, the edges of this sheet should not be completely sealed because it is desirable to have some air circulate in back of the print to further prevent moisture from collecting. Furthermore, thin pieces of cork or felt should be glued to each of the corners on the back of the frame away from the wall. This further provides for ventilation.

Several different types of glasses can be used to protect the print. Ordinary window glass usually has a green tint to it, which may prevent seeing the print colors as they were intended by the artist. Therefore, a clear glass should be used in most instances. Non-glare glass also can interfere with observing a print, but sometimes can be used over watercolors without unduly interfering with what the artist intended to convey.

Large Posters

During the 19th century, some very large posters, often the size of people,

were made that create special problems for conservation. These posters should not be rolled, but rather stored flat and they require a backing to prevent their brittle bodies from becoming mangled. The paste described above is put over the entire back of the poster. A backing material is then applied while the poster rests on a flat surface, and pressure is put to bear until the back surface of the poster is glued to the front surface of the backing material. Muslin and linen have sometimes been used to back posters, but the pressure applied during the gluing process can sometimes push the texture of the cloth through the front surface of the poster and this is undesirable. A better backing material would be a large sheet of mulberry paper with characteristics as similar to the poster as possible, so that expansion and contraction of the two materials with changes of humidity and temperature will not create stresses that might result in tears. If the poster is still strong enough and you understand its chemistry, it might be advisable to try chemically deacidifying the poster first.

Storage

Always follow a few simple rules when storing paper artifacts. Keep the artifact away from direct sunlight or other source of ultraviolet light so that it does not become bleached or discolored. Keep it in a pollution-free environment with a relative humidity of 50 to 65 percent. A lower humidity unduly dries out the paper and a higher humidity invites attack by microorganisms. The temperature should be kept at less than 75 degrees, because any chemical deterioration will take place faster the warmer the environment. Keep the paper separated from acid papers. Harmful chemicals can spread from one to another in contact like a contagious disease. Prints should be stored horizontally with glassine or mylar sheets between them.

CHAPTER III

DEVELOPING THE RIGHT TYPE INTO THE PICTURE OF HEALTH (PHOTOS)

The Frenchman, J. Nicéphore Niepce, produced a photographic image on paper in 1816 by exposing light-sensitive photographic salt. However, at that time he was unable to find another chemical process that would prevent the continued interaction of sunlight with the photosensitive material. The image was therefore lost over time, and his research continued. In 1822, he produced the first permanent photograph. The process was called heliography, and was perfected by 1826 so that a metal plate could be etched when chemicals on its surface were exposed to sunlight. Initially, bitumen was put on the surface of a copper plate, and after exposure the bitumen was exposed to iodine vapors in order to enhance the figures. The shadows consisted of bare copper, while the lighter areas were made up of hardened bitumen. Eventually, tin replaced copper to form a better quality heliograph.

In the year 1829, L. J. M. Daguerre, a painter, formed a partnership with Niepce. Daguerre had been experimenting with the light-sensitive nature of the chemical salt, silver iodide. Somewhat by accident, Daguerre discovered that an iodized silver upon which a camera image had been projected would bear a distinct, somewhat permanent image if fumed with mercury vapor. His new invention, called the daguerreotype, was described in publications in 1839. A copper plate was silver-plated, buffed to a high luster, then fumed with iodine. Eventually bromine was also used to further sensitize the plate. Initially, daguerreotypes required several minutes of exposure in bright sunlight to ade-

quately instill an image upon the plate. Further refinements provided an adequate image after only a few seconds. The image was developed by placing the exposed plate over a cup of heated mercury at about 75 degrees centigrade. Unfortunately, mercury vapor is poisonous and many young photographers in the middle of the 19th century were afflicted with mercury poisoning because of their dedication to their work. Sodium thiosulphate was used to fix the image on the plate and gold chloride was used to tone it.

Calotype

Fox Talbot discovered a process whereby paper saturated with silver chloride could be exposed to produce an image. It was fixed with either sodium chloride or potassium iodide. The image produced, however, was a negative image. Further refinement of Talbot's method in 1839 revealed that silver iodide and silver nitrate could be used and fixed with sodium thiosulphate. The Calotype was developed in gallic acid. The paper on which the image appeared could then be waxed or oiled, another light-sensitive piece of paper placed in contact with it and exposed, and then developed and fixed to produce a positive print. Talbot took great pains to patent his process in England, and protection of these patent rights prevented the widespread use of the Calotype in the United States.

Understandably, one of the limiting factors in producing a good quality print from the Calotype process was the lack of transparency of the paper which was chemically treated. In the search for a more transparent base medium to hold the light sensitive chemicals, glass plates became a prominent substrate. Initially, albumen (egg whites) was used to bind the chemicals to the surface of the glass plate. However, albumen also lacked appropriate transparent properties, and prints produced from Calotypes or albumen-coated glass plates lacked clarity and detail.

Ambrotypes

In 1851, another Englishman, Frederick Scott Archer, developed a new process which displaced the popular daguerreotype. A thick liquid produced by dissolving nitrocellulose in a mixture of alcohol and ether was used as the medium to hold iodide and bromide. The liquid was poured on a sheet of glass and allowed to flow evenly across the plate. As the alcohol and ether evaporated, a thin sticky transparent film was formed on the plate of glass. A solution of silver nitrate was then poured over the chemical-bearing collodion to form silver iodide and silver bromide, which now made the plate light-sensitive.

The mixture lost much of its light-sensitivity as the plate dried. Therefore, to be practical as a photographic medium, the plate had to be prepared, exposed in the camera while it was wet, developed, fixed, washed and dried within about one hour. The image was fixed with a solution of potassium cyanide instead of sodium thiosulphate. Because of the speed with which a photographer had to work in using the wet plates, also called ambrotype, mobile darkrooms in the form of tents, wagons

and laboratories on wheels, made their rounds drawn by horses across the country. The ambrotype image is actually a negative that appears to be positive when viewed against a black medium.

Tintypes

Somewhere around 1856, a gentleman photographer sat down with a glass plate negative in his hip pocket—hence the tintype was invented. The tintype essentially was the same photographic entity as the ambrotype. However, glass was replaced with an iron sheet that had been painted black. Sometimes tintypes were called ferrotypes or melainotypes, depending upon whether you preferred the Latin word for iron or the Greek word for black.

Tintypes were varnished to protect their surface. Because of the dark background immediately below the exposed light-sensitive salts, little light was transmitted from underneath the photographic image, and hence it almost always appears as a positive.

"Chocolate tinting" was used around 1870 by photographers to produce a warm-colored background that was more aesthetically pleasing for portraits. Whites in tintype, nonetheless, appear as a dull gray and never offer a full contrast with the dark tones that are present. Tintypes were sometimes colored by buffing-on transparent pigments over still tacky varnish. Ambrotypes were also sometimes colored in this way.

Dry Plates

In 1881, the dry plate negative was invented by impregnating gelatin with

With light shining at a glancing angle, a daguerreotype appears to be nothing more than a mirror.

silver bromide and depositing a thin layer of the gelatin on a glass plate. These plates could be stored dry for a relatively long period of time, inserted into the camera when needed and then re-stored for some time before processing.

Dry plates were produced at the factory and sold to photographers—a welcome relief from the hectic preparation, use and processing of wet plates.

Later Developments

Since this book deals primarily with arts and artifacts dating from the Victorian period, only slight mention will be made of developments that took place around and after the turn of the century. Although some glass plates continue to be used today, the ease of being able to roll film and keep significant quantities of it available in a small space led to the development of plastic strips on which light-sensitive chemicals were deposited. The first strips were made from a clear plastic called nitrocellulose, which was extremely thin and had a tendency to curl up and wrinkle easily, but which would not shatter upon dropping as a glass plate would. Nitrocellulose, however, is inflammable and many accidents were caused by spontaneous combustion of this material. Eventually, nitrocellulose-base negatives were replaced by other plastics that do not chemically react quite so violently.

Papers For Printing

Three types of papers basically have been used for printing photographs. The first type is albumen paper, which was developed around 1855. A solution of albumen was used to hold sodium chloride to the surface of paper and sold in this form to photographers. A photographer, as he needed to make prints, floated the paper face down in a solution of silver nitrate. The silver nitrate solution reacted chemically with the sodium chloride paper to essentially impregnate the paper with silver chloride. The paper was then dried under a yellow light and put in a special frame in direct contact with the negative which was to be printed. The frame was exposed to bright sunlight, and the procedure was referred to as "the printing-out-process". The printing paper was removed after a period of time, washed in water, toned with a gold chloride solution, fixed in sodium thiosulphate and then dried. The papers came in convenient sizes which were referred to by various trade names for the convenience of photographers and customers.

In 1891, printing-out papers were developed which used either collodion or gelatin to hold a light-sensitive emulsion on the printing paper. Although printing-out papers were processed similar to albumen paper, they have a thicker base and generally have a higher gloss with different characteristic colors in the print. The tones range from maroon to sepia.

In 1880, developing-out papers were invented. They offered advantages over printing-out papers in that they provided a print much quicker with less bother to the photographer. In general, printing-out papers required several hours for exposure and processing, while developing-out papers required only 30 minutes. These papers were promoted by Eastman Kodak and shipped from the factory with the light-sensitive layer fixed to the paper. Developing-out papers essentially had the same advantage over printing-out papers as dry plates had over wet plates used for producing negatives. Either silver chloride, silver bromide or a combination of these two chemicals was used to produce early developing-out print papers. The bromide-type continues in use even today.

Stereographs

Stereographs were made using all the various photographic techniques available from about 1856 until about 1920. Their popularity rose and fell as the whims and styles of the day changed. Stereographs were made by taking a picture with a camera that had two lenses mounted side-by-side, about the same distance apart as human eyes. After a print was made from the negative, the right and left printed pictures were switched and mounted on a card so that they gave the impression of being seen with human binocular vision. The earliest stereographs were flat, but later ones were curved about a vertical axis through their middle. They were viewed through a device, call a stereoscope, which required both eyes to focus separately on the respective pictures and gave the psychological impression of a three-dimensional image.

How To Tell If It's The Right Type

Calotypes are extremely rare, and most Americans probably never will have any opportunity to attempt to identify one of them. However, their appearance as a waxed or oiled paper negative

should quickly attract any observer's attention.

Daguerreotypes, ambrotypes and tintypes often are found in small cases made of either celluloid or paper with a velvet lining and a gold-plated brass embossed-foil border. Under this border, a plate of glass covers the picture. Some form of cutout bezel or mat covers the daguerreotype under the glass plate. The silver-plated copper sheet upon which the picture appears will be found under this mat. The surest way to identify a daguerreotype from all other forms of photographs is to remove the copper plate picture from its encasement. However, sometimes it is advantageous to identify one without removing the picture from its encasement. A daguerreotype will appear as either a positive or negative image, depending upon the direction of incident light and the direction from which the photograph is viewed. Alternate positive and negative images can be seen by turning it through several angles. However, a piece of white paper held in front of the daguerreotype to make a 90-degree angle with it should change a negative image into a positive image when viewed with overhead lighting. Similarly, a black piece of paper reflecting the overhead light onto a positive image will turn it negative, because it will minimize the reflected light.

Ambrotypes generally consist of two pieces of glass within the encasement. Under the cover glass and mat will appear another glass plate on which the image is deposited. An ambrotype is a negative that appears positive when a dark material is placed behind it. The

Many early photographs were preserved in fancy cases.

For an ambrotype, the contents of the case included (1) a foil frame, (2) a bezel, (3) a glass plate, (4) the photograph with blackened reverse.

Before: A daguerreotype of an elderly woman. The photograph has considerably tarnished.

Held to the light at a certain angle, a positive daguerreotype picture turns into a negative.

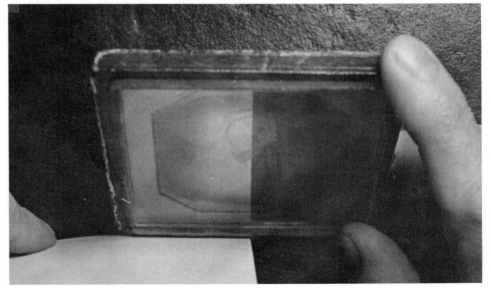

Holding the daguerreotype over white and black paper will cause part of it to appear as a negative and part as a positive.

33

Some ambrotypes were not painted on the back. When placed over white paper it appears as a negative.

When placed over black paper an ambrotype appears as a positive.

Instead of a sheet of black paper behind it, the back of some ambrotypes was painted black. This one is still partially stuck to its wrapping paper.

image is on the side of the glass plate on which the collodion has been deposited, and this should be the side closest to the viewer so that the image will not be reversed. A sheet of black paper generally will be found behind the ambrotype, or, in some cases, black paint on the back side of the glass.

In some cases, black paint mistakenly was placed over the image. Although this painted surface generally gives the image additional protection, it also requires anyone to view the image through the glass as though it were reversed in a mirror.

Dry plate negatives can sometimes be found encased as ambrotypes. They differ only slightly from ambrotypes, but in general are found in glass plates that are considerably thinner and have even-cut edges that were made at the factory. The surface coating on the plate is smooth and uniform, and has a dark gray-black hue in reflected light. Color gradations will range from clear to black. The wet collodion ambrotype, however, will show patterns where the collodion has been swirled, and some of the covering will be nonuniform where it has been either overly deposited or is entirely missing. In reflected light, the collodion side will appear a light tan or gray. Since the silver image on either a dry plate or ambrotype can be scratched easily, the photographer often coated the surface with a layer of varnish to give it some protection.

Tintypes are most often found in fancy but inexpensive paper framing and matting. However, they are also sometimes found in small enclosed cases

covered by a glass plate. An ambrotype reversed in the case so that the collodion side of the glass plate is away from the viewer and immediately in front of a black medium will appear exactly as a tintype. However, when placed appropriately, the tintype can easily be identified, because it is almost impossible to find an angle at which a negative image will appear. This is so because transmitted light cannot be reflected from the background and through the image on the plate so easily. The tintype image is formed directly on the black metal surface, while an ambrotype image is the thickness of the glass away from its black background.

Life And Death Through Chemistry

Chemistry provides amazing miracles that either contribute to our survival or bring about our demise. Chemical reactions within the human body between food substances produce the products of energy to sustain life and proteins to build new cells. Man also through his technology introduces detrimental chemical reactions with which he must cope. Automobiles emit incompletely combusted gases in the form of carbon monoxide and hydrocarbons. Carbon monoxide is directly harmful to man and can cause death if ingested in sufficient quantities. Hydrocarbons interact with sunlight to produce what is commonly called smog. Breathing smog, in turn, can cause heart and lung problems. Other materials interact with light through the miracles of chemistry; namely, silver, or in particular, silver chloride, silver bromide and silver iodide. Each of these chemicals

34

has a certain sensitivity to light which causes it to darken when interaction takes place.

Putting these chemicals on some substrate forms a photographic plate. When a camera focuses light in an orderly fashion to form an image upon this photographic material, an image forms in the chemical with the likeness of the projected object. By dissolving and washing away the chemical which does not interact, and then preventing the reactive chemical from further reacting through the use of another chemical, we have as a result a permanent picture. Or do we? The activities of both nature and man produce other chemicals that find their way into our environment. These chemicals can bring about the demise of a photograph, just as poisons can bring about the demise of humans. We need to study the physiology of each of the various forms of photographs to determine which chemicals act as poisons and shorten their lifespans.

Medicine For Daguerreotypes

Recall that the image on the silver surface of a daguerreotype is brought out through the formation of an amalgam of mercury vapor with silver. The amalgam alloy to a certain extent can be described as a solution of the two metals. Most people are familiar with the carbon dioxide bubbles that are dissolved in liquid soda pop, and know that if the soda pop is heated the bubbles come out and no longer remain in the liquid solution. Similarly, when heat is applied to a daguerreotype, or to any silver mercury amalgam, the mercury evaporates. When this happens, the image is reduced and becomes fainter. For this reason, daguerreotypes should not be stored in a heated place, such as near a furnace vent or in the attic.

Excess hypo left on any photographic print with age will tend to discolor and stain that print. Luckily, with daguerreotypes, hypo is easily washed off the metal surface and most likely will not have caused damage over the years. However, some stains may have been caused by an inattentive photographer. Not much can be done with these stains, because the chemical damage to the photograph may be irreversible.

Sulfur in the atmosphere in the form of sulfur dioxide or hydrogen sulfide can react with a silver surface to produce a tarnish. Silver reacts with sulfur to form silver sulfide, which does not look silver, but rather has a black appearance. An obscure daguerreotype can be caused either by tarnish on the surface of the silver or by dirt that has been deposited on the glass plate in front of the daguerreotype.

The first step in restoration requires disassembling the daguerreotype. The photographic plate with its accompanying decorations must be taken apart and thoroughly cleaned. Using a small but sharp screwdriver, very carefully pry the photographic plate cover, glass, mat and sheet metal framing from its protective case. Handle the cover glass carefully so as not to rub it across the surface of the daguerreotype, which might produce a scratch due to grit that has been wedged in between. A scratch across the image cannot be removed without further damage to the image. The sheet metal framing can be peeled from the back forward to allow removing the sandwich of daguerreotype plate, glass and mat in between. The glass plate should be washed both front and back with a mild detergent or, even better, a good window glass cleaner. If the glass is cracked or broken, it should be replaced with glass of comparable thickness that is as clear as the original glass and containing minimal tint. The daguerreotype itself should be handled only by its edges, and the fingers should never be placed on the silver surface of this valuable aged photograph. Oil from the fingers can chemically react with the surface to produce splotches, or may act as a shield to prevent the appropriate chemical interactions described in the restoration process to follow.

During their lifetime, daguerreotypes were more than likely displayed in houses heated with coal burning stoves or furnaces. The coal undoubtedly contained some sulfur, and the burning of the coal resulted in sulfurous gases which in either large or small concentrations permeated the environment. Even today in many urban areas, burning coal by industrial installations or power plants produces the sulfur dioxide that chemically interacts to bring about the deterioration of many materials. In fact, sulfur dioxide reacts with air and any present atmospheric water vapor to form sulfuric acid, which brings about even further material deterioration. In order to remove the tarnish from the daguerreotype, the conservator needs to decide whether he wants to take his life into his own hands and use potassium cyanide or use a chemical known as thiourea. Thiourea is present in many commercially available silver cleaners which are used to remove tarnish from silverware or coins. One product that contains a predominance of thiourea is called Tarn-X. Thiourea provides a direct chemical interaction with the tarnished surface to remove the tarnish, and no abrasion is necessary. Any silver cleaner that requires rubbing in any form should not be used. Appropriate solutions require only dipping the tarnished silver object into the liquid for a short period of time and then washing.

Use rubber or plastic gloves or tongs to handle a daguerreotype by its edges, since chemical solutions can irritate the skin. First, wash the daguerreotype in mild detergent solution to remove surface dirt. Use of a dishwashing detergent advertised not to leave water spots will work best. Then, rinse the daguerreotype thoroughly in cool running water to remove all traces of the detergent. It should then be immersed in the tarnish-removing thiourea solution. When it becomes obvious that the tarnish has been removed **and no longer,** remove the daguerreotype from the solution and place it in cool running water for about one minute. Again wash the daguerreotype in the detergent solution to remove any traces of the chemical, and then rinse in distilled water. Distilled water is used so that any of the chemicals used in treating the water do not remain after the water evaporates to cause water spots. It is important to protect any coloring on the daguerreotype (which may have been applied through the plating of other metals or through the use of pigments in some form of varnish) that has not been removed with the tarnish. Immediately dry the daguerreotype with a hair dryer. Any spots that might appear are caused by some impurity in the water. A few drops of Kodak Photo-Flo, or another wetting agent such as Basic-H, in about a quart of distilled water makes the rinse water wetter and allows it to flow off the photograph more easily to reduce the chances of producing water spots. If no coloring is apparent on the surface of the daguerreotype, there is no need to be concerned about dissolving the varnish or other resins which might be used as the adhesive for the pigment. In that case, the print should be removed from the distilled water, shaken carefully to drip off as much water as possible and then immersed in pure ethyl alcohol. The ethyl alcohol will absorb moisture from the surface of the photograph and it then can be evaporated using the hair dryer so that no water spots will appear. Be sure to use a fresh supply of ethyl alcohol, because even pouring this liquid through moist air will cause it to absorb moisture.

Clean the metal mat and foil frame with the solution used for removing the silver tarnish, then rinse and dry.

Any markings found on the back of the daguerreotype or within the case should be noted and indexed before the daguerreotype is reassembled. Even if nothing appears on the back of the photograph, this condition should also be noted to prevent unneeded disassembly that might result in possible harm to the historic picture.

Place the mat over the daguerreotype and then the clean glass over the mat. The assemblage must now be sealed to prevent dirt and chemicals, as much as possible, from working their way under the glass to the surface of the picture. Place Permalife paper cut into strips wide enough to fit over the side of the three layers and then folded over about one-eighth inch both front and back around the perimeter. Use Jade 403 adhesive on the inside edge of the Permalife paper. This paper and adhesive will not cause chemical deterioration of the daguerreotype. The corners of the paper can be snipped so that the one-eighth inch overlap can be folded down across the front of the glass plate and the back of the daguerreotype. The sealed picture can now be placed back into its metallic foil frame and reinserted into its carrying case.

If a photographic reproduction of the daguerreotype is desired, it should be made before the glass plate is sealed over the metallic plate. The photograph can be made with a camera focused to take a picture through a pinhole in a piece of black craft paper. Since the surface of the daguerreotype is silver and mirrorlike, it would reflect the image of the camera onto the negative being produced. The black paper with the pinhole prevents this and allows an unobstructed picture to be made.

Operating On Ambrotypes

Occasionally, the cover glass of an ambrotype is cemented to the negative glass plate. No attempt should be made to pry the two plates apart because all that will result will be either damage

After: The tarnish from the daguerreotype has been partially removed from the left side and the center to reveal the contrast between restored and unrestored portions.

Before: A daguerreotype of a young woman.

After: The young woman is considerably more visible with the tarnish removed.

to the glass itself or damage to the photographic image. If the glass plates are not cemented together, the ambrotype should be disassembled in the same manner as the daguerreotype described above. The cover glass should be cleaned with a dry cloth. No rubbing or cleaning should be attempted on the side of the glass plate with the photographic image. The black background should be replaced with a black polyethylene film. Black polyethylene can be found at a hardware store or cut from a black plastic trash bag. Polyethylene is non-reactive and should not deteriorate the old photograph. If the ambrotype's image is to be placed back into its case on the side of the glass farthest from the viewer, then a mat needs to be made to separate that image from the black background so that it will not be hurt by direct contact.

Clean the mat between the two glass plates away from the work area so that flakes of dirt do not contaminate the glass plates. Cleaning the mat with chemicals should be avoided, so that no chemical residues will be sandwiched between the glass plates. Any facts or dates found inside the ambrotype or their absence should be recorded before reassembly. The ambrotype should then be reconstructed in the same manner as the daguerreotype.

Occasionally, an ambrotype's surface was protected by the photographer with a layer of varnish over the collodion. With age, the varnish sometimes will fracture and perhaps peel away. There is no easy way to restore such a photograph without taking a chance of gravely injuring the image. However, a glass plate can be taped over the peeling varnish to prevent it from dislodging from the photograph. The tape used should be 3M acrylic polyester 850. This tape will not give off gases with age that may injure the photograph. In some cases, a plastic spray, such as Krylon or other plastic fixatives used to preserve pastel drawings, can be used. The philosophy of most conservators would be against such practice since it is irreversible.

Because the nitrocellulose base of the collodion in these wet plate negatives makes certain their eventual demise, each negative should be duplicated with modern materials to insure preservation of the photograph for future generations.

Treating Tintypes

Extensive restoration of tintypes is usually not necessary since they are varnish protected, and with normal precautions have easily lasted through their 100-year history. However, surface dirt can be removed by washing the tintype in a mild detergent such as is used for washing dishes. The tintype should then be rinsed in distilled water and dried. That is all you need to do.

Occasionally, one will find tintypes with the varnish flaking. These incidences are most unfortunate, because the solvents used to reamalgamate the varnish also are solvents for collodion. Therefore, attempts to stop flaking or to restore the varnish will result in removing the image from the tintype. Therefore, this type of restoration should not be attempted, and the tintype should be placed under a cover glass and taped

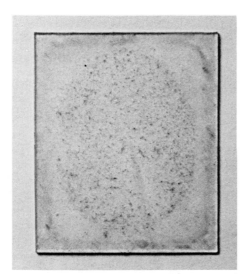

This cover glass had accumulated decades of grime. Cleaning it will aid in viewing the photograph beneath it.

This tintype is housed beneath a dirty cover glass.

in that position to avoid further deterioration.

Doctoring Dry Plates

The gelatin base on dry plates is more easily affected by chemical residues than the collodion base on wet plates. Chemicals may be found in the form of residues left after the developing process, chemicals present in the storage area of the dry plates, or simply chemicals in the atmosphere. Immersing a dry plate in any liquid after its years of aging can cause a shock to the emulsion that can result in thousands of tiny fractures of the photographic image. If this has not happened, clean only the glass side of the dry plate the same as the nonphotographic side of a wet plate is cleaned. If the emulsion has cracked, there is danger of wiping some of the image off the glass plate. Or, perhaps, some of the image has already lifted. A special glue must be concocted to place part of the image back into its original position or to prevent the fractured emulsion from lifting off the glass plate. An old lady once gave me her secret formula for doing dry plate restoration, but I have difficulty in remembering the magic words that were supposed to be said over the potion. In the absence of the black magic, the following formula can be tried. One tablespoon of plain Knox gelatin should be dissolved into one-fourth to one-half cup of warm (not hot) distilled water. Add to this mixture one-fourth teaspoon of ammonium hydroxide (household ammonia) and one-fourth teaspoon of Kodak Photo-Flo or one drop of Basic-H. Strain this mixture through four layers of cheesecloth

to remove any lumps. Then use the solution to reglue the flaking chips of emulsion, or simply coat the entire gelatin surface of the plate to prevent fractures from eventually lifting. Never use this solution if it is more than two days old, but mix a fresh batch.

Healing The Wounds of Prints

All prints on paper can suffer from yellowing or staining caused by residual hypo attacking silver within the photographic image. Chemicals from the paper or cardboard also can attack either the photographic image itself or the paper on which it is mounted. In the case of albumen prints, Kodak film cleaner can be applied with a cotton ball to remove dirt and some stains. The print should then be swabbed with methyl alcohol to remove any resulting streaks. Simple dirt can be removed from albumen prints by using distilled water and Basic-H (one teaspoon Basic-H to one pint water).

Printing-out and developing-out papers can suffer the same staining and discoloring maladies. These papers can be reprocessed to remove residual chemicals, but all papers with a gelatin base should first be treated with Kodak SH-1 hardener to prevent damage to the photograph during the reprocessing.

The Nitrocellulose Demons

Nitrocellulose as a base for photographic negatives was used as early as 1889. But the changeover from glass plates to flexible negatives by photographers took a long time afterward. Use of nitrocellulose sheet film was widespread only between 1913 and 1939.

Because most nitrocellulose film products were used after the turn of the century and therefore after Victorian times, their treatment is really beyond the scope of this book. But because of the great dangers involved in handling and storing nitrocellulose products, a few precautions will be offered.

Nitrocellulose is extremely flammable. Excessive heat, sparks, or in some cases even spontaneous combustion will put the entire mass of film into flames. Nitrocellulose film should be stored in well-ventilated areas in temperatures no higher than 70 degrees.

Nitrocellulose decomposes over time. Nitrocellulose film products have been known to last from 20 to 65 years, depending upon the chemical purity of the nitrocellulose itself and the physical properties of the film, such as thickness. The thicker the film product, the more difficult it is for gases trying to escape the film to be released by it. At first, nitrogen dioxide and other gases are given off. Any available moisture will transform the nitrogen dioxide into nitric acid. Nitrocellulose film first yellows, then becomes tacky, liquifies, and finally turns to powder. During any of these stages, the gases given off can stimulate other nitrocellulose products in its chain reaction of decay. The gases can also harm other photographic materials and even eat paint off the shelves on which the material is stored.

Nitrate-based films were produced for some lines of products until 1951. Dealing with these products can be somewhat dangerous, and therefore a text treating their safe care should be consulted.

Preservation

Many dumb mistakes are made in storing photographs and negatives that will eventually bring about their demise. Use of rubber cement, clear tape, or rubber bands to hold photographs together in bundles or mounted on cardboard will inevitably result in discoloration and staining. The sulfur present in the rubber products and adhesive in the cement, as well as sulfur and other chemicals in the cardboard, will react with the chemicals in the emulsion on negatives or prints. Glass plates should not be stacked up in horizontal planes, because the result will be scratching and nicking of the emulsion surface or perhaps even breaking some of the glass plates under the weight of their neighbors above them. Glass plates should be stored in a vertical plane.

A few simple measures can go a long way toward preserving photographs from premature deterioration and demise.

1. Isolate all nitrocellulose negatives. This will insure that any nitrocellulose decay will not cause a chain reaction in other nitrocellulose materials and that the fumes will not cause the deterioration of other photographs.

2. Control relative humidity to less than 50 percent. Humidities much higher than this will lead to the growth of mold and fungus. Moisture in the air can combine with excess hypo left on photographs, which will then reactivate and cause staining.

3. Store in temperatures below 70 degrees Fahrenheit. Since there are always some chemicals present in the environment to react with the chemicals

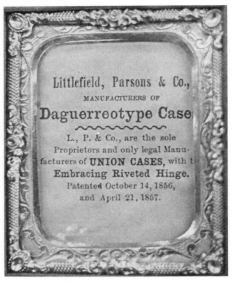

Old photographs were rare and treasured possessions housed in cases befitting their value.

Before: This paper case is faded and brittle.

After: Liquid shoe wax has been used to restore the color and resiliency of this case.

in the photographs, the temperature should be maintained at a level that will not accelerate chemical activity. Chemical reactions take place at a rate proportional to the absolute temperature. The higher the temperature, the faster the rate of reactivity.

4. Keep the photographs away from dust and dirt. Dirt can only mean that a photograph will have to be cleaned, and thus take a chance on damaging it. Even if it is not cleaned, simple movement can cause physical damage by the abrasive action of dust particles.

5. Keep a collection of photographs away from chemicals that might be corrosive. Do not store the collection in a basement near where paints and solvents are stored. Do not keep the collection near a fireplace, especially if coal is burned.

6. Separate negatives so there is no chance of them sticking together if the humidity should get out of control.

7. The best way to store prints is under polyester or acetate sheets. Photograph albums with these sheets are now available and provide for the easy viewing of photographs without the hazard of chemical contamination or damage due to excessive handling or mishandling.

Restoring Daguerreotype Or Ambrotype Cases

Basically, two types of cases were used to store and display mid-19th century photographs. One was made from embossed paper and the other from a hard rubber or black celluloid-like material. Photographs were expensive possessions, not easy to come by, and required a specialist to produce them. The cases in which they were kept were, therefore, fancy and interesting in themselves.

The rubber-like material is generally durable and seldom requires restoration. Paper cases sometimes have dried out and cracked, and require either cosmetic or structural work. A liquid (not solid) shoe wax (not polish) can be used to rejuvenate the case and add color to worn areas. Kiwi shoe wax is excellent. Several applications may be necessary.

Hinges were usually made of black cloth. Torn hinges can be replaced by using black "twill tape", a cotton product used for reinforcing seams in sewing that can be found in the notions section of most department stores or supermarkets. Remove the old cloth hinges with a razor blade, trim the new cloth and glue it into place using Jade 403 adhesive.

PHOTOGRAPHIC APPENDIX

One of the largest suppliers of conservation materials (including 100% rag paper and adhesive) is:

Process Materials Corporation
301 Veterans Boulevard
Rutherford, New Jersey
07070

Permalife envelopes for storing negatives and other Permalife products (paper, etc.) can be purchased from:

Talas
104 Fifth Avenue
New York, New York 10011

CHAPTER IV

WORKING WITH MOLDS (MOLD MAKING AND CASTING)

Very often a decorative roundel, handle or other part of a piece of furniture is missing. Gilded antique frames often take a beating in transportation and a section of the molding may be broken or lost. These problems are easy to deal with, considering the wide variety of modern materials available to the conservator. Basically, a mold is made from a similar object and a new piece is cast. This chapter will deal both with the materials available for making molds in various situations and with the materials available for casting the new object.

Missing Molding On Frames

Many frames made during the Victorian era had highly detailed plaster designs on the surface which could easily have been broken or chipped sometime during their 100-year lifetime. The frame need not be ruined nor discarded, because it can be restored to its original appearance. First, a section of the frame must be found that is similar to the one that has the piece missing. An impression is taken using one of three materials.

Alginate

Alginate is a substance which, when mixed with water, cures in a few minutes time into a gelatin-like mass. It is smooth. It is cool. And it quivers. The material can be bought from a dental supply house because dentists use it to take impressions of teeth. It can also be bought in a craft supply house, because it is also used for making casts of plaster and wax objects. The appendix at the end of this chapter will provide sources for this mold-making material.

Alginate is a powder. It does not have to be heated, but merely mixed with water to start the chemical reaction which causes it to solidify. However, the solid is very pliable, making it easy to remove the cast object from the mold. The dental version is usually flavored with spearmint, because it ends up being poured into somebody's mouth. Unless you are trying to take an impression of some antique bridgework, the flavoring is not necessary. Cost of this material is somewhere between $3 and $4 a pound, and a pound can be used to make a number of molds with a volume equivalent to this book. Alginate molds must be relatively thick so that they are not deformed when material is poured into the case. Use putty or modeling clay to build a waterproof dike around the section of the frame you want to reproduce. The dike should be about one-half inch deeper than the highest portion of the design.

Various instructions on the alginate container tell how to mix it with various proportions of water to achieve different consistencies. These instructions sometimes hamper your ability to make a proper mold. The important thing is to get a mixture that will allow the alginate to flow, and then quickly pour it into the dike. Spending time trying to get perfect proportions will result in the mold never being made. Alginate once mixed must be poured within seconds or it will cure while you are mixing it. Even though I have had considerable experience with this material, occasionally I still find that it hardens on me

Putty can be used to cover the openings to prevent the mold material from filling hollows or recesses. (A)

The original must be set firmly in place against a flat surface with a cardboard dike built around it. Masking tape will prevent the loss of mold material through small openings. (B)

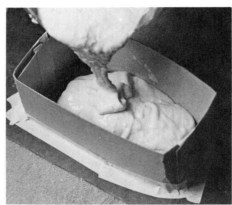

The alginate is ready to pour when it has the consistency of pancake batter. (C)

If properly mixed, there will be no clumps as appear in this photo. Jiggling the mold for a few seconds will help to remove air bubbles. (D)

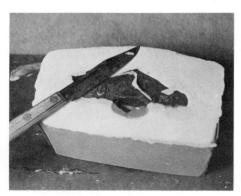

In a few minutes the dike can be removed and the edges trimmed with a knife. (E)

The mold with the original removed. (F)

while I am pouring it. The warmer the water, the faster it sets up. The more it is stirred, the faster it sets up. After you have tried it a couple of times, you will be amazed at how quickly the chemical reaction takes place.

Another amazing thing about the compound is how well it flows into the smallest cracks and crevices even though it appears to be a very viscous medium. When poured, it has the consistency of thick pancake batter. Yet, a little tamping to remove air bubbles allows it to quickly flow into places where you would think that only a liquid with the viscosity of water could go.

Basically, the steps for using this material should be as follows:

1. Spoon as much alginate powder into a plastic, glass or ceramic cup as will be needed to make the mold.

2. Under a tap, allow a small amount of water to flow into the cup. Pull the cup away and stir quickly until the water has been thoroughly absorbed into the alginate.

3. Add a little more water, pull the cup away from the faucet and continue stirring with a wide spoon for maximum mixing.

4. Repeat the process until the alginate has taken the consistency of thick pancake batter with no unusually large lumps or powdered areas that have not been dissolved.

5. Immediately pour this thick compound, using the spoon to hasten its flow, into the diked area.

6. Give it three or four minutes to fully cure.

7. Remove the dike and gently lift the mold.

The alginate should have flowed so that you have a flat surface on the bottom of the mold. When inverted and placed on a table, the mold should be able to support plaster or whatever material is poured inside. The casting should be done almost immediately, because the alginate will shrink and lose flexibility upon drying. If plaster of paris is to be used, follow the instructions on the package for mixing. Pour the liquid plaster into the mold, smooth its back surface with a piece of cardboard or other scraper and allow it to cure. This should be only a matter of minutes until the casting can be removed from the mold.

Alginate molds can be reused a number of times, provided that they are kept from drying out. I have stored them for several months under water in a glass jar. Use a couple of drops of formaldehyde to prevent fungus from attacking this organic material. If a casting substance will take more than a few minutes to cure, the alginate mold should be surrounded with wet rags and perhaps covered if the covering will not contaminate the casting. The alginate, upon drying, will shrink fully 50 percent into a white, unpliable, brittle, plaster-like material.

Moulage

Moulage is a unique material which makes a mold of consistency similar to alginate. It costs about $11 a small two-pound package to make molds that can be reused, melted and re-formed a number of times. Moulage is a wet, gelatin-like material that melts when

An alginate mold can be preserved for several months if kept sealed under water.

45

Moulage looks like soggy popcorn. (A)

Moulage is melted in a double boiler at a temperature more than 150-degrees Fahrenheit. (B)

After the first coat, moulage can be built up in thick layers with a spatula. (D)

Then a dike can be built and the mold completed by spooning in thick layers of moulage. (E)

subjected to temperatures in excess of about 150-degrees Fahrenheit. It comes in a crumbled form in a plastic bag to keep it moist. Moulage crumbs are heated in a double boiler until they form a consistency of thick pancake batter.

The same process of building a dike around the object for which an impression will be made is sometimes desirable to contain the mold and minimize the amount of material required. Moulage flows like liquid when warm, but upon cooling returns to its gelatinous state. It also will lose its moisture and shrink if allowed to dry out. A mold made from moulage and a mold made from alginate, sitting side by side, look and feel very similar. The alginate mold, however, can be used again only to cast other objects within that mold, and care

must be taken in its storage to prevent its drying out. A moulage mold can be remelted and cast into another mold.

Moulage will not stick to anything when cool, not even to hair. It is used in the medical profession to make molds of diseased organs. It can even be used to make molds of people's faces while they are still alive. Rather than pouring moulage to make a mold, it is best to first brush it over the desired area. Brushing insures that no air has been trapped to form bubbles that will prevent the smallest detail from being reproduced. Brush the moulage on in increasing thickness, taking care to insure that the material stays warm. After it cools, it will not stick to itself. If you want a very thick mold, you can use wire screening for reinforcement, but be careful that the screening material does

Hot moulage is applied with a brush, working it so that no air bubbles are trapped. (C)

Liquid rubber is brushed on so that air bubbles are worked to the surface.

It will cure in air, or it can be heated in an oven or with a heat lamp to vulcanize it.

not penetrate the entire thickness of the mold down to the object. When the mold is about one-half inch thick, you can pour the rest with warm moulage similar to pouring the alginate. Allow the entire mass to cool before removing the mold. Use a fan or rags soaked in cold water to hasten the cooling process.

If the moulage is to be melted and made into a new mold, it should first be cubed into small chunks for faster melting. Almost any knife is suitable to cut it. It may be necessary to add a small amount of water upon reheating to replace lost moisture. Moulage improves as a casting material after the first few remelts and can be used about 100 times.

Liquid Rubber

Liquid rubber is a rubber-base material dissolved in an ammonia-base solvent. It comes either in a pink variety, which cures into a bright red form, or a white variety, which cures into a tan or brown form. Liquid rubber cannot be

poured into a thick mass because the outer surface will cure and prevent the inner volume from curing. It does not solidify and make a usable mold in a matter of minutes as does alginate or moulage. It does, however, form a permanent mold which can be used hundreds of times, and requires only storage with no additional precautions. If the proper procedures are not followed to make the mold, however, and it does not cure properly, after some time it deteriorates into a useless, oozing mass.

Sources for rubber mold-making material are listed in the appendix at the end of this chapter. One manufacturer of the white rubber liquid recommends that one coat be brushed on and allowed to cure before a second coat is applied. Some distributors of the red rubber liquid recommend that it be vulcanized in the oven between coats. I have found that it may take 12 hours or more for one coat of red liquid rubber to cure, if not heat-treated with a heat lamp or the oven. If raised to a temper-

A dike is built around the completed mold.

Plaster is poured into the dike to form a "mother".

The "mother" supports the mold from beneath and prevents it from deforming.

Before: The top of a Corinthian pillar needing restoration.

After: Molds were made of existing pieces and reproductions were cast to replace missing pieces.

ature of about 110 degrees, the job is done in less than half an hour. Of course, there will occasionally be objects that are too big for the oven or too delicate to be heated, in which case air curing is the only alternative.

Care should also be taken with this material because of the ammonia base. It can discolor finishes on wood and even stain some woods badly if allowed to penetrate through the surface. I once used the red liquid to make molds of faces that were on some rosewood chairs. It removed the lacquer finish. It did not discolor the wood and it was a simple matter to retouch the chairs but, nonetheless, I should have anticipated the effect and didn't.

I also used the red liquid once to make molds for a set of plaster castings to decorate plaster ceilings. The molds were made over several thicknesses of newspaper on top of an oak table that had been varnished with a walnut-colored varnish stain. The ammonia from the mold-making compounds seeped through the many thicknesses of newspaper and stained the oak table with black rings representing the doughnut-shaped mold. So, although this material presents some significant advantages if many pieces are to be cast, it also presents some significant disadvantages, or at least potential disadvantages, that must be dealt with intelligently.

Liquid rubber should be brushed onto a surface with a cheap brush that probably will not be suitable for reuse. Try to remove all air bubbles from under the liquid rubber. A very thin coat is all that is necessary at first. The brush should be immediately washed in warm

running water to remove as much liquid rubber as possible.

If the item is small enough to be placed in an oven and will not be damaged by spending some time in 110-degree heat, the oven should be prewarmed and the item placed there until the rubber has vulcanized. The vulcanization process takes only a few minutes, depending upon the thickness of the mold, and has been completed when the pink liquid rubber turns bright red or the white liquid turns a deep tan. Remove the object and apply another thin coat of liquid rubber. Repeat the heating process. Continue this process until about one-eighth inch of thickness has been formed. This should be sufficient for small molds and so you can end the process and manufacture a "mother".

If the item has considerable bulk, it may be desirable to reinforce the mold to hold a large amount of casting material. With the next coat of liquid rubber, embed strips of cheesecloth, wire screening or fiberglass cloth trimmed to the approximate size of the object into that coat of liquid rubber. Brush on additional liquid rubber and then vulcanize the mold again. The reinforcing process not only strengthens the mold but makes it possible to apply a generous thickness of liquid rubber—up to more than one-eighth of an inch at one time. Use a spatula to put the mold-making compound into position and smooth it. A completed mold is flexible, and when removed from the object, its shape will have to be restrained so that it does not distort the casting.

To hold the mold in this shape, a

"mother" is constructed. A mother is simply a rough cast plaster receptacle into which the mold can be placed without distorting it while the casting is poured and cured. The area around the mold is diked with modeling clay. Plaster of paris is mixed and poured so that the finished section is at least one-half inch thick. When the plaster has hardened, the mother is removed and the mold is also removed. The mold can then be placed in the mother and casting is ready to begin. For unusually large mothers, strips of canvas can be embedded in the plaster while it is being poured to reinforce it.

Fixing Frames

What are the necessary steps to manufacture a new piece of molding to take the place of a missing piece on a frame? First, a mold is made either from alginate, moulage or liquid rubber as described above. Plaster is then poured into the mold and a piece cast. Usually, plaster of paris will do to make the missing piece because it was very often used to make the original. But, of course, the original did break and you may wish to make a piece that is stronger than the original.

Other forms of plaster are available that harden into a more durable mass than plaster of paris. Dental plaster is one such compound. Dental plaster is usually yellow as opposed to the pure white plaster of paris. Your dentist, hopefully, would be willing to secure some of this material for you, which is usually sold in 25-pound packages at a cost of about 50¢ a pound. The thicker and less liquid the plaster when it pours, the stronger will be the final product. However, thicker plaster does not flow as well as thin plaster, and the detail in the design may be somewhat obscured. For small molds, a vibrating table can help greatly in getting the plaster to flow into the smallest cracks and crevices. Using a stick or a spoon to massage the surface of the wet plaster will work sometimes. This process is called "floating" and draws water to the surface while, at the same time, allowing the more dense plaster to sink. Use gravity to your advantage and try to make sure that all air bubbles are out of the plaster before it begins to cure.

Other materials are used to temper or harden a plaster. White craft glue comes in a highly concentrated form. Eight ounces of glue are mixed with one gallon of water. This milky liquid is then used instead of water to mix the plaster. It significantly aids not only in hardening the plaster to make it chip resistant, but also helps to form a very smooth surface. It essentially acts like a glue to permeate the plaster, while not interfering with the water-plaster chemical reaction that causes the curing process to take place.

After the plaster reproduction has cured, it can be removed from the mold. If it is still moist, care must be taken in handling the surface or it will easily crumble. Heating it in the oven for a few minutes can remove a significant amount of its moisture, and it will noticeably lose weight when this is done. Sandpaper or a file should be used to carefully smooth the back of the reproduction and remove any excess plaster,

Before: The decoration on a gilded frame with a piece missing in the lower left-hand corner.

so that the reproduction will take on the exact shape and thickness of the original. If the sanding is done while the object is still moist, the plaster will crumble easier, but greater care must be taken in its handling. Sanding after the object has been thoroughly dried requires less care but will also require more time.

The object can be glued in place if it is to be permanently affixed to a flat surface. If the surface is irregular, plaster or some other adhesive may be better. A small amount of plaster of paris can be mixed and placed on an irregular surface. Press the reproduction into place, wipe away the excess plaster oozing from the edges and clean surrounding surfaces with a damp excess plaster oozing from the edges and clean surrounding surfaces with a damp cloth. Liquitex modeling compound also can be used for this purpose. It does not require mixing, but will require additional time for drying. When the repair is complete, the reproduced area can be gilded by following the instructions in the chapter on gilding.

Composite Pulls

Many pieces of Victorian furniture

A similar design is found elsewhere on the frame, and prepared so that an impression can be taken of it.

50

A mold is made.

A plaster casting is made, trimmed, and affixed to the appropriate place on the frame.

After: The design is gilded to blend in with the rest of the frame.

A composite pull is being cast in alginate.

The reproduction is removed from its mold, sanded on its back and finished on its front.

Which is the original and which is the reproduction?

have pulls that appear to be made of walnut and that required some wood carving skills to manufacture. Close examination of many of these pulls will reveal that they were not carved, but, indeed, were cast from a composition material. Many decorations, plaques and roundels were also made in this manner and applied to pieces of Victorian walnut furniture.

The original pieces were made by mixing sawdust, or some other cellulose-based material, with glue and then pressing this composition into a mold under pressure. The molds were most likely metal, and some heat-treating process may have been used to hasten the cure of the composition. I have been unsuccessful in my research to find the secret used in making most of these composition materials, but with trial and error I have been able to duplicate their appearance with some of the readily available materials in art and craft supply stores. To duplicate a pull or roundel, first prepare a mold of either liquid rubber or alginate. Moulage can also be used, but some of the mold will be contaminated and, therefore, will not be reusable. If moulage is used, this contaminated portion must be trimmed from the rest of the mold and discarded before the moulage can be remelted and made into another mold.

The process is somewhat complex as will be seen, but the end-product is well worth the effort. A new material available is called Sculptamold, which is a cellulose-type material embedded with dry glue. When mixed with water, it assumes a papier-mâché type of consis-

tency. Supposedly, the material will harden upon drying to form an object that can be carved or sanded. I have had significant problems in using the material as a casting medium, because it never dries thoroughly at the interface between the casting and the mold. The remainder takes a great deal of time to dry. Plaster, on the other hand, is easy to cast, but does not have the texture or feel of a composition pull. Here is the secret. Make the concoction by mixing dry powders as thoroughly as possible. These dry powders are three parts dental plaster mixed with two parts Sculptamold, plus two parts of brown tempera powder that will give the casting a simulated walnut color. Use plaster hardening liquid instead of water to mix the casting batter. Pour it into the mold, float and jiggle it to remove all bubbles and allow to cure. So far the process is easy, and now the real art begins.

Sculptamold in and of itself when colored with the tempera may have been suitable to formulate the casting, except for the curing problem mentioned earlier. Dental plaster helps to solve this problem, but the cellulose in the Sculptamold does not chemically react with water and will hold a significant amount of moisture as the casting cures. If you pour casting batter into a rubber mold, the rubber will not permit moisture to seep through it and all curing will have to take place through the top surface of the casting. If you use alginate, you find an apparent paradox. The casting must be dry enough so that moisture will flow from it, yet, at the same time, the alginate must be kept

An escutcheon has been broken. The missing pieces have been lost, making repair impossible.

In lieu of a better alternative, the escutcheon is replaced by a reproduction cast from an impression made from an escutcheon elsewhere on the same piece of furniture.

moist or it will shrink. Actually, the problems balance to a certain extent, because as moisture evaporates from the outer edges of the mold, it will be replaced by moisture that is absorbed out of the casting batter. There is a little trickery involved, though. You must ascertain when 90 percent of the moisture has left the casting batter, leaving a relatively well-cured casting, while making sure that enough moisture is left in the mold so that it can be flexed and removed from the casting before it dries enough to be cemented to it. Perhaps the safest technique is to use the rubber mold with its plaster mother. Once the batter has been poured into the mold, the entire package is placed in an oven to bake at about 120 degrees until the batter has thoroughly dried. An indication of drying will be the change in color of the batter from a deep rich brown to a light brown.

After the composite pull or roundel is removed from the mold, it may be baked further to remove remaining moisture. Its weight, and thus its feel, after it has given up that moisture will be very similar to the composition pulls of old. Sand its back smooth so that it can be glued into place. Use a file and sandpaper to trim any excess away from the edges. If any fibrous material makes the surface slightly fuzzy, your fingers should be enough to push it back into place.

The casting can be further strengthened after it is thoroughly dry by allowing it to soak overnight in a verathane penetrating sealer that is normally used as a wood finish and is available at most paint stores. Place the casting on wax paper until dry after wiping excess vera-

thane oil away first. If it is necessary to deepen the color further to match other pulls on the same piece of furniture, a varnish-base walnut stain will do the job. Simply brush it on the surface, let it dry and add additional coats if necessary.

Metal Casting

Occasionally, you will need to cast metal pulls or handles. The problem here is that molten metals must be poured into the mold, and so gelatin, moulage or liquid rubber are not appropriate as mold-making material. They would simply melt or burn. Although the original pulls may have been made of brass or steel, some available metals will allow duplication, but will not require extensive equipment or a foundry cupola in the back yard.

Half-casting is the easiest technique to use, which will produce one surface 180-degrees of a metal article while the other side remains flat. If only one side is to show, this method is wholly appropriate. You can make a plaster mold of this type of item by first varnishing its surface, laying it flat in a pan or a tray and pouring plaster over it. The varnish separation between the item and the plaster allows you to remove it. Molten metal can then be poured into the plaster.

Sometimes, however, plaster poses considerable difficulty in separating the metal item from it, because neither is flexible. A material called "Polyform" has the consistency of clay and can be molded with the fingers easily after it is worked for a few minutes with the hand. The material can be pushed over a piece of metal and held for awhile to take the

An original cast iron pull.

shape of that metal. As the Polyform becomes slightly stiffer and less gooey, it is easily removed from the metal object. Furthermore, it remains pliable to the extent that it will flex enough to release the object being molded. Polyform can be baked in an oven at about 300 degrees for a half-hour to render it permanently hard, yet slightly flexible. I have found that instead of baking it, pouring molten metal into it allows it to be the perfect mold-making material without such deterioration due to the heat.

Without equipment to produce extremely high temperatures, it will not be possible to duplicate metal items from brass or steel. However, lead can be cast, and so can another metal called babbitt. Babbitt is a nickel-lead alloy that melts at a higher temperature than lead, but at a low enough temperature to be turned into the molten state with a propane torch available from a hard-

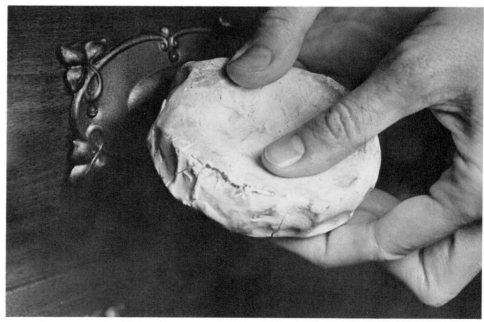

Heat resisting material is used to make an impression.

Molten lead or babbitt is poured into the impression.

ware store. Either lead or babbitt metal can be melted in a small coffee can or, better yet, in a cast iron ladle designed for lead casting. For small items, the flame from the torch can be directly applied to the metal until it turns liquid. To melt larger quantities of metal, supplementary heat will need to be provided by a stove top or other means. Simply pour the melted metal into the Polyform mold and allow it to cool. If the metal is very hot, it may scorch the Polyform surface, but the mold should be suitable for several castings, nonetheless.

Use a file to trim excess metal from the casting and smooth the back surface. Then, using the techniques for electroplating, certain metals can be plated over the casting to give it the appearance of something else. If the electroplating process for the metal you desire will not work, an appropriate-colored enamel will disguise the metal adequately. I have an old sideboard that has copper-plated cast iron pulls. Several of the pulls were missing, and I used this tech-

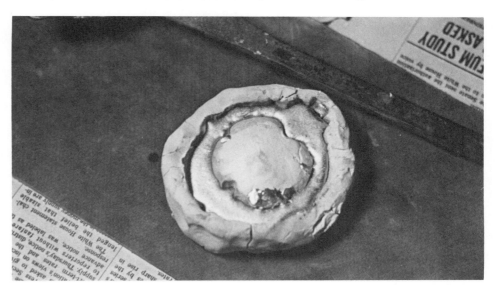

The hot metal is allowed to cool on an insulated surface.

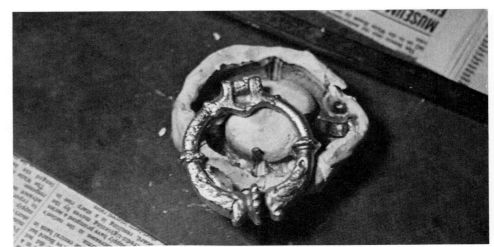

The casting is removed from the impression.

nique to cast new versions out of lead. The copper had worn off the old cast iron in certain places. By first painting the lead castings black and then using copper enamel, I was able to duplicate the finish to the extent that visitors are now defied to tell the difference between the originals and the reproductions.

Lost Wax?

The lost wax process is used to cast small metal objects, particularly jewelry. A number of texts are available dealing with this subject, and so a detailed treatment will not be given here. The tech-

nique is not especially useful in antique restoration, because it is necessary to reproduce an already available item three-dimensionally in a piece of wax. Of course, two molds can be made, one for each half of an article, and then those molds used to cast wax. The two wax halves are fit together and finished into a three-dimensional replica of the item. Additional channels are added in wax from small segments of the item to other small segments to insure that there will be a way for metal to flow in the casting, and that metal will be available to all extremities of the article. The

After: The reproduction is finished and appropriately affixed.

item is then cast into a chunk of plaster, being sure that two wax extremities are available to the periphery of the plaster mold.

After the plaster is cured, the mold is placed in an oven and heated until all the wax has melted. Be sure to place the item so that the molten wax will run free of the plaster. Molten metal is then poured into one opening and air escapes through the other opening. After the metal fills the entire mold, it is allowed to cool. The plaster is then broken away and a three-dimensional replica of the original item has been made of metal. The additional channels that were added to facilitate the flow of molten metal are cut away, and the item is finished by appropriate filing.

Polyester Resin

Polyester resin is a clear plastic liquid that becomes solid through interaction with a catalyst. A few drops of another liquid facilitates the chemical hardening of the polyester resin. Dyes are available to color it any shade desired, either in a transparent or opaque form. In fact, one coloring agent will render the polyester resin iridescent and duplicate the mother-of-pearl effect. Therefore, this material is useful in duplicating the effect if mother-of-pearl cannot be found. Polyester resin can be cast and then cut, sanded and polished to any desired shape and size within certain limits. Castings less than one-eighth inch thick take a very long time to cure, if they cure at all. Castings thicker than two inches sometimes pose problems in curing because of nonhomogeneity of the curing process. Curing produces heat which, in turn, hastens curing of adjacent sections. If one area is heated or cooled greatly relative to an adjacent area, strains may be set up and warping or cracking can result. The instructions on the container should be suitable to begin experimentation with this substance, and experience should be the guide in all subsequent projects.

Imagination is the only limiting factor in what can be done with this material. It can be made to look like marble and even ivory. But, remember that it is merely a plastic and should be treated like plastic. During its curing, the material also produces noxious fumes and presents a fire hazard, so it should, therefore, be used only in a well-ventilated area.

MOLD APPENDIX*

Polyform is available from:
Polyform Products Company
Schiller Park, Illinois
60176

Polyester casting resin is available from a number of sources, but one brand name is called Clear Cast and is manufactured by American Handicrafts Company. Their General Offices are located in Fort Worth, Texas, but they have retail stores in most major cities across the country.

Alginate can be obtained through dental supply houses under the name Jeltrate. One manufacturing company is the
L. D. Caulk Company,
Milford, Delaware
19963.

Alginate casting material, under the trade name Mix-A-Mold, is distributed by:
American Art Clay Company, Inc.
4717 West 16th Street
Indianapolis, Indiana
46222.

Sculptamold is also available from American Art Clay Company, Incorporated.

Plaster hardener is no longer available, but can be made by mixing craft glue with water before adding to dry plaster.

Liquid rubber mold-making material is available in the red form from:
Bersted's Hobby Craft, Inc.
Monmouth, Illinois.

Liquid rubber mold-making material in the white form, under the trade name Mold Tex, is available from American Handicrafts.

Various rubber for making molds are available from:
Deep Flex Plastic Molds, Inc.
Fort Worth, Texas
76110

They have both a shrinking and a non-shrinking variety called "Mold-Lene" which is available in gallon quantities only.

*Almost all of the above materials are available from local hobby or craft supply stores. If they cannot be secured there, write to the manufacturer for information where they can be obtained.

CHAPTER V

HOW TO BUILD UP YOUR BUST AND OTHERWISE KEEP YOUR MARBLES (MARBLE)

The wide use of marble as a structural material and medium for the decorative arts began several thousand years ago in ancient Greece. Far before the dawn of modern technology, the Greeks excavated, transported, cut, sculpted and polished great stone slabs into temples and statues, many of which have lasted until today. Gods, goddesses and athletes were the subjects of most Greek statues. Since this book deals with modern techniques utilized to restore old artifacts, it is interesting to note that it is also modern technology that has brought about the deterioration and even destruction of many treasures that have lasted scores of centuries.

A case in point can be exemplified by the Greek Parthenon which was begun in 447 B.C. The Parthenon is chiefly constructed of marble on the Acropolis at Athens. It was built as the chief temple for the Goddess Athena. The Parthenon is believed to have remained intact as built by the ancient Greeks until about the 5th century A.D., when it was transformed into a church dedicated to St. Sophia. In the following century, it was dedicated to the Virgin Mother of God. During this time certain alterations took place that did involve some damage to the original sculpture; which might be expected since the character of the old Greek art was definitely not Christian in nature. In the middle of the 15th century, Athens was captured by the Turks and the Parthenon was converted into a mosque.

The building remained in an essentially unaltered state until the fourth quarter of the 17th century, when the Turks converted the ancient temple into a powder magazine. During a bombardment by the Venetian army in 1687, a shell caused an explosion that blew out the middle of the temple. In the ensuing years, what remained of the building slowly deteriorated and the art work was sent to England in 1816. Now, much of that work can be found in the British Museum, the Louvre and other museums. Despite the weather, the wars and the looting, the Parthenon still stands in Greece as a symbol of an ancient culture. The greatest present threat to the survival of this masterpiece is air pollution. As you will see later in this chapter, marble will dissolve under the influence of even weak acids. Acid mist in the air pollution caused by industry and traffic in the vicinity of what remains of the Parthenon, has caused the marble to deteriorate considerably. Although the structure has been partially dismantled, dismembered and bombarded over the centuries, the greatest threat to its survival is the direct deterioration of the substance of its artistry.

Going back to ancient history, we can find the origins of many of the subjects of Victorian statuary. When the Romans conquered the Greeks, they not only moved hundreds of marble and bronze statues to Rome for garden decorations, but also brought along many Greek artists who were employed to instruct Roman artists in the techniques of sculpture. Although many of the Roman works were copies of Greek masterpieces of mythological origin, a number of works depicting Roman dignitaries were also produced. After the decline of the Roman Empire and the lack of artistic activity through the Dark Ages, we find

A renewed interest in Roman archaeology during the 19th century inspired the creation of marble statuary fashioned after mythological characters.

An oval marble-top table.

sculpture emerging with Christianity as its significant theme. Characters from the New and Old Testaments were recreated in marble from the 12th century through the Renaissance. The culmination of talent and craftsmanship throughout this period is probably exemplified by Michelangelo's Pieta.

Michelangelo's genius inspired him to begin a new period in art—baroque. During this period, we find little regard for marble as a fragile stone. We find deep undercutting in three-dimensionality to the point where we may no longer see a stone representation, but rather the subject of the artistry itself. We also find exaggerated decorations and style for the sake of style, with no regard for embellishments in relation to human proportions.

A renewed interest in Roman archaeology during the latter part of the 19th century inspired a new period called Neoclassicism. Excavations from Pompeii provided an inspiration to once again recreate figures from the mythological past. These interests continued into Victorian Europe and America, where we also find sculpture of prominent heads of state. As affluence broke away from the dominion of monarchies to the realm of industrialists, we also find created in marble the busts of their loved ones and family members.

Besides being a material for conveying artistic imagery and constructing monuments during all these years, marble also found its way into incorporation as parts of furniture. When Napoleon conquered Europe, he instructed his architects to design for him a new style

of furniture befitting someone of his rank. These architects found themselves recreating the regal characteristics of the empires before him. Marble increasingly became a commonplace adornment of furniture until the middle of the Victorian era, when new technology made it possible for people of even modest means to purchase stylish marble-topped parlor and bedroom furniture.

Getting To Know The Patient

Now that we know the origins of the use of marble as an artistic medium, and the chronology of the manner in which it was used, it is time to study the physiology of marble as a stone and medium in some modest detail so that we have some insights into the precautions that must be taken to preserve and repair antiques made from this marvelous stone. Marble is classed as a metamorphic stone whose origin is limestone. Limestone was formed millions of years ago from the debris of animal skeletons, shells and coral that was built up over periods of many years from sediment in areas where these animals thrived. Most limestone deposits are rich in the fossilized remains of these animals.

The technical term for limestone is calcium carbonate. Calcium carbonate is almost pure white in color, but limestone deposits may be many different colors depending upon the types of impurities that find their way into the calcium carbonate. For instance, iron oxide (common rust) can give the limestone a reddish or brownish tone. Other impurities can color the stone green, yellow, gray, pink, a cream color, or even black. The primary uses of limestone in our modern society are as crushed rock for rural roads and to manufacture other materials such as concrete. This latter material is formed by subjecting limestone to extreme heat, thereby driving off some of the carbon dioxide from the calcium carbonate, yielding calcium oxides. This material is also called lime, and when mixed with sandy clay and burned in a kiln, forms the material commonly known as portland cement.

Limestone is subject to chemical and physical changes under common geological stimuli. Marble is formed when limestone is subjected to extreme heat or pressure or both. The material crystallizes and takes on a translucent character. Under microscopic examination, particles of marble with few impurities might appear to be transparent; that is, they allow most of the light incident upon them to pass through with little reflection. Material that is opaque in nature does not allow light to pass through at all. Translucency is the property of a material to allow some but not all light to pass through it. Marble has a translucency and appearance of depth all its own because light incident upon it passes through many of the crystals in the outer extremities of the rock to be reflected at the surfaces of small crystals inside. So, although we can touch only the surface of a piece of marble, the light we see that forms the image in our eye is reflected not only at the surface of the marble but up to approximately one-half inch under the surface. This translucent character of marble is its most difficult property to reproduce, and is oftentimes not attempted even in museum-quality restorations.

Marble as we understand it, then, is the compaction of many small crystals of limestone that are sufficiently close together to allow the material to be polished. Marbles may be found in many places throughout the world, including Italy, France, Germany, South

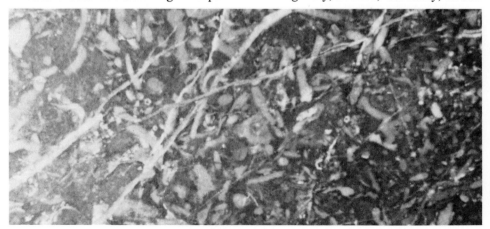

Impurities resulting from the deposits of other minerals give grain and color to marble.

America and the United States. Marbles of various geographic locations have become known for the different types of impurities and, therefore, colors and characteristics imparted to them in these locales. Many of the buildings in Carthage and Rome were built of marble that was quarried in Algeria. This stone has been called onyx marble, because it is clouded with yellow and brown to produce a very rich effect. Carrara marble is commonly understood to be the purest marble and is colored snow white, although it may contain an occasional vein of another material such as quartz. This marble is found in the Alps and had not been discovered at the time of the Romans, but was employed by Michelangelo in some of his finest works. Carrara marble has generally been the choice of most artists for stone sculpture.

Much of the white-veined marble that we find common to the better pieces of Victorian furniture was brought out of quarries in Italy during the 19th century. Thus, it is very common to find Victorian furniture of typically American style, made of native American walnut or even oak, topped by a piece of imported and exotic Italian marble. It is not likely that the demand for Italian marble decreased in the United States in the latter part of the 19th century, but rather economics dictated the marble on a lot of American furniture of the Eastlake style. This marble from the central United States is sometimes called "Napoleon gray", and at times has a pinkish-gray cast to it. It appears to be more of a granite than a marble.

In ancient times, the term "alabaster" was used interchangeably for "marble". It refers to crystallized and compacted calcium carbonate, just as the term marble is applied today. However, in modern times, the term "alabaster" is applied to a different mineral called gypsum or calcium sulphate. Marble cannot be scratched with the fingernail, but alabaster can. It is usually a yellowish, pink or white color that has the advantage of not being influenced by acids as marble is. Alabaster is found chiefly in deposits under the beds of salt lakes. Alabaster has also been used for statuary and the decorative arts, although it has not been employed as a construction material. By subjecting it to high temperatures as in boiling water, it can partially dehydrate and take on a more opaque appearance similar to marble.

The techniques that will be described in the remainder of this chapter with regard to marble can be applied, in many cases with a great degree of success, to alabaster. Common sense should dictate how these techniques, when applied to marble, can be altered to provide the greatest success with alabaster. Since this book is not concerned with ancient antiquities, but rather artifacts of the 19th century, we will not discuss techniques necessary to remove incrustations or other problems associated with the burial or aging of pieces of marble over centuries. We will be concerned with care and restoration of certain marble works of art and pieces of marble associated with furniture.

When An Ambulance Isn't Available

When we purchase a piece of marble statuary or a piece of marble-topped furniture away from home, our first concern is to get it to our residence without causing any more undue damage or additional wear than it has already encountered. Since, in general, we can't afford to purchase an extra airline ticket for our marble statue to accompany us on an airplane, or an ambulance isn't available with a bed so we can strap down our piece of delicate marble for long distance transportation, we have to resort to standard ways of getting it from one place to another. For pieces of flat marble, it is important to remember that marble is heavy yet relatively soft. It is brittle. It will chip. It will crack, and may ultimately break if subjected to undue stress. Flat slabs should be transported, if at all possible, on edge. Since most marble slabs are less than one inch thick, the marble's weight on edge would have to be enough to break through many inches of material, instead of just one if the slab were lying flat. It is not always possible, however, to transport a slab in an upright position in an automobile. If it is absolutely necessary to place the slab in a flat position, care should be taken to make sure that no obstructions, points, ridges or other protrusions are underneath the slab. Blankets or foam rubber should be placed under the slab so that the inevitable vibrations in transportation will be spread across the greatest possible surface area to minimize the impact upon any small area.

Many antiques are bought within a few miles of home and it is not practical to crate and transport marble slabs for those short distances. I have moved slabs of marble on scores of occasions over several hundred miles and have yet to lose a patient. If more than one slab must be transported at the same time and it is not practical to put the marble on edge, no two heavy pieces of marble should be placed one on top of the other, but rather spread out over a flat surface with padding as described above. In emergencies, newspaper in layers of about one-eighth inch thick can be used. When pieces of marble may be only a few square inches in area, they may be transported with more ease in almost any position, but should be well insulated and padded from each other in order to avoid unnecessary abrasions.

Transporting marble statuary is a bit more difficult. One sure way is to hold a 100-pound bust in your lap. But a bust on the lap has a tendency to put one's legs to sleep. In case of an unfortunate accident, a bust in the mouth may also be very uncomfortable. If transportation over a short distance is all that is necessary, the statue may be wrapped in blankets and propped from underneath by soft but firm pieces of plastic, wood or foam rubber, in such a way that it will not vibrate or rotate or rest with any of its weight upon any sharp places or extremities.

Ancient techniques of marble sculpture dictated that the shape and characteristics of the stone be taken into account before any sculpture was performed. That means that the sculpture could probably be rolled down a hill without suffering any substantial damage other than abrasions and minor scratches. However, Michelangelo started the school that continued through the 19th century, in which the artist tended to forget that he was carving the resemblance of some familiar form in a stone that had less than familiar strength. Although this new technique was fortunate for the sake of art, it was unfortunate for the sake of transporting the work of art.

The only sure way to transport a piece of marble statuary any distance, without personal care, is to crate it in a strong wooden box. The statue or bust is placed in the crate with wooden braces on all sides, bolstered against substantial areas to prevent any movement whatsoever. These wooden braces should be covered with cotton and tissue paper to prevent any direct abrasion or staining of the marble. It is important to try to brace the marble along all flat sides so as to spread out over the largest possible area any concussion that may be encountered. The fit of such bracing should be so snug as to prevent even the slightest movement of the stone.

After the last brace is put in place, a small wedge, also covered with cotton and tissue paper, should be tapped into position to make sure that all is as snug as possible. This wedge and all braces should be screwed into place to insure that none of these supporting members is jarred loose. Straw is not suitable packing material because it may contain organic compounds or mold that could attack the marble under some circumstances. Likewise, newspaper is not a suitable packing material for marble because the inks used may, on occasion, stain the marble.

If crated marble is stored for any length of time prior to transportation, the crate should be disassembled and checked to make sure that none of the packing material has warped, stretched or contracted in any manner that would allow the statuary to vibrate in its container.

Marble Hygiene

Unless you are going to keep your piece of marble statuary in the sterile atmosphere of an operating room, it is most likely that you will, at some time or other, have to face removing accumulated dust from the object. Because a cloth has a tendency to rub dirt into the porous surface of marble, it is recommended that a feather duster or camel's hair paintbrush (clean and unused, of course) be used for this task. Flat slabs on furniture that have been protected with a wax finish can be dusted with a cloth just like a piece of wooden furniture. If, however, it has not yet been polished and finished, the brushing method is preferred.

Because a piece of marble may be unusually soiled, it may be necessary to wash it as opposed to merely dusting it. This can be done safely, but a number of precautions must be taken. First of all, remember that marble is a composite of compressed pieces of limestone that have been crystallized into tiny crystals called calcite. Calcite is found in many different crystalline shapes, and although these crystals lie close enough together to allow us to polish the marble to a high

A feather duster or camel's hair brush should be used to keep marble sculpture clean.

Many marble objects such as this pedestal can be disassembled into a number of pieces.

The several parts of the pedestal.

Marble should be washed with a mild cleanser and distilled water in a plastic tub.

shine, enough space is left between the crystals to leave the marble porous. Most liquids put on marble can penetrate for some distance below the surface. It is extremely important to avoid even the mildest acids in polishing marble. Acid tends to eat away at the finished portions of the marble and make it additionally porous.

If the marble happens to be stored outside or in an unheated area for any length of time, moisture may accumulate in acid-damaged areas to expand when subjected to frost and perhaps permanently damage an otherwise good piece of marble. Our first tendency, then, would be to use clean water without the use of any additional chemicals. But in many areas of the country, water may be found to be slightly acidic. A small amount of ammonia or alkali added to tap water would neutralize any slight acidity, but we also have to worry about other chemicals and trace materials found in tap water that may have a tendency to stain the marble. It is very common to find iron in water from many of our water supplies and this iron may, over time, have a tendency to stain a piece of white marble red or brown. Therefore, the safest step is to use distilled water.

If you use distilled water, it is important to use a container that won't contaminate the water. Therefore, an iron bucket or galvanized pail is not the appropriate receptacle. A plastic bucket or glass container, however, is wholly acceptable. A small amount of soft soap or detergent can be dissolved in a comfortable quantity of warm distilled water, and a few drops of ammonia added to this mixture is all needed to remove most dirt and grime. Many all-purpose cleaners found in grocery stores these days, when diluted with distilled water, are also acceptable. The marble should be washed a small area at a time with a soft cloth or brush of synthetic or natural bristles (provided that they are softer than the marble and will not scratch it). If nylon or plastic bristles are used, try rubbing an unimportant section of the marble first to make sure that they will not scratch.

Statuary should be washed in small segments beginning at the top and working down the piece. After washing a small area and rinsing that same small area, it should be immediately dried to remove any residue of the soap solution that might remain and have a tendency to collect dust. Commercial marble cleaners are available that are soap-free and will not form any undesirable residue or scum buildup. One such product is produced by the Carthage Marble Corporation in Carthage, Missouri. After a piece of marble has been cleaned, it can be rinsed with distilled water over its entirety, and dried.

Correcting A Bad Complexion

One of the first tendencies in trying to remove a stain of any nature from an object would be to consider mild household substances that we use in other situations for stain removal. Two substances in common use for certain cleaning situations are vinegar and lemon juice. **DO NOT** use these on marble. Vinegar contains acetic acid and lemon juice contains citric acid. Both of these will damage marble. If either of these liquids, or any fruit juice for that matter, is accidently spilled on unprotected marble, immediately wash the surface with a dilute solution of ammonia and water to neutralize the acid. Then use plain distilled water to remove any residue that might remain. Too much ammonia or any other alkaline material used to neutralize the acid may react with impurities in the marble to produce some other discolorations.

Although we may never remove all stains in marble, there are some that can be taken out without much difficulty. Before attempting to remove any stain, examine the marble carefully to make sure that the stain in not a natural pigment of the marble. All marbles are not pure white in color and many have a cream-colored hue. Do not try to remove this natural color from the marble in an attempt to turn it into something that it is not.

Some forms of pigmented grime that have been deposited simply by scraping with a razor blade or fine abrasive. Care should be taken not to abrade the marble but only the built-up layer of pigmented substance.

A liquid rubber can be used in an attempt to remove some of the substance from below the surface in the pores of the stone. Such rubber is bound in an ammoniated solution and used by hobbyists to make molds for casting plaster. One such compound is called Liquid Latex and manufactured by Mold-Tex. It can be purchased from many of the American Handicraft stores or other hobby stores across the country. This mixture is white when wet and dries to a yellowish brown when cured. Do not use the red material called Liquid Rubber which contains a pigment of its own that may stain the marble.

A brush can be used to paint on the white rubber compound. It is then allowed to cure. A thin coating of only about 1/32 of an inch is all that is necessary. The material adheres to itself and may adhere to the substance which has gone into the pores of the marble to stain slightly below the surface. When the rubberized compound is peeled off in a layer, hopefully it will bring some of the pigmented material with it. This procedure can be repeated several times in hope that more of the pigmented substance will be pulled loose from beneath the outer plane of the marble. This method, however, will not remove any stain that has penetrated below the surface layer of pores.

If whatever caused the stain is a greasy or oily substance, such as butter, there is a chance to remove some of that material by applying an organic solvent that will put some of the staining material into solution. Then you must remove that solution before it penetrates any deeper into the marble. One way to do this is to place some lighter fluid (benzine) over the stained surface and put some blotting paper over this area to soak up the solution of lighter fluid and staining material. This technique is best used on a flat slab that can be turned upside down with the blotting paper underneath, hoping that gravity will help remove the solution from the marble rather than cause it to penetrate further. Use of this technique on an irregular surface like statuary is questionable, because it may remove some of the exterior stain and decrease its intensity, while at the same time allowing some of the stain to penetrate further.

Stains sometimes may be caused by the growth of mold, fungus or algae on the marble. In this case, treatment with an ammonia solution can often correct the problem. Spraying with a disinfectant, such as Lysol, may also help, and spraying with formalin should also kill any such growth and facilitate its removal. Any growth of this nature will be near the surface of the marble and will not have penetrated deeply. A simple washing or the use of the above described rubber peeling technique may prove helpful.

In some cases where the stain has penetrated no more than a very small fraction of an inch below the surface, but out of reach of the methods described above, it may be necessary to grind the surface of a slab down and repolish it to be rid of the stain. This should only be done if you cannot live with the stain. Using abrasives for polishing will be described later in this chapter. On a piece of white statuary, only damage and loss of value to the figure will result from grinding or polishing. Therefore, applying a cosmetic in the form of a little chalk dust may be appropriate to cover a stained area to make it less obvious.

Warping

Upon occasion, marble has been known to warp. Most notably, marble used on fireplaces or mantles, when subjected to extreme heat, may bend in one direction or the other depending upon the alignment of the calcite crystals within the marble. The calcite crystals will expand varying amounts in different directions even with the same amount of heat. There is no known way to remove the warp in marble that has been damaged by some form of high temperature. I have heard of marble that had sagged in the center during its storage in damp areas between two supports. Although the cause of this type of warping is not explicitly known, the only suggestion I can make is to hold the marble in similar conditions, but flipped over so that the problem has a chance to correct itself. Another solution might be simply to buy a new piece of marble.

Granulation

Marble exposed to extreme heat can dehydrate and take on the consistency of a sugar cube. Such damage is extremely serious and impossible to satisfactorily repair. If the marble piece is of very high value, it might be worth an attempt to consolidate the material so that it does not further decompose or fall apart. To do this, slightly heat the stone slowly so as not to cause any thermal shock that would crack the marble. High temperatures should be avoided. The stone should be allowed to heat throughout to the point that it is warm to the touch.

A solution of paraffin dissolved in ether can then be applied carefully in hope that the paraffin will penetrate deeply enough to consolidate the impaired area on hardening. Of course, you cannot use an open flame to heat the stone or any other extreme direct heat method because of the extreme inflammability of ether. As the ether evaporates, a more concentrated solution of paraffin can be applied until pure liquid paraffin may be brushed on the surface. Be sure to use appropriate ventilation to avoid the toxic danger of inhaling ether. The consolidated piece is then allowed to cool and the excess paraffin is removed. Most likely there will be a color difference between the area treated and the healthy marble. Colored powdered chalk may be used to minimize any color difference.

Repairing Broken Marble

Small pieces of broken marble or chips may be replaced on the main body of a slab or artifact by very carefully applying epoxy to the broken piece and fitting it to the main section. The secret of performing this task successfully is insuring that all dirt and foreign matter has been removed from the chip or broken piece so that it will fit perfectly into the void that was created when the piece of marble was broken. In addition, it is extremely important to remove all dirt from the edges so that the crack will not show on the surface of the marble after the repair is made. This point is very important and should be emphasized once again; take much care to clean, as described earlier, the edges of the two pieces of marble to be joined together so that, at most, only a hairline crack is visible and the break is not obvious. Many pieces of marble have small hairline cracks inherent in the marble as a natural flaw and, therefore,

small cracks visible due to a repair will not be obvious provided that the edge is cleaned appropriately before repair and excess glue is not allowed to harden along the seam of the crack while drying.

Any appropriate epoxy glue is acceptable for this job. Most epoxy resins will have a label on the package indicating that the epoxy is appropriate for use on marble. On pieces that have been repaired earlier, not using the above procedure, and a seam is outstanding, it may be appropriate to grind away the uplifted edge of the section of marble which stands higher than the other if the glue cannot be dissolved and the piece removed. Fill any void left with wax or paraffin to smooth the contour. This process will be described later in this chapter.

If the marble has been broken into two or more large pieces (weighing more than about one pound each), then it may become necessary to insert a dowel or two to add enough strength to the piece to prevent rebreakage. The appropriate process for doweling is described in the chapter concerning doweling of wood. The only difference here is that you must use stone drilling bits to drill holes in marble, and the dowels must necessarily be metal rather than wood. Steel or iron dowels should not be used, because moisture which might be absorbed through the marble can cause the dowel to rust and stain the marble from the inside out. Instead, a metal not subject to moisture deterioration should be used, such as stainless steel, or perhaps even aluminum if the pieces to be joined are thick enough to use a strong rod.

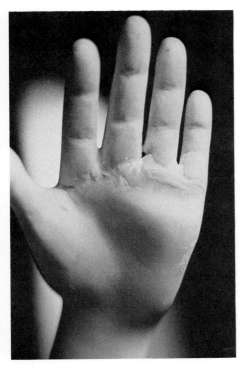

Before: The fingers on this marble hand were repaired with plaster by an unknown repairman.

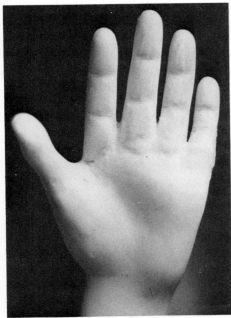

After: Wax has been used to conceal the repair.

Concealing Cracks And Filling Small Voids With Plastic Surgery

Cracks may be concealed and small voids filled-in with wax or paraffin. These materials may be colored with dyes that can be purchased in most hobby shops, or made very inexpensively by shaving off small sections of crayon a little at a time into a melted wax mixture until an appropriate color is reached. One of the secrets for reproducing the texture of marble is to add an appropriate base agent, such as chalk or plaster of paris or some other available ground material, to the wax while it is hot to produce a granulated yet smooth texture after it is dry. The purpose of using wax is to preserve the translucency of the object being repaired. If the voids are filled carefully, excess wax can be scraped away or carved on a piece of statuary (or simply sanded and polished if a flat surface), so that it is difficult to tell that the void is not a natural imperfection in the marble.

If you are lucky enough to be able to color the wax correctly, it is possible that a repair can go unnoticed. It is important to experiment with different mixtures of wax, coloring and base powders to try to match the consistency and color of the marble being repaired. Small amounts of wax can be heated in a small container. When the mixture is melted, varying amounts of these different materials can be mixed and compared, only after hardening, to the marble that is being prepared for repair. Patience is the key to success. Document trials and errors to help "zero-in" on the appropriate mixture.

Old obvious repairs can be concealed using wax mixtures without disturbing the soundness of the repair.

Wax may not be appropriate if greater strength or durability is required, or in a warm climate. Then repairs with plaster of paris are acceptable. However, when using plaster, it is impossible to reproduce the translucency of the marble. Thin areas with white surrounding the marble will be apparent if repaired with plaster, and these types of repairs should be attempted only if the owner will be satisfied with small opaque sections in an otherwise translucent piece (many museums are satisfied with plaster repairs).

A substitute for plaster of paris is a modeling compound manufactured under the brand name of Liquitex. This compound is produced by mixing together an emulsion of some type of resin with ground marble. Although one might presume that the ground marble adds the effect of the translucency to the mixture, it does not. It has the advantage over plaster of paris of taking longer to set up and may be applied in small amounts without having the mess of mixing it with water. Both plaster of paris and the Liquitex modeling compound can be colored with food coloring. Liquitex compound has the additional advantage over plaster of being appropriate for colored marble, even though extensive experimentation in coloring the compound will be necessary prior to its application. It is also important to allow the compound to cure with its coloring before being satisifed that the color will match, because the

69

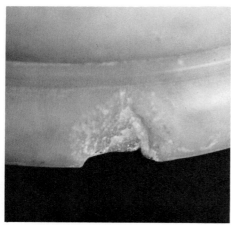

A large chip in the edge of a marble pedestal.

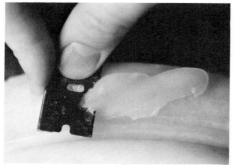

Different color waxes are melted together to match the area being repaired. When cooled, the repair is trimmed so that it blends with its surroundings.

The nose on this face was broken at the tip. Modeling compound has been sculpted to replace it.

coloration changes as the compound hardens.

If the marble is slightly yellowish in color, dental plaster from a dental supply house or perhaps your neighboring dentist, can be mixed with plaster of paris to provide a yellowish tone. Plaster of paris usually is pure white, while dental plaster is generally yellow. The dental plaster also has the characteristic of curing much harder than plaster of paris. Chemicals that add additional strength to plaster can be purchased from a hobby shop. Another compound that is yellow in color and can be purchased from most hardware stores, perhaps even in grocery stores, is called water putty. This material is essentially a yellow plaster that dries with amazing strength.

If small areas are required to be repaired, the putty or plaster can be mixed to the consistency of clay and applied, allowed to cure, and then trimmed, sanded and polished to the appropriate finish. If large sections need to be repaired, it may be easier to build a dike around the area to be repaired with clay that adheres to the main piece and the plaster poured into the dike. Of course, you have to have some skill at carving or sculpting once the material has hardened in order to bring it back to the shape of the marble piece being repaired. For a flat slab, this simply means skill at sanding. Statuary requires some additional skills.

Some synthetic marbles are made by mixing some sort of plastic resin with ground marble or other ground material. One trade name for large slabs of this material is Corfam. Corolay of California also casts this mixture into elaborate and artistic plastic-stone boxes and other decorations. Polyester resin can be purchased from hobby shops almost anywhere to cast clear plastic paperweights and similar paraphernalia. The liquid plastic is poured into a mixing container, a few drops of a catalyst are added, any other materials that might be appropriate, such as coloring agent or a medium to simulate the texture of marble (like plaster, sand or ground marble), mixed together, and then poured into a mold. It is necessary to dike the area on a marble object prior to pouring so that the resin will not run all over. A form of paste used to be manufactured that could serve a similar purpose, but it is no longer available. One brand of this type of resin is called Clear Cast. It is important when casting this material to make sure that the object upon which new synthetic marble is going to be added is in a position such that the resin may be poured up to the required depth and thickness without spilling. The thicker the mold, the shorter the curing time and the less catalyst required.

Some polyester resins will yellow with age and should be avoided. If these are the only ones available, a slight anticipation for this change in color can be made. Using too much catalyst will cause the plastic to shrink unnecessarily and form a harder plastic that may pull its edges away from seams where the material is cast. Although you might anticipate that shrinkage would cause a problem on curing, it has not proved to be an obstacle in my restoration ventures.

The top of the hat on this bust was missing and was replaced by a polyester resin.

A close-up of the hat reveals the repair. The area below the dotted line is marble. The area above the dotted line is polyester resin.

Some years ago, a newlywed friend of mine walked into a laboratory, in which I was working, with a piece of pie that his new wife had made for him. It was apple pie and since this was the first time she had cooked for him during their married life, he wanted to preserve the piece of pie for posterity. We decided to make a paperweight by casting the piece of pie in a block of solid plastic. Unfortunately, the mold we made had a slight defect that allowed air to get in through one corner of the casting to the pie in the center. After a few weeks, the pie began to decay inside the paperweight, but my friend was unmoved by this and continued to boast to other acquaintances that the paperweight on his desk contained the first piece of pie that his wife had ever baked for him.

Polishing

The only piece of antique furniture that has come down to me through the family is a three-drawer marble-topped chest which belonged to Grandma Polka. Grandpa Polka purchased the chest of drawers from a used furniture dealer in 1905. The three-drawer Victorian walnut chest had a coat of paint over it, including a coat of paint on the marble. Grandpa fixed it by adding a new coat of paint. When I finally talked Grandma out of the chest, it was a real challenge to restore its original appearance. A picture of it sometime later surprised Grandma, because she had never seen the bare wood herself.

So far as the marble was concerned, the first step was to scrape the aged paint off by delicately shaving it with a single edge razor blade. That seemed

to work well, but needless to say, there wasn't much shine left on the marble when the task was completed. Unfortunately, using a stripper would allow the pigment to go deeper into the marble and, therefore, had to be avoided.

The next job was to decide either to take the marble slab to a professional stone finisher, who would have charged about $1.50 per square foot for polishing, or to do it by hand. Since this was a family piece, I decided to do the job personally. For this purpose, tack a piece of emery cloth of no less than 220 grit around the bottom of a flat board that more than extends across the width of the piece. The board insures that all polishing done is absolutely flat. In long, even strokes in one direction and then at right angles to it (not moving in circles), move the emery cloth on the board back and forth across the marble surface. When it has an even but most likely dull sheen to it, it is time to switch to a finer grade of emery cloth. Four-hundred grit is the next grade to use, then 500. Water can be used with these grades to keep the emery cloth from loading, which would prevent the necessary cutting action. The slurry formed can easily be wiped off the edges of the marble.

The final step is to use 600-mesh emery cloth without wetting the surface of the marble. Using water with this fine polishing cloth will cause the cloth to plane over the thin film of water and prevent any cutting action. Many would think that the next logical step would be to use a powdered abrasive such as rottenstone, but my experience indicates that rottenstone will produce a duller

Before: Grandma Polka's chest of drawers complete with painted marble. A razor blade was used to scrape the paint to create the stripe in the middle.

An ogee edge.

After: Grandma Polka's chest of drawers after restoration.

finish than 600-mesh emery cloth. However, you could use an appropriate powdered abrasive of tin oxide applied and rubbed in a circular motion with a felt pad.

Apply a sealer finish when polishing is complete. Compounds are made by commercial firms for this purpose. They protect the marble from stains and also give it a high polish. Some restorers have recommended the use of lacquer on interior marble finishes, but this practice can cause problems when the lacquer begins to chip or flake. Any high-grade, hard paste wax should serve the purpose.

Cutting and Grinding

Professionals cut marble with abrasive wheels and cooling liquids, or with wires containing abrasives on their surface. But surprisingly enough, for small jobs, you can use a band saw with a wide-toothed and wide-pitched blade. You must be careful to feed the marble very slowly, and have a piece of wood underneath the marble to prevent chipping on the bottom side. Abrasive sabre saw blades, hacksaw blades and circular saw blades can also be bought to cut marble, but they do have a tendency to wear out before too long. The edges of a slab of marble can be beveled easily by using a belt sander, beginning with a coarse grade of sandpaper and progressively working to finer and finer grades. It will probably be necessary to finish the polishing by hand. But, fancy edges such as the "ogee", which is a typically concave followed by a convex curve over the edge of a piece of Victorian marble, can be done with ease only with the equipment of a professional stone-cutter.

Removing Scratches

Shallow scratches can be removed by using the techniques suggested above for polishing, only utilizing them in a localized sense. Use only the roughest grade of sandpaper necessary to remove the scratch first, then follow with progressively finer grades of emery cloth and eventually polish with tin oxide.

CHAPTER VI

PAINTED TONGUES AND NON-RELATED PROBLEMS (OIL PAINTINGS)

The easiest way to avoid a painted tongue is not to put the brush in your mouth. However, most problems involving the art of painting do not lie in preventing a painted surface, but rather how to preserve the paint as it was placed by the original artist. Some paintings that are thousands of years old, made by cavemen on stone walls, call still be found throughout Asia, Europe and America. The paintings that have been preserved, with the natural berry-colored pigment formulated by prehistoric artists, were lucky enough to have been placed in environments suitable for such preservation. We do not find paintings in other areas simply because they were either never there or the ravages of time have brought about their demise. As civilization progressed, man learned that he could put his impressions on some medium that was more suitable for placing in his living room than on a stone wall. Our objective, therefore, is to find ways to conserve, prepare and preserve the media chosen by yesterday's masters. The problem is complicated by the alterations which we have made and will make to the future environment in which these media must exist.

Major schools of art with varying materials, techniques, styles and subject matter have prevailed from time-to-time in various locations throughout the world. The Flemish, the Dutch, the Germans, the Spanish, the Viennese and Florentines, the English, and others had well-established schools of art with a multitude of masters in each. Conserving paintings made in many of these schools can present problems that are beyond the scope of this book to deal with. The materials used by many of these masters would now be hundreds of years old, and can pose problems to which many other books must be devoted to solving. However, the paintings of approximately 100-years vintage, from the time of the Victorians, in general, pose less severe and less complicated problems. We will limit ourselves to these problems and their solutions.

Cleanliness Is Next To Godliness

Although it is always advantageous to prevent dirt and grime from contaminating the surface of a painting, it is not always in the best interest of either the painting itself or the art world to employ the first available mechanism to remove soil. It was not until the beginning of the 20th century that conserving and restoring art works was approached scientifically and methodically. Of course, as time progresses, old paintings become older, as well as new paintings becoming old, and more attention must be paid to these art works to prevent unnecessary deterioration. The standard primitive method of cleaning paintings over the past several hundred years has been simply to scrub them as any other piece of furniture, wall or floor would be scrubbed. The abrasive action of brushes and rough cloth over the years has caused pieces of paint to be ground away, never again to be replaced. Some old prescriptions for cleaning included scouring with such abrasive materials as sand. One method described in an old text reveals that a canvas painting should be washed with soap and water, then placed on edge and rinsed with a hard stream of urine until all the soap is removed.

Even today, there are many prescriptions for restoring color and resiliency of paintings by soaking them with linseed oil. Although the linseed oil can bring out the colors of various pigments, the result will be an eventual darkening of the entire painting as the oil darkens with age. At the same time, the oil has a tendency to pick up dirt and dust floating in the air and hold them on the surface of the painting, providing a greater challenge for future removal.

To properly restore paintings, it is necessary to have some knowledge of physics, chemistry and art. Chemistry is necessary to understand the workings of time and age within the painting itself, as well as to understand the effects of various chemicals and solvents that may be applied to the painting in an attempt to restore it. A knowledge of physics aids in some of the analysis to determine how a painting may have been altered over the years, and it also helps us to understand the workings of nature that may bring about deterioration of a work of art, even if undisturbed by man. The knowledge of art, including technique and style, is useful to identify areas of the painting that have been altered, as well as to help restore a painting, using as close as possible the technique of the original artist.

Cuts And Bruises

Occasionally, a painting on canvas is accidentally hit by the handle of a broom, a baseball or the corner of some sharp object and a dent results that makes the

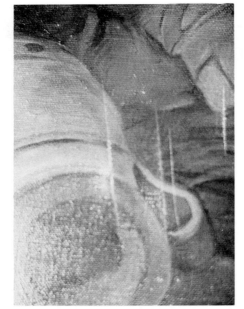

These scratches were caused by bumping the painting against a sharp object.

painting unsightly. To remove the dent, the painting should be taken out of its frame and placed face down on a sheet of waxed paper, and the canvas then should be moistened from behind lightly —definitely not soaked. A blotter should be placed over the dent and weights placed on top of the blotter. The blotter should be replaced by another clean, dry blotter about every half-hour until it appears that no more moisture is being drawn from the canvas. As the moisture is removed, the canvas should shrink in the dented area and once again take on its original shape. The last blotter and its encumbering weights should remain in place overnight.

Occasionally, a rip or tear may result in the canvas from any number of accidental reasons. This rip or tear will require more masterful techniques (described later) than the simple removal of a dent, and should be bandaged temporarily pending some of the experience that can be gained later in this chapter. Use masking tape on the back of the canvas to keep the rip or cut from spreading. No adhesives should ever be placed on the front of the painting, because its removal may also take off some of the paint. In addition, chemicals in the adhesive, whether the tape is on the front or back of the painting, could eventually affect the pigments or resins. Therefore, such taping must be considered only a temporary measure.

Anatomy Of A Painting

During Victorian times, paints were placed on glass, wood, cardboard, canvas, metal and other substrates to hold the likeness or image which the

(A) Canvas, (B) size, (C) gesso, (D) paint, (E) varnish, (F) wax.

A stretcher is kept taut by wedges tapped into slots in its corners.

artist attempted to convey. In some cases, the choice of materials was a good one and the work of art has endured until today. In other instances, the choice was poor and perhaps the work of art has long since deteriorated. The most common, yet the most complicated restoration, involves paints placed on cloth. The knowledge and experience gained from understanding the problems of conserving these works of art can readily be transferred to dealing with paintings on other materials.

In this chapter, we will deal primarily with what has been referred to as "oil paintings". For the most part, these paintings have been placed on material that we commonly call canvas. Canvas can be made from cotton, hemp, jute or flax. Canvas made from flax is known as linen. Some Oriental paintings were put on silk. In addition, canvas was sometimes placed over cardboard to make a surface very convenient for the artist, but which causes special problems for future preservation and restoration. Eventually, the cardboard under the canvas will deteriorate and need to be removed so that the canvas on the surface can be restored and preserved. During the 19th century, the use of academy board, which is a form of pressed fiber, was also used and most likely will present significant restoration problems. However, most paintings of a quality worthy of the time and expense of restoration have been placed on canvas pulled tight over a frame called a stretcher.

A stretcher has four sides that more or less float over two wedges placed in each corner behind the mounted canvas.

The wedges, when tapped into the stretcher, put considerable tension on the canvas. In general, some water-soluble adhesive, such as rabbit skin glue, is painted over the surface of the canvas to size it. Some form of ground, such as zinc oxide and chalk or gesso, is applied to form a base on which to place the pigments. The painting operation itself may consist of one or more coats put on with a brush or spatula, or perhaps some even more exotic technique. After the painting had dried (at least we hope after it had dried), a varnish may have been placed over the surface of the paint. On some occasions, paintings were not varnished. Varnish, however, is desirable to finish any old painting and aids considerably in preserving the paint. Occasionally, paintings were waxed, either in place of varnish or on top of varnish, to give them a finish either to the liking of the artist or the owner of the painting.

Color

Paints are made up of pigments suspended in some form of bonding agent. This bonding agent can be an oil or a varnish, it can be made from egg yolk and water which is referred to as tempura, it can be a watercolor where the color is suspended in gum arabic, or color suspended in some synthetic substance such as an acrylic resin or polyvinyl acetate.

Color comes from pigments which, in general, are found in nature and can be either organic or inorganic. Blacks and browns in the past have been formed from the use of lamp black or derivatives of coal or tar. Various shades of yellow have been extruded from cattle urine, with variations in intensity depending upon the types of plants that had been fed to the cattle. A certain shade of red has been obtained from ground cochineal, which is composed of the dried bodies of the females of an insect that lives on cactus plants in tropical America.

Most inorganic pigments are composed of the oxides or sulfides of various metals. For instance, azure is made from copper carbonate, while a shade of red familar to many is made from rust or iron oxide. There are a number of sources for white, including zinc oxide and lead oxide.

Throughout history, depending upon the location and time of an artist, only certain combinations of these materials were available. The lack of discovery of certain chemical techniques for refining various pigments, the unavailability of natural resources, or simply the lack of discovery of the material greatly influenced the number of pigments available to the artist. One would definitely not expect to find the use of an acrylic resin in a Rembrandt masterpiece. Similarly, no European painting could have employed the use of cochineal before the discovery of the Americas. A chemical analysis of pigments, therefore, can help greatly to identify when and where a painting likely was done or, alternatively, when and where it could not have been done.

The resins used to bind pigments are, in general, refinements of other workings of nature. Shellac is a sticky substance produced by the lac bug. The substance is soluble in alcohol and has been used occasionally to make paints. Some soft resins are made from colophony, also called rosin, a residue remaining after distilling the turpentine obtained from various species of pines. Dammar is another soft resin obtained from trees in the East Indies which also has measurable durability. Copal is a fossil resin that can be mined and used to make varnish or paint. However, it darkens with age and is extremely hard and insoluble, posing significant problems for certain types of restoration.

Getting It Together

Consolidation is the term conservationists use to describe reattaching paint that is either in the process of falling off the canvas or already has done so. Paint can flake away from layers of paint beneath it or from the ground over the canvas for a number of reasons. In the restoration process, an adhesive first must be concocted to glue the flaking paint back to its substrate. One of the primary rules of restoring any art or antique work is not to do anything that cannot be undone. Experience has taught us that future generations may develop techniques more sophisticated than our own to do a better restoration job. The adhesive to use for flaking paint is comprised of 75 percent beeswax and 25 percent dammar resin or rosin. At times, I have found it difficult to locate dammar resin, but have always been able to find rosin. Chunks of rosin are placed in little cloth bags that baseball batters use to help keep their hands from slipping on the bat. Be sure to try a sporting goods store during or just prior to baseball season to get some rosin

78

A number of BB holes are obvious in the front of this painting.

From behind, a magnification shows how the threads from the support have been broken.

bags, which can be emptied and their contents used for a number of conservation projects. If the flaking is not very serious, the beeswax alone may be adhesive enough provided that extremely warm temperatures are not found in your location.

Use a sheet of mylar to insulate the flake of paint from the direct heat which is to be applied to it. A bit of wax or the adhesive should be melted and dripped behind the flaking paint. The use of a heated spatula is, in general, the method employed by many conservationists at this point, but I use a temperature-controlled soldering iron with a special spatula tip. The heated spatula or iron is placed over the mylar sheet or strip that is in contact with the paint. Upon heating, the paint becomes soft and pliable and can be pressed against its ground where the wax or adhesive then melts. When the flake becomes flexible enough, it should be pressed flat, held and allowed to cool.

Occasionally, paint will become dislodged from the ground in a form other than what is commonly known as flaking. For instance, cleavage is a malady diagnosed as the loss of bond between the ground and the canvas. Instead of a small flake falling from the ground, the paint blisters and possibly cracks over a significant section of the canvas. This problem is cured only by lining, which will be described later in this chapter.

Puncture Wounds

Tears, holes and punctures can originate from various accidents or careless habits in the presence of old paintings—

or even new ones. I once restored a painting that apparently had been stored in a basement some distance behind a target used by a youngster for his BB gun range. The 100-year-old painting had 12 BB holes in the canvas, which not only ripped threads apart but pushed surrounding areas of paint through those holes. The painting was successfully restored with barely a trace remaining of the off-target collison of the projectiles. First, any of the cloth or paint pushed from the front to the back of the canvas in the tear or hole must be gently moved forward to the front of the canvas once again. It may be advisable to warm the paint in this area slightly to make it a bit more flexible. From behind the canvas, any threads that can be matched should be aligned as closely as possible to their original positions. Frayed edges hanging to the sides should be trimmed. A tear should be flattened similar to the manner in which dents are flattened as described earlier in this chapter. A patch must now be placed on the back of the canvas.

Use a level working surface in a well-lighted area. Place a sheet of soft cloth or felt over the working area and spread the mylar sheet across the top of this pad. Place the painting face down on the mylar sheet. The beeswax and rosin adhesive used to consolidate flaking can be melted and brushed on the back of the canvas liberally, but not in such great quantities that it runs. A piece of new canvas should be cut large enough to more than cover the area needing repair. Fray the edges of this patch so that it does not have a sharp boundary that might be visible from the front after

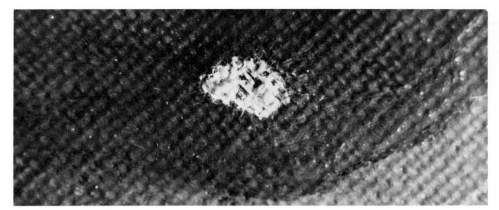

Before: A gouge resulted in a hole and the loss of paint surrounding the damaged area.

A hot mixture of rosin and beeswax is brushed over the damaged area on the reverse of the painting.

A canvas patch with frayed edges is placed over the puncture, and more melted rosin and beeswax is brushed over it.

A warm iron is used to seal the patch in place.

The void in the front of the canvas is filled with gesso. Another piece of canvas is pushed into the wet gesso to give it a texture of woven threads.

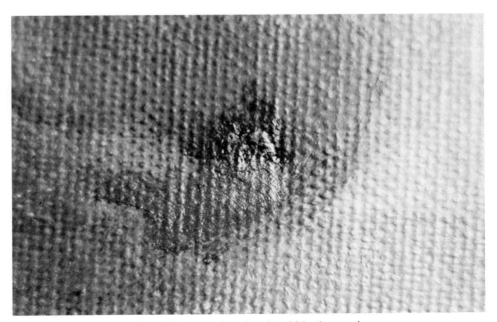

After: The gesso is painted to hide the repair.

Crazing on an old oil painting.

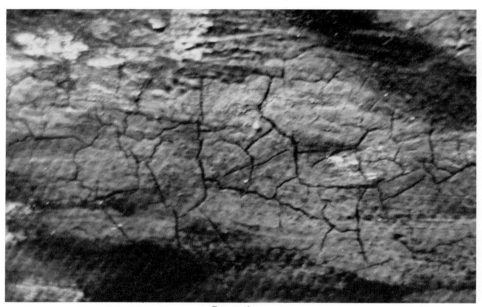
Craqueleure.

the patching process. Place some of the wax-rosin adhesive upon the patch and fix it over the hole or tear so that the axis of its fibers are aligned with the axis of the fibers in the original canvas. Apply heat from the back, perhaps with an electric iron, and apply mild pressure while the patch and adhesive are allowed to cool.

After the patch has been made, the painting must be observed from the front to determine if any paint or ground has been lost thus leaving a void in the surface. Any void should be filled with gesso, putty, or even plastic wood to reconstruct the ground to just below the surface of the surrounding paint. In this way, retouching paint can be applied over the reconstructed ground so that the painting does not have the appearance of having a hole in it. If the paint is thin, use a piece of canvas to leave an impression in the new ground medium or use a small tool to fashion simulated seams to give the new ground the appearance of being composed of threads. When the new ground is dry, it should be varnished to seal it. The painting is ready for retouching when the varnish is dry. Some hints on retouching will be offered later in this chapter.

Paintings Can Be Bugged

Insects occasionally find their way into either stretchers or canvas. If the painting is not to suffer, the insects must be eliminated. Because of the wide variety of insecticides used, it is very important to find one that does not have chemical properties that will cause even greater damage to the oil painting. You need to determine the vintage and types of materials used in the painting. The insecticide can either be brushed on or fumigated.

The Old Physical Examination

Just as with human beings, examinations of paintings are sometimes left until some disease or damage has resulted in overt symptoms. An examination can determine whether a painting has been abused, left alone or repaired adequately or inadequately sometime in the past. Check the surface of the painting for dust and dirt. Surface dirt may be either loose or holding fast to the surface and may require cleaning.

Check the surface to see if it has been varnished. Varnish discolors with age and may hide the true colors of the painting underneath. If moisture has invaded the varnish, a bluish white discoloration may appear called "bloom". If a grayish opaque discoloration appears on the surface, it is probably blanching, a problem caused by a residue of varnish remaining from a time when someone attempted to remove the varnish but did not do a complete job. A minute

network of small cracks covering the painting is a sign of age and is called crazing. Crazing can be apparent in the varnish but may have permeated into the paint beneath it. Craqueleure are wider or deeper cracks that usually permeate the paint layer due to age. Crazing or craqueleure do not detract from the value of a painting, providing they are dealt with by a conscientious conservator so that they do not work to destroy the painting.

As paint ages, it continues to dry and lose its resiliency. Oil paints can take from 25 to 100 years to dry—or even longer. Moisture and variations in temperature that contract and expand the canvas can cause the paint to crack once it has aged and lost its flexibility. For this reason, it is important to control temperature and humidity for the painting's optimal environment. Air should be free to circulate behind the painting, so that moisture does not have a tendency to condense and penetrate the ground from behind.

Occasionally, the artist is the culprit who causes deterioration of the painting surface. Paint applied so thick that it cannot dry uniformly will result in surface cracking, even while the paint beneath is somewhat wet. Placing paint over an undried ground is usually disastrous, since the paint does not bond to the ground and will eventually separate from it. Varnish placed over wet oils can cause a similar problem, since the varnish may harden and prevent the oils underneath from drying properly. Where the oils do dry, they have physical properties different from areas where the oils remain uncured. These nonhomogeneous areas expand and contract differently, which may result in stress across the painting.

Diagnosing The Disease

Cleavage is the loss of bond between the ground and the canvas that causes the painting to appear as though it has a boil. The boil may spread or eventually crack. The canvas will probably have to be relined to cure this ailment.

During the 19th century, bitumen (a substance prepared from coal tars) was used because of its attractive transparent properties to form a glaze on paintings. It was also used in shading. Unfortunately, bitumen melts easily and may flow on the surface of the painting if subjected to heat from a fireplace or even sunlight. Bitumen never dries completely. Its melting and subsequent coalescence can form a surface similar to alligator skin above the rest of the pigments. Future conservators may learn to deal with this problem, because the state of the art is not capable of doing so at this time.

Wrinkling can result when the surface of the paint dries without allowing the paint underneath to dry. Although the surface may be acceptable if the painting lay flat, it is normally hung vertically and the wet paint underneath can run and sag. Turning the painting upside down will let the runs and sags go in the opposite direction, but will not permanently cure the problem.

Moisture present in the ground when the paint was put over it or moisture that has been absorbed through the back of the canvas can cause flaking. Although most flaking can be prevented, it does happen and can be dealt with reasonable well.

Blisters occur on paintings just as they occur on human skin. Fires or extremely high temperatures can cause the rapid volatilization of the resins within the paint, causing it to become puffy and sometimes leaving nothing but a bare crust on the surface of the blister.

Abrasions can occur through inadvertent scratching or intentional but misguided restoration. Abrasions almost always require retouching—challenging the artistic talent of the conservator.

Medical History

Paintings should be checked for evidence of any previous restoration. Hopefully, a responsible conservator would have made notes relating to his work and perhaps even documented that work with photographs. However, this is usually not the case, especially for work that was done prior to the availability of formal education in the area of conservation. Things to look for include the loss of detail caused by applying solvents that were too harsh in a previous cleaning attempt. The use of lye, for instance, could have all but destroyed certain sections of the painting. Check for abrasions and overpainting. Some evidence of overpainting can be found with the use of ultraviolet lamps or the simple observation of craqueleure, if it is apparent. The craqueleure in an overpainted area will usually appear different from the craqueleure in the older resins. Check also for inpainting or retouching. Use of cleaning solvents may not affect older paint, but may dissolve overpainting or inpainting if special tests are not done before beginning the cleaning process.

Checking the Support

The canvas support should be examined for tears or dents. Evidence of fungus or infestation should be dealt with accordingly. It is also possible that the canvas is rotting. This symptom should alert the conservator to exercise extreme care in any movement or handling of the canvas. Check to see if the canvas has been lined. Check to make sure that the stretchers are true and not warping. Warped stretchers will require replacement.

Sunlamps

Sunlamps or ultraviolet lamps, preferably in the form of fluorescent tubes, can be used to determine otherwise invisible characteristics of the painting. In a darkened room, a fluorescent black light can be moved above the surface of the painting so that the visible light reflected can be observed and perhaps photographed. Under a black light, varnish fluoresces a yellow-green. Overpainting fluoresces purple. Unvarnished areas will appear to be brown.

Heat Lamps

Infrared lamps can be used to penetrate the surface of the painting to see what lies beneath. Infrared light passes through surface dirt, varnishes, glazes, and even upper layers of paint to what lies beneath. Areas of the painting that otherwise would not be visible be-

cause of dark discoloration or shading on the surface can now be seen. Signatures that lie beneath decades of grime can be found, while they remain obscured if viewed only through regular light which is reflected at the surface of the painting.

X-Rays

The use of x-ray equipment is somewhat beyond the scope of this book, since such equipment is not available for the normal household. X-rays penetrate deeply through the painting, emerging in intensities proportional to the lack of absorbing materials in the painting itself. The use of lead in pigments within the painting will cause x-rays to be absorbed in that area. Layers of stratification that otherwise would not be detected can be found through the use of x-rays. In recent years, x-ray photographs have been used to find older paintings hidden under more recent paintings.

Lab Tests

Chemical analysis can also be valuable in determining the age of a painting and its condition. Chemical analysis can be performed on pigments to help identify the possible origin of the painting or to eliminate impossible origin. Some chemical techniques may be used to determine which solvents can best be used to dissolve varnish without harming the paint beneath.

Cleaning

The history of cleaning paintings is sometimes grim. The use of sandpapers, solvents, soap and urine, as described earlier, make it easy to understand how so many works of art have been lost or ruined over the years.

Surface cleaning is usually a noncontroversial item and consists of removing dirt and grime from the top of a varnish. If the ground is bound in oil and the varnish is stable so as to prevent moisture from detaching the paint from the ground or the ground from the canvas, surface cleaning is probably advisable. Apply synthetic detergent and water judiciously. I have found that Formula 409 (found in almost any grocery store), diluted with water to a strength that is just enough to quickly and easily dislodge dirt, provides the needed effect.

A cotton ball dipped in the Formula 409 solution can be used to swab a small section of only a few square inches at a time on the painting which is put in a vertical plane. Swab with very little pressure to prevent abrasion. The surface dirt should loosen quickly and begin to run under the influence of gravity. Use a clean swab to collect this scum and then throw it away. Even stains caused by tobacco smoke usually can be removed by this technique.

Some other materials claiming to be specially concocted oil painting restorers can be bought in art supply stores. I have been disappointed by most of the materials that I have tried. They have very little detergent action and require

The left side of this painting has been cleaned, while the right side is still covered with discolored varnish.

considerable rubbing to dislodge surface dirt. Although they may smell good because of the presence of camphor or some other substance, they should probably be used only to clean the dirt from the surface of a painting that has not been varnished. They are not strong enough to thoroughly clean a varnished painting and are probably a waste of time.

To Clean Or Not To Clean—That Is The Question

Removing surface dirt and grime is almost always desirable. Cleaning a painting really just refers to removing the discolored surface varnish and applying a new varnish. Throughout the years, there have been some severe and serious arguments as to whether or not the patina should be removed from an oil painting. Patina on most other antiquities is found to be a desirable element that enhances its value. Aged shellac on a piece of American Empire mahogany furniture increases its value. However, when it comes to oil paintings, any blanket of color or obscuring film prevents seeing that work of art as the artist intended it. In the past, many conservators have felt very strongly that anything such as the yellow or brown hue of aged varnish which typifies the age of the work of art should not be tampered with. However, now it is widely accepted that a work of art should be viewed as the artist intended it to be viewed—and so it is necessary to remove old and discolored varnish.

The length of time that it takes for varnish to discolor depends upon the environment and the type of varnish used. It takes most paints 30 to 35 years or longer to dry and become insoluble. Considerable difficulty will be found in trying to strip the varnish from the surface of any recent painting. To be successful, the paint must be considerably insoluble to the solvents that will easily dissolve the varnish. Basically, varnish has either a spirit base or an oil base. Spirit varnishes are made from soft resins dissolved in alcohol or turpentine. They are brittle and pose very little trouble to an experienced conservator. On the other hand, oil varnishes are made from such hard resins as copal or amber. They are melted in oil at high temperatures and are quite insoluble, posing a challenge to anyone attempting restoration. Dealing with copal varnish has tried my patience more than dealing with any other conservation problem in the past 10 years.

Testing

Before proceeding with removing the varnish, it is necessary to find a solvent that will do the job without damage. In general, a section of the painting that is light in color should be found where the removal of a little pigment will not be apparent. Test in an area of about one square-inch, and definitely no more, by applying solvents with cotton swabs. Solvents most often used include ammonia, turpentine, acetone, cellusolve, various alcohols, and toluene.

It is necessary to find a solvent or mixture of solvents that will not dissolve the paint, while causing the varnish to dissolve into a jell so that it can be removed readily. Because of the use of bitumen or different types of resins in various paints, it may be necessary to test over each different pigment. Testing should be done in good, even light so that any minor changes in the painting surface can be seen at once. Unimportant places in the painting should be the first areas to be tested. This includes the area that may have been protected by the edge of the frame and will not be visible when the painting is reframed.

After the painting has been surface cleaned and all loose paint has been fixed so that it will not flake with minor contact with a cotton swab, the cleaning process is ready to begin.

Getting A Feel For It

It is advisable to practice on inexpensive, unimportant paintings before proceeding to greater challenges with more serious consequences. Experience will teach you that what you hear as the cotton swab moves across the painting and what you feel can guide you toward doing an excellent job of restoration. When cleaning, cotton swabs should not be rubbed across the surface of the painting. They should be rolled. The swab should be dipped in the solvent and rolled between the thumb and the index finger over the varnish. Watch carefully for any displacement of pigment from the painting onto the swab. Blues, reds and greens are easy to see developing on the swab, while darker colors, such as brown, can easily be confused with the discolored varnish being removed. Be especially careful on those darker colors. Varnish dissolving and being lifted onto the swab feels as though the swab is being rolled

through a mixture of a creamy consistency. After the varnish has been removed, a clean swab will feel as though it is being rolled over a coarser surface. Similarly, the sound of lifting varnish can be described as smooth, while the sound of the swab rolling over paint is more raspy.

About one square-inch at a time should be cleaned. As soon as a cotton swab becomes dirty, discard it and use a new swab. If any paint dissolves, the area should be wiped with cotton immediately to remove the solvent before it does additional damage. Then, dilute the solvent with some other solvent that will neutralize its action.

Lining

I have seen paintings lined, relined and relined again. In fact, I have seen as many as five linings backing an original canvas. The purpose of lining is to give additional support to a painting, if the original canvas has deteriorated and is subject to breaking or collapsing. Hypothetically, the canvas will need relining every 50 to 75 years. For very old paintings, it might be necessary to remove one or all of the linings under the original support before a new lining is put on. But for 19th century paintings (the ones that we are addressing in this book), it is not likely that more than one lining is now present and, therefore, we will not deal with removing old linings.

The following steps should be followed in applying a lining to an old canvas.

1. The painting should be dusted both front and back with a feather duster or soft brush. A vacuum

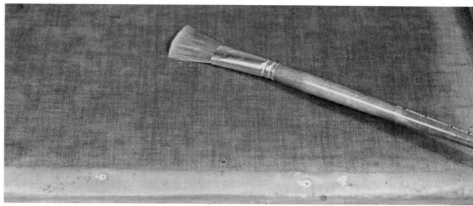

After removing the painting from its stretcher, it should be cleaned both front and back with a soft brush or feather duster.

A simple restrainer is made onto which the lining is tacked.

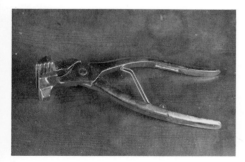

Canvas stretching pliers are used to pull canvas over stretchers and restrainers.

Rosin and beeswax are melted together to make an adhesive.

cleaner can be used to remove lint and heavy dirt from the back of the canvas, but should not be used on the front because of the danger of drawing in loose paint.

2. The canvas should be removed from its stretcher very carefully. If the canvas needs lining, it is because it is old and deteriorating. Care should be exercised not to damage it any more than necessary during the removal process.

3. The bent edges of the canvas should be straightened and flattened so they do not fold back on themselves when the lining is applied. Frayed edges should be trimmed.

4. Some schools of thinking suggest that a canvas should be lined first and cleaned later. My personal experience is that this practice is all right provided that a large amount of insoluble dirt has not become embedded in the varnish. The heating and pressure applied during the lining process may cause some of this grime to penetrate into the surface layer of paint. Therefore, a very dirty painting should be cleaned prior to lining.

5. The canvas used for lining should be as close in consistency to the original canvas as possible. This is necessary because changes in temperature and moisture will always make a canvas expand and contract. Lining with a like material will assure that the lining and the original canvas will expand and contract with the same proportions. The lining must be placed on a restrainer, which is a simple frame made from soft

The adhesive is poured onto the lining, and a warm iron is used to attach it to the reverse of the oil painting.

Turpentine is used to clean the adhesive from the front of the painting. Other solvents may be used to remove the old varnish.

Before: A painting should be lined to aid in the repair of many small punctures.

lumber and is larger in size than the painting to be lined. The lining is stretched over this restrainer in the same manner that a canvas is placed on its original stretcher with a special stretching tool.

6. If the painting has areas of impasto, that is areas of built-up paint, that can be damaged by the application of pressure to the canvas, a facing will be needed. A facing can be made by using strips of tissue paper and a mixture of flour and water to build up other areas of the painting so that they are all of a uniform thickness. This facing is removed after the painting is lined and all residue of the flour paste is washed away. However, most 19th century paintings will not present this problem. Use a large enough work area and cover it with felt or some other soft cloth. Place a sheet of mylar large enough to cover the work area over the felt, and place the painting face down over the mylar. Mylar is used because it is heat resistant and will not melt and adhere to the surface of the painting; **do not** use polyethylene.

7. A mixture of six parts beeswax and four parts dammar or rosin is heated in a double boiler. Usually, I pour the contents into a can, which I then set in a pot of boiling water. The mixture is stirred to be made homogeneous and then brushed while hot on the back of the original canvas.

8. The new canvas, on its restrainer, is placed over the old canvas. The mixture of beeswax and rosin is poured thinly onto the back of the lining. It should be poured in strips that crisscross horizontally, vertically and across the diagonals of the canvas. An iron is now used to melt the mixture further and apply enough pressure to embed it through the lining into the old canvas. One square-foot at a time should be worked. Enough heat should be used to melt the lining adhesive, but not so much heat that the adhesive runs freely. The iron should be kept moving and not left on one spot—overheating can damage the paint beneath.

9. Work should begin at the center and proceed toward the edges of the painting. That way, excess material can be driven out at the edges and any bubbles that may form between the two layers of canvas can be eliminated.

10. Turn off the iron and continue to move it across the canvas as it cools. The bond will be completed as the waterproof beeswax and rosin mixture becomes hard.

11. Examine the canvas for any unbound areas, reheat the iron and repeat the process until these areas have adhered.

12. After everything is cool and the lining has been completed, the painting and lining should be cut from the restrainer.

13. The painting can now be placed back on its old stretcher, or new stretcher if necessary. For very large paintings, it might be necessary to place the painting as well as the lining on a restrainer to avoid wrinkles and bubbles while working.

14. Turpentine can be used to dissolve any rosin and beeswax that may have penetrated to the front of the painting. Be sure to make some tests first, but for the most part, turpentine is a weak enough solvent that it will not damage any paint. Therefore, cotton balls dipped in turpentine can be used to readily dissolve and remove the adhesive similar to surface cleaning.

Vacuum tables are used by professional conservation units of significant means. The lining is placed on a large flat table with a number of holes in it. The adhesive is placed on the lining and the painting is placed face up onto this lining. The table is heated to melt the adhesive and a vacuum is drawn from underneath to pull the two canvases together. Such sophisticated mechanism, however, is not necessary. I have lined canvases as large as 5x9 feet with the use of an ordinary household iron. A steam iron with holes in the bottom has a tendency to collect and accumulate the adhesive. This may not be a significant problem unless the iron is lifted and placed aside while you are busy examining the painting. The adhesive will run out of the holes and boil off the heated surface, causing it to smoke. An iron can be fitted with a flat plate underneath so as to accomplish this task, but it is not really necessary. Using an iron exclusively for lining paintings may be advisable to prevent stains on the family laundry. However, using turpentine with care can clear all of the resin and wax from an iron, so that its use really should not provide an obstacle to the housewife or househusband, as the case may be.

Retouching

People's taste in art as well as their morality changes with time. Nudes painted at sometime in history may have appeared offensive several generations later. Accordingly, an individual dubbed the "Pants Man" was hired to add fig leaves to appropriate personal places on paintings. He wasn't really retouching, he was overpainting—he was painting something over what the artist intended to be there. The art of retouching is intended to duplicate the original effect that the artist had designed. A good job of retouching means that the area will not be detectable to the casual observer at least and to any observer at best. Great care must be taken to mix paints so that the retouch pigments identically match the pigments in the original painting. This task is extremely difficult because most oil-based pigments darken with age, and although they may be undetectable when the retouching is done, will stand out like a sore thumb in later years as they dry. Because of this, egg tempura should be used for most retouching. It does not change much in color as it cures.

After: The painting has been lined, cleaned, repaired and varnished.

91

Revarnishing

One of the most common varnishes used during the last century was dammar varnish. There is now a synthetic material that has greater durability than dammar, but also possesses most of the desirable characteristics such as the removability of dammar. It is called Kammar. It is a Krylon product produced exclusively for use as an oil painting varnish. Varnishing should not be done immediately after retouching or overpainting. The paint should be allowed to dry first—usually a matter of months or perhaps as long as a year. Some art stores sell temporary varnishes that can be applied before the paint is completely dry in order to protect it from dirt. These varnishes may be used, but are no substitute for a good coat of varnish after the paint has dried sufficiently. Varnish enhances the colors of paints and gives the picture additional contrast. Varnish keeps the paint clean and protects it from the ravages of today's polluted environment. Be sure that the varnish used is removable—avoid copal varnish. Document the type of varnish used for reference by a future conservator. If solvents for the varnish are listed on its container, make a note of these and attach the documentation to the back of the frame to further help the conservator.

Varnishing is the final step in the restoration of an oil painting. The painting should be placed flat and the varnish should be applied by spraying. Varnish can also be brushed on, but there is always the danger of losing some bristles or leaving brush marks on the surface of the painting. Usually, brushing on varnish leaves a thicker layer than necessary to protect the painting. This coating, as it discolors with time, will further obscure the colors placed by the artist. Any mechanism that produces a fine varnish spray is suitable. A pressurized can, air brush, spray gun and compressor, or new electric sprayer will do. The varnish should cover the painting evenly and be applied with whatever instructions available with the varnish suggest. Two or three thin coats of varnish will afford more protection than one thick coat. When the varnish is dry, the painting is ready for reframing and hanging.

This photograph shows the reverse side of a painting by Victor Mueller. The reverse should always be photographed before it is patched or lined if the artist has done something noteworthy on it.

In this painting, "The Temptation of St. Anthony", the old gentleman is having trouble resisting the temptation because the "Pants Man" had not visited.

CHAPTER VII

TURNING OVER A NEW LEAF (GILDING)

Gilding essentially means the art of spreading gold or silver over the surface of an object to decorate or protect it. Gilding is mentioned often in the Old Testament, and can be traced back as a decorative art to the ancient Egyptians. The Greeks and the Romans were known to gild artifacts, as well as the ceilings in many of their buildings.

In addition to laying gold leaf, gilding can be done chemically by applying amalgams of mercury and gold to other metals, or by using a solution of aquaregia (a combination of hydrochloric and nitric acids) and dissolved gold to decorate porcelain.

The term "gilding" can refer to applying gold paint or gold putty or any other form of decorative art that turns another surface metallic. However, the terms "gold leafing" and "gilding" are often used interchangeably, and this chapter will deal primarily with the application of real or synthetic gold leaf. Gold leaf is a sheet of real gold beaten extremely thin. Gold is unique among the metals in being able to stay strong enough to remain intact when only a few molecules in thickness. In certain light, gold leaf is partially transparent. It is only a few millionths of an inch thick. A synthetic material, having somewhat the appearance of gold leaf but slightly more red in color, is called composition leaf. It is an alloy of copper and zinc, and is usually at least three times as thick as gold leaf.

At the present time, the market value of gold is more than $200 an ounce, in contrast to the $32 an ounce official price in the United States earlier in this century. Needless to say, buying gold even in very small quantities for decoration can amount to a small fortune. Unfortunately, I do not have any photographs of my early gold leafing attempts, and I have not been able to afford real gold in the past 10 years. Nonetheless, I will describe first the process used for applying real gold leaf, and then will follow that discussion with instructions for applying composition leaf.

Cleaning

Most items appropriate for gilding are made of wood or plaster. The object must first be completely cleaned and free of loose dirt and dust that can possibly contaminate either the working area or the gold leaf when applied later. The object should be dusted and, if possible, vacuumed to remove any loose dirt. Next, any parts of the object that are loose or broken should be repaired.

Before: A frame needing repair must be made ready for gilding.

A separated corner must be reglued.

Corner clamps are used to insure that the sides make right angles.

A missing chip must be repaired.

Plaster is used to fill the void.

It is then sanded and shaped to blend in with the rest of the frame.

A thin coat of gesso is brushed over the entire frame.

After it has dried, 0000 steel wool is used to remove any excess gesso.

More than one coat of gesso may be applied, with steel wooling and sanding between coats.

Smooth

The next step is to provide as smooth a surface as possible with the material of which the object is made. "Quicksand", which is a composition sponge covered with an abrasive, is perfect for sanding both curves and flats. It takes the place of a sanding block for flat surfaces, and is pliable enough to be used on substantial curves. For very irregular surfaces, steel wool is appropriate; 0000 steel wool is one of the finest that can be bought and should be used on all the higher surfaces of the object without overly destroying any detail. Be careful not to oversand, which can cause loss of detail and actual defacing of an artifact. Remove all gold leaf, if any remains from an earlier deposition.

Applying Gesso

Gesso is a mixture of chalk or some other type of whiting material in glue. Sometimes, it is colored through the use of various pigments, all of which can be bought at an art supply house. Gesso, in general, is white, but as a substrate for gold leaf it is often colored red, so that any small cracks that might appear do not have to be covered up with leaf but rather allowed to show for an antique type of effect. Gesso can be bought in any art supply store, and the brand marketed by Liquitex is excellent. Keep it warm so that it will be viscous and flow freely. It should be brushed on thinly and not allowed to puddle in areas of deep recession or carving. If necessary, it can be thinned with water for easier brushing. Allow it to dry for one or two hours, or follow instructions on the package. After drying, use 0000 steel wool to remove any excess gesso and additionally smooth the surface. More gesso is applied in a similar fashion to the first coat and the entire steel wooling process is repeated once again after the gesso has completely dried. The process is then repeated once more, only this time the gesso is applied only to the most raised portions of the design. Applying gesso to the lower portions will fill in the detail and cause the designs to be not quite so outstanding. Allow the last coat to dry for three hours and then use 0000 steel wool to smooth the whole surface.

Shining Or Not So Shining Example

Now is the time to decide whether or not the object being gilded is to have an outstanding shine and polish, or have more of a flat gilded finish. In general, only the most outstanding features are burnished to a bright shine, while the rest of the object is given a matte finish to provide some contrast. In fact, deeply recessed areas are not at all easy to gild with gold leaf, and are usually gilded instead with some form of gold lacquer or enamel. The most obvious convex and concave parts should be brought to a bright shine. Apply one to two coats of shellac to the matted areas, and steel wool with 0000 steel wool in preparation for an oil size.

Areas that are to be given a truly metallic appearance will be burnished. For this, a burnish size must be prepared and it's made according to the following recipe. Add one ounce of granular rabbit skin glue to a pint of cold water and let it stand for about eight hours. Then place the glue solution into hot, but not boiling, water as in a double boiler. Be sure that the container in which the glue solution is mixed is of pyrex or some other appropriate glass or porcelain that will withstand heat without cracking. The glue solution should be warm to the touch but not overly hot, because overheating destroys its adhesive qualities. Then, red burnish size (made from clay) that is purchased from an art supply store is added in the proportion of one part by volume to three parts by volume of the warm glue solution. After mixing, strain through a fine mesh, such as a nylon stocking, into another receptacle. Stir the size every few minutes to keep it homogeneous and keep it continuously warm.

After all loose dust from sanding the gesso has been vacuumed from the object to be gilded, the red clay size and glue solution is brushed on thinly to completely over the gesso. Do not wipe the brush against the side of the receptacle in which the size was held, because globules may form that dry upon cooling and sink back into the size and cause lumps that will generate problems by tearing gold leaf if applied to the object. Stroke the brush in one direction and not back and forth over the gesso. Each completed application should be allowed to dry for about a half-hour, and 0000 steel wool is then used to smooth it. Three coats, with alternate steel wooling after drying, should be sufficient.

The smoothness of the gold leafing will be determined completely by the smoothness of the size. Any lumps or bumps in the size will not disappear simply by placing gold leaf, only a few millionths of an inch in thickness, on top of it. Similarly, rough spots or unpolished areas will not be made as smooth as polished metal by placing a thin gold film over them. Use 600-grit silicon carbide abrasive paper to very gently polish the surface of the burnish size. It is only necessary to polish the high spots, and you should take as much care to apply the abrasive paper as though you were sanding a baby's behind. Burnish size is soft and can be sanded completely through if too much pressure is applied. A smooth stone or agate burnishing tool can be used to further polish the size after sanding.

Oil-type size is a varnish base liquid that is brushed over the shellacked areas to prepare them for gold leafing. Either quick drying or slow drying oil in size can be purchased through many art supply houses. Instructions on the container should be good enough for an expert application.

Turning Over A New Leaf

Apply the burnish leaf first, because you might mar the burnished prepared surface while gold leafing the matted areas. First, a gilder's tip, which is a thin flat brush a few inches wide and made of very fine hair, is lightly brushed across your own hair to give it an electrostatic charge. It is then laid across a piece of gold leaf about one-quarter inch from the edge of the leaf. Since the gold leaf is metal, it becomes polarized and attaches itself to the gilder's tip by means of electrostatic attraction.

A solution containing seven parts distilled water to three parts of denatured alcohol is formulated ahead of time. This is known as the gilder's liquor. A watercolor brush is used to apply this liquor quickly to the spot intended to be gold leafed. The area should be thoroughly moistened with light swift strokes of the brush. If the area dries before the gold leaf is applied, more liquor should not be added until the burnish size has been completely dried—otherwise, some burnish size may be worn away from the softening and friction.

While the size is still wet, the gilder's tip with the gold leaf attached is moved over the wetted area, down towards it, in a motion that attempts to lay the leaf flat over the area in one motion. The gilder's tip is then stroked away, leaving the leaf in place. The wet size should hold the leaf fast. If the leaf tears and does not cover the area completely, another leaf should be immediately picked up and put over this area.

Use a soft camel's hair brush to push any portions of the leaf not in contact with the size down flat on top of it.

The watercolor or sable brush has probably picked up a few particles of red size. If it is immersed into the alcohol liquor again, it will contaminate the liquor. Brushing the gilder's liquor over a new section of size will probably result in traces of size being deposited on gold leaf that has already been laid, thus causing a thin film that dulls the finish on that gold leaf. Therefore, as soon as the leaf has been laid and pushed into place, rinse the sable brush in clean water and immediately dry it in a terry cloth towel. Change the water if it becomes noticeably dirty. Ordinary tap water will do. The entire process is then repeated until the leaves have been laid and the whole object has been gilded. Whisk the camel's hair brush lightly over the entire object to remove any loose particles of leaf that have not adhered to the surface.

Spots will undoubtedly appear where the gold leaf has not attached. Apply the gilder's liquor to these spots sparingly, so as to overlap already gilded areas if possible. A small piece of leaf is then put over this bare spot and pushed into place with the camel's hair brush. Be careful not to apply too much liquor to a recessed area and create a pool. If this happens, a tissue or some other absorbent material should be used to dry the pool—gold leaf should not be placed over it. Some areas in deeply recessed carvings will not be accessible for laying gold leaf. Don't worry about these areas; they should be gilded with liquid gilt (gold paint) after the burnishing has been done.

A steel or agate burnisher is used to rub a gold leaf, and essentially iron out any seams created by overlapping metal. The gold is soft and so thin that burnishing causes these areas to fuse. Hold the burnisher the way you hold a pencil and rub with moderate pressure over the gold-leafed area. Too great pressure may tear the gold leaf, and too light pressure will result in a dull, unburnished appearance.

If lines can be seen between the strokes, you have been moving the burnisher too fast. Burnishing is a slow, tedious process that requires patience,

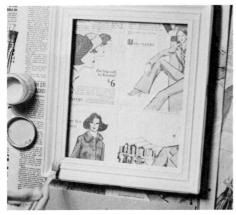

A sealer is used to further smooth the gesso finish.

The sealer is steel-wooled after it has dried.

An oil-type size is brushed on to hold the composition leaf.

and the burnisher must be moved only a small distance with each stroke. The length of the stroke should be one inch or less and should be methodically done, either from left to right, right to left, top to bottom, et cetera. Be careful not to break the foundation of the object near any sharp corners.

After the burnishing is complete, gold leaf should be laid on the areas that were designed to have a matte finish. The oil-type size is applied according to the directions on the container. Cover only an area that you can gild in about an hour or less. In one to two hours after the oil size is applied, it should become tacky. Push a dry finger onto the tacky surface and pull it away quickly. If a sharp click is heard, the surface is ready for gilding. If the surface still feels wet, test it again after it's allowed to dry a little longer. It should not be allowed to dry completely, however, because the gold leaf would have no adhesive to cling to. When the entire area to be matte gilded has been covered with gold leaf, the camel's hair brush should be used to insure that the leaf has made appropriate contact with the surface wherever possible. Then short gentle strokes should remove any overlapping that was necessary when applying the leaf and brush away any loose particles. Small bare spots can be covered with these particles, and large bare spots should be covered with new leaf.

The burnisher should not be used on the leaf applied over oil-type size. Briskly rub soft cotton or flannel cloth over the gilded surface after the oil size has

thoroughly dried—which should take about 10 to 12 hours.

Patent leaf can be applied to flat surfaces without worrying about a small breeze pulling the leaf away from the gilder's tip. Patent leaf is simply gold leaf attached to a tissue backing. Patent leaf is cut to the shape and size desired, placed over the oil size and pressed on gently. Simply rub your finger across the back of the tissue to attach the gold leaf, then lift the tissue away from the leaf, using the point of a knife if necessary.

Gilding With Composition Leaf

Composition leaves measure about five and one-half inches square, are thicker than gold leaf, and are applied with a technique similar to the application of gold leaf over a matte surface.

Gesso is used to build the foundation over the area to be gilded. It is sanded smooth after drying in a manner similar to preparing the surface for real gold leaf.

However, instead of applying a clay base size over the gesso, use an oil-type size, which can be either quick or slow drying. Care should be taken to insure that the size does not pool. When the size has dried to the appropriate tackiness (tested the same as matte size), composition leaf is applied to the entire surface. This is done by carefully applying each leaf with the fingers aided by a knife, or perhaps more easily by using a plastic gilder's tip. A plastic gilder's tip is a small plastic sheet rubbed by a cloth on its underside to become electrostatically charged and capable of lifting

After the size reaches the desired tackiness, a plastic gilder's tip and static electricity are used to lift the composition leaf.

The leaf is placed over the tacky size.

Overlapping leaves cover the entire frame.

After: A soft cloth is used to burnish the leaves and remove left over fragments.

composition leaf. It works about the same way a hair brush is used to move gold leaf.

Lay the leaves adjacent to each other with a slight overlap. If your touch is gentle enough to use your fingers, make sure the leaf is lifted with its adjacent tissue between the leaf and your fingers. Then after laying the leaf over the sized surface, use your fingers in a manner similar to applying patent leaf, to get the composition leaf to hold fast. Remove the tissue immediately after the leaf has been applied.

Since composition leaf is much less expensive than gold leaf, an additional layer may be applied to insure that the entire surface will have gilding material available to it for burnishing. Composition leaf is thicker than gold leaf and must be pressed more firmly into contact with the size to get it to stick. Allow the project to dry for about 12 hours, and then use a soft cotton or flannel cloth to rub away excess leaf. Bare spots are then patched by resizing the ungilded areas and applying new leaf when the appropriate tackiness has been achieved. Use a brush to make sure that the leaf has come in contact with the tacky surface beneath it. The project is then burnished by rubbing with a flannel cloth with soft strokes until all wrinkles have been removed. A top coat of protective varnish or lacquer will be necessary to keep the composition leaf from discoloring.

Before: This picture shows the edge of a frame before the next composition leaf is applied.

The applied leaf clings to the frame, but is not in complete contact.

After: Subsequent to burnishing, the leaf acquires the texture of the surface beneath it.

CHAPTER VIII

BREAKING UP IS HARD TO GLUE (FURNITURE REPAIR)

I am always amused when reading columns in publications that deal with antique furniture. Someone always asks the question, "How old is it?" And the expert in the column always answers, "Well, it might be a reproduction, but it could be old. Does it look 100 years old?" I have seen museum pieces of Victorian furniture preserved in homes that basically look like they were made yesterday, aside from a little fading of the upholstery and darkening of the varnish. I have also seen furniture that was made yesterday look like it was 100 years old after being exposed to certain groups of children who were not taught to respect other people's property. In fact, being around that type of children makes me age about 100 years.

Sometimes antiques are abused or misused. Other times, unfortunate incidences that are somewhat unavoidable require the hand of a skilled conservator.

These handmade dovetails indicate that this piece of furniture was likely made before machine-made dovetails became prominent in the latter part of the 19th century.

Bruises

Someone trips over a loose rug and plants a steel-toed shoe directly into the leg of a piece of fine Victorian furniture. Dennis the Menace plays carpenter and plants his hammer onto the leg of a piece of fine Victorian furniture. Or, perhaps, you're out for a quiet evening of bridge and when you return, you find that the house had been attacked by Indians and there is a target arrow stuck in the side of your bookcase. What to do?

A blow with a blunt instrument crushes cellulose fibers in wood and leaves an impression. We know that wood expands when it is moistened. The effect is especially pronounced in absorbtive soft woods. Although it does not work very well on oak, there is a technique for removing dents in most other woods used for Victorian furniture. A cloth or paper towel should be soaked in water and placed over the area of the dent. After the wood has absorbed moisture for about 15 minutes, a steam iron or steam kettle is used to place hot steam either directly in contact with the wood itself or with the cloth over the dent. The water will make the wood fibers expand somewhat, and the heat increases the effect. If the area that has been dented does not raise to the level of the surrounding wood, the piece is allowed to become nearly dry, and the process is repeated two or three times if necessary. It is possible that the dent can even raise to a level above the surface of the surrounding wood. In this case, it is sanded flush once again. Of course, the steaming process may destroy the finish on the wood, and so severe dents should

Before: Careless use of a hammer on this walnut leg caused the numerous dents.

102

Cloth or tissue soaked in water is placed over the dents so that the wood can absorb ample moisture.

Steam is then applied to the injured area. More water can be applied if necessary.

After: When the grain is raised, the wood can be lightly sanded to make the dents disappear.

be removed before a new finish is applied in the refinishing process.

Deep gouges in the wood can be repaired a number of ways. Shellac stick can be heated and melted into the gouged area, and then smoothed while warm to take approximately the shape of the piece under repair. It must then be sanded and finished to blend in with the surrounding area. Plastic wood is also a good material for filling in these areas, but will be apparent unless the color matches the color of the wood very closely. Plastic wood is sold in a variety of colors. In general, it cannot be stained and, therefore, it is important to buy the appropriate color, although it can be tinted somewhat with aniline dyes.

A very deeply-gouged area can first be filled with water putty, which is a form of plaster that becomes rock hard upon setting. Plaster of paris could also be used. This area then is covered with plastic wood or stick shellac to blend in with the surrounding area. Waxes can also be used to fill these voids, but they are soft and will not endure if pressure is applied, especially in a warm environment.

Before: The gouge in this rosewood chair requires filling.

Shellac sticks come in many colors. A set of 12 can handle most jobs.

The shellac stick is melted with a heated spatula or soldering iron to fill the void.

After: If the shellac stick has been matched to the wood, the repair is barely visible.

Blotches

Sometimes wood is inadvertently stained in contrast to the type of staining discussed under the chapter on refinishing. Ink often is accidentally spilled on a desk top. The spiller does not react fast enough, because he panics and does not know what to do about the spilled ink. Therefore, the spillee, or the desk in this case, becomes stained until someone as smart as you, who has read this book, comes along to change the situation. Most old inks were made from berry juices. Strong oxidizing agents will chemically react with the materials in those juices to remove the pigment. In a sense, we will be bleaching the wood similar to bleaching clothing to remove stains.

A few oxalic acid crystals, which can be purchased at the local pharmacy, are dissolved in one cup or so of water until no more will dissolve. A brush is then used to cover the entire wood area surrounding the stain as well as the stain itself. Additional oxalic acid is then brushed into the stain repeatedly until it disappears. This process will work remarkably well unless carbon black has been used in the ink. Other bleaching agents, like hydrogen peroxide, can also be used, but oxalic acid does the job quickly and effectively. It forms a dust made up of small oxalic acid crystals on the surface of the wood upon drying, and you should avoid inhaling this dust if you do not enjoy sneezing or coughing. Other than these precautions, the solution is relatively safe to handle. A damp rag is used to wipe the surface and remove the dust after the stain has been removed. If the area has become so white that it does not blend in with the surrounding wood, simple household ammonia brushed on sparingly will darken the wood. When it is dry and wiped with a damp cloth to remove any

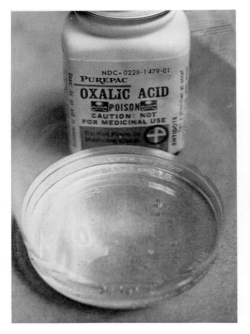

Oxalic acid crystals can be dissolved in water to form a mild bleach.

Before: Ink was accidentally spilled on the burl walnut trim of this desk.

106

Oxalic acid solution is brushed over the stain and surrounding area.

After: The stain has been bleached and the wood refinished.

remaining residue, the area is sanded lightly and a new finish applied.

Loose Screws

Screws through hinges, or between any two pieces of wood for that matter, sometimes strip the wood within the boring and no longer make a good fit. Sometimes a larger diameter screw can be used to once again make the joint secure. However, there is an old trick, which most people know, for making the old screws fit again. The first time I tried it, I was still in college and had an old upright oak piano that had a loose panel. Someone told me to take some wooden match sticks and shove them into the hole after the screw was removed and then turn the screw back in. It almost worked. There are two additional things that the friend should have told me. One, break the heads off the wooden matches first; and two, put some glue into the hole to insure that the matches don't pull out when you yank on the piece to put out the fire.

Another way to deal with this problem is to fill the hole with plastic wood and allow it to cure. A new hole can then be drilled and the old screw put into place, resulting in a joint that is as secure as the original.

Removing Warps

A simple technique can be followed that is successful for removing nearly all warps (except for my sense of humor). Remember once again that moisture causes wood to expand. If you moisten one side of a flat board and not the other, the moist side will, of course, expand while the other sides does not. Conversely, if a board has moisture in it and one side is subjected to dry heat, more moisture will be lost by that side of the board than from the other side. When either of these situations occur, the only result can be warping. That is, either an expansion of one side of the board by absorbing moisture or the contraction of the other side of the board by loss of moisture. The concave side is always the moisture-deficient side.

The remedy for this problem is to introduce additional moisture to the concave side of the board and possibly, at the same time, try to remove moisture from the opposite side. Placing the board in the sunlight with its face down on a wet lawn or a pile of wet rags uniformly spaced along the board should do the job. It may help to place some weights on the convex side to help flatten it. The heat from the sun will dry the top side of the board, while there should be ample moisture available for the concave side to absorb.

You can use your imagination for accomplishing the same purpose. However, be sure that your imagination includes the addition or subtraction of moisture from the appropriate sides of the board. I have seen people try to flatten table leafs, or other warped panels, simply by applying weights to the rounded side and gluing or screwing boards across the grain on the underside to act like splints to hold the panel flat. It doesn't work. The forces that caused the board to warp in the first place are very strong and may well pull the screws right out of the splints or cause the panel to split. Besides, who wants to ruin a perfectly warped panel by adding ugly splints?

Split Panels

Over the years, as temperature and humidity changes, panels of wood expand and contract following the laws of nature. The best way to preserve antique furniture is to stabilize the environment in which it must remain—this means humid heating during the winter and air conditioning during the summer. Temperature and humidity should remain as uniform as possible the year around. In fact, stability of temperature and humidity is probably even more important than exactly what the temperature or humidity is. Constant changing of these two variables causes the dynamics that introduce stress into wooden artifacts. Sections of wood do not look the same, because various factors influence different portions to grow at varying rates. The composition of a board may not be uniform, because of the availability of various nutrients while the board was still a growing tree as its roots moved down through different layers of earth.

These varying conditions result in one section of wood being stronger than another section, and also results in one area of a board being slightly more hygroscopic than another area. These factors, coupled with changing environmental conditions, can cause a board to split either partially or totally. Furniture made from lumber that is not seasoned properly before manufacturing can result in split pieces. Lumber either has to be kiln dried or seasoned over several years to dry to the point where it is suitable for use in furniture. Seasoning must also be done in such a way that air is allowed to circulate uniformly around the board or log. The ends have to be protected so that they do not lose more moisture than the rest of the log, or the entire piece of wood will be ruined. The syndrome is referred to as shake, which is a conglomeration of cracks and fissures that propagate through the wood.

Sometimes split board can be glued back together before the split propagates all the way through. The board should be separated slightly to get enough glue into the split and then clamped very tightly to hold the split together. Excess glue should be wiped from both sides of the board and the joint allowed to dry. The best glue to use is either white glue, such as Elmer's glue, or Weldwood glue mixed fresh for this purpose. If the factors that caused the board to split in the first place have not been eliminated, it is very possible that it will continue to split. In fact, the glue joint may now be stronger than the section of the board that has not split, and the split may propagate down along the grain in that direction. Hopefully, the source of the problem will have been eliminated and the repair should be permanent.

If the board has split all the way through, simply gluing it back together will not provide sufficient strength for it to hold. Simply gluing it back together would be called making a butt joint. I have repaired antique tables where the tops were not doweled together, but rather glued by placing consecutive boards side by side, making adjacent butt joints. As one or the other boards dried more than its adjacent companion, they simply split apart, leaving a void where they were once snuggled closely together. To fix this type of table top or any panel that has split all the way through, it is necessary to dowel the panel sections together.

Doweling is the technique of joining two pieces of wood by means of a small hardwood shaft, called a dowel, placed perpendicular to the grain in the panels. Of course, there are other applications when the dowel can run parallel to the grain in the wood. Doweling can be accomplished by drilling a hole parallel to the surface of the wood where the hole is slightly larger or the same diameter as the dowel rod. A pin called a dowel pin is inserted into the hole. The dowel pin is a small metallic item, that somewhat resembles a thumbtack, with a stocky head. The head is placed into the hole that has been drilled, and when the board is positioned against it, the pin point makes an impression on that board so you know where to drill the hole. Another hole is then drilled in that second board the same size as the one in the first board, and just deep enough so that the small section of dowel rod that has been cut will fit into that space created for it when the two boards are butted against each other and glued.

Glue is put into each of the holes and the dowel cut to size. A small groove should be cut along the length of the dowel to permit glue to escape from the hole if too much as been put in. Dowels should be placed at least every foot along the length of two boards that are to be butted against each other. Legs and arms on tables and chairs will also be joined occasionally by means of dowels where the dowels are placed only inches apart.

There are much neater ways to join boards these days than through using dowel pins. Various doweling jigs are available from lumber yards or woodworking supply houses that do a lot of the thinking for you. When the two pieces of panel or, alternatively, two boards are joined, both the front and back surfaces of the adjacent pieces should be flush with each other. Unless the dowel goes in directly perpendicular to the axis of the joint, the two boards cannot be made to join properly, especially if more than one dowel is used. The doweling jig insures that the hole is drilled perpendicular to the axis of the joint, and also insures that the hole is placed approximately in the center of the board edge. More importantly, the jig insures that the distance from one edge to the hole on one board is exactly the same as the distance from the same surface to the hole on the other board. Another advantage of using a doweling jig is that the depth of the hole being drilled is readily apparent, and therefore more controllable. Illustrations in this chapter substitute for the thousands of words necessary to give an adequate explanation of this process.

The first step in doweling two boards is to draw a line across the edge that is to be joined at the point where the dowel will be placed.

The doweling jig is aligned with the mark on one of the boards.

The jig is adjusted so that the hole is centered properly for the thickness of the board.

The dowel size is chosen and the correct size hole is drilled. The process is then repeated for the other board.

Glue is placed into the holes and a dowel inserted.

Several dowels may be used if desired. Glue is applied to the edges of the two boards to be joined and they are clamped together until the adhesive has cured.

Broken Or Shattered Pieces

Unfortunate incidents sometimes completely shatter a piece of furniture. Or, perhaps, a piece has been lost. In these cases, a new piece must be carved to replace the missing one. This book cannot give you the talent to do wood carving, and if significant talent is required you may wish to seek that talent in a local woodworking or wood carving shop. If such talent cannot be found, call someone in Amana, Iowa, where just about everyone knows somebody who knows something about woodworking.

The most important part of making repairs of this nature, if talent is not the major obstacle, is finding a suitable piece of wood that will blend both in figure and color with the surrounding area. Sometimes this is impossible, and staining, bleaching or otherwise deepening the color of one or both pieces may be required. If possible, repairs on old wooden furniture should be made using pieces of old wood instead of new wood. I have found no way to take a section of walnut that was cut about five years ago and make it resemble a section of walnut that was cut over 100 years ago. The older wood is always mellower and richer in color, even if the newer woods can compete in figure. I have repaired

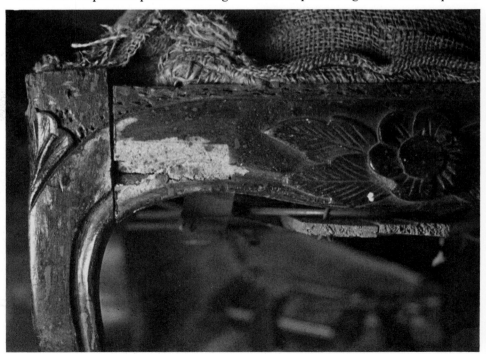

Before: An old amateurish repair on this ottoman completely ruins its appearance.

112

two ends of an ottoman that were shattered. It looked like someone weighing 800 pounds had jumped on it. The time and trouble to make the repair was worth much more than the value of the ottoman, but the damage was so extensive it posed a challenge that could not be passed up.

Broken or split legs on furniture should always be fixed immediately. Because of the weight bearing down on the legs or feet, a crack can propagate upwards to destroy the entire leg. This is especially true on chairs—the pieces of furniture that get more wear and tear than anything else. If a foot is split, it normally requires amputation and replacement by another foot. Oftentimes, the same is true for furniture legs. Of course, that is probably the worst that can happen, unless the piece of furniture collapses and becomes further damaged. Therefore, attempts to glue or join the broken pieces should be attempted.

After: The damaged section is replaced by a piece of new wood.

113

Before: A damaged rocker arm is repaired by planing the damaged area until it's flat and gluing another piece of wood to it.

One surface of the applied piece is planed until it blends with the adjacent surface of the arm.

After: The remaining surfaces are planed until the arm is nearly as good as new.

The old walnut foot above is too badly damaged to be sturdily repaired. The replacement foot below it has been turned on a lathe.

Before: So long as the pieces from this old chair are kept together, it is not a lost cause.

After: The chair has been refinished and reglued to be as good as new.

Taking Care of Your Seat

We would not think of putting our entire weight on a desk or table or bookcase or dresser or armoire, and then immediately removing that weight and putting it on again, then off again, and so forth. This is exactly what we do to our chairs. They take more abuse than any other piece of furniture, and for that reason break more often. Any chair that is not repaired when the first sign of wear and tear becomes apparent will be inviting an even greater pain in the seat.

Some people know how to sit in antique furniture, while others don't. Even some who know how to sit, as well as get in and out of a piece of 100-year-old wood, can't help but rest a 200-pound body on such a fragile structure. The Victorians were mostly small people who seldom exceeded five feet six inches in height. The chairs were made lower to the ground than our modern chairs, and our smaller ancestors did not anticipate that we would cherish their furniture so much that we would put them in our houses to abuse them.

If a chair is even slightly wobbly, all loose pieces should be disassembled. All the glue must be scraped from all the separated glue joints down to the bare wood. New glue will not hold old glue; it must make contact with wood. Putting the chair back together again must be done in one step. One arm cannot be put on with hope that an adjoining leg will fit neatly into the puzzle. After all the glue joints are cleaned, glue is placed on these joints and the entire chair is once again assembled before the glue dries. The chair must then be clamped using any necessary combination of web clamp, pipe clamp, furniture clamp or tourniquets. Pressure must be placed on all of the joints, just as in making any other wood glue joint, so that the bond is as permanent as possible. Lack of clamping will result in a broken glue joint.

In addition to the store-bought type of clamp, strips of inner tubes can be used to apply pressure in appropriate areas. Similarly, clothes line can be used with a dowel rod inserted to tighten the clothes line as you would tighten a tourniquet. The dowel is then brought into alignment with the rest of the rope and tied down with a separate piece so that it does not loosen.

I can't overstress how important this operation is to the survival of a chair, so I will emphasize it once more. The chair should be taken apart to dissociate all loose joints by using a rubber mallet if necessary. All old glue should be removed from all old glue joints. New glue is placed on these joints and the entire chair is assembled in one step standing on a level surface. Pressure is put on all of the glue joints by whatever mechanisms are available to insure a tight fit, and such pressure must remain until the glue has dried. White glue will work, but because of the stress that chairs must cope with, a fresh batch of Weldwood glue is probably most appropriate.

I had a pair of prize Victorian rosewood gents chairs with elaborately carved faces and flowers on them. One day, I noticed an arm to be loose, both at the joint where it met the seat frame and leg as well as the dowel joint where the back of the arm joined the back of the chair. I was very careful getting in and out of the reupholstered piece to make sure that I did not further damage the chair, and hoped that I would soon have time to repair it. My father came to visit and, of course, picked that chair to sit in. I, being a jogger, am built like the frail Victorians except for being somewhat taller. Dad, on the other hand, is about the height of the frail Victorian, but is built more like two professional football players. I sat on the floor in front of the fireplace during that winter evening, talking about anything, but thinking constantly that I should have

repaired that chair arm. About the time that I had decided to say something about it, dear Dad decided to stand up. I heard a crunch that sounded like all my knuckles had cracked simultaneously. Dad stood there, looking ever so slightly embarrassed, with a refinished, reupholstered rosewood chair arm in his hand. All four dowels had been broken. It was quite some task to cut the old dowels away from the pieces, align new holes and insert new dowels that would make the joints fit appropriately. I could have avoided the entire affair by regluing that arm when the dowels were still intact and the arm was not in hand.

Belt clamps (A), bricks (B), C-clamps (C), pipe clamps (D), and whatever other means of tension available are used to apply pressure to reglue a chair, all at one time.

Loose pieces are removed with a putty knife.

Old glue is brittle and unsightly, and must be removed before regluing.

Coarse steel wool or sandpaper efficiently removes old glue.

Small spring clamps can be used to apply pressure to glue small pieces. Pieces of cardboard are used to prevent the wood from becoming marred.

Going Around In Circles

All perfectly round pieces, such as spindles and similar decorative items, must be manufactured on a wood lathe. This book is not the appropriate place to give instructions on how to master the techniques on a lathe. However, lathe work is a lot of fun, and it is very satisfying to see exquisite work produced by your own hands with such little effort. Many high schools and vocational institutions offer nighttime adult education classes in woodworking. Some of them emphasize the use of the lathe, and I suggest that if you have the time available you take the course, if nothing else to give you some peace of mind by doing something productive with your hands.

Shattering Experiences

This section is not designed to teach you how to do anything, but rather to give you confidence in the job that must be done. Regardless of how badly damaged a piece of furniture is, there is always some hope for making the necessary repairs. To cite an example, I'd like to share an experience that occurred a number of years ago. I had finished stripping paint from a small three-drawer walnut commode. The drawers had nicely carved fruit pulls. A molding around the face of each drawer ran across the top and bottom of the drawer

Can you tell which of these oval moldings was reconstructed from more than 50 splinters?

118

and was joined on both left and right sides by half circles. The paint had been very stubborn and required one of the commercial strippers that raised the grain of the wood. Considerable sanding was necessary. In order to do the best job, I decided to remove the moldings from each drawer. The moldings came off two of the drawers just fine, so that I could get my power sander onto the flat face of the drawer. However, the molding in the third drawer was a little more obstinate.

I delicately placed my chisel next to one of the brads holding the molding in place, and when I lifted the chisel, the molding shattered along its length into about 50 pieces, many of which were much smaller than toothpicks. I was immediately plunged into the depths of depression. As I moaned and groaned over my stupidity, my wife came to see what the problem was. She is a master at jigsaw puzzles and seeing all those dissociated slivers lying on the floor did not faze her one bit. To my utter amazement, she used a magnifying glass and tweezers to put all those little bits and chips together again, gluing them as she went, until the molding was restored to its original form. We still have that commode and I can't remember, nor can I tell, on which drawer the molding was shattered.

A very dear friend made a gift to us of her mother's porcelain dresser set. In the exchange of hands, the set was dropped and several of the pieces shattered on the floor. Unfortunately, my wife was not around to vacuum the dust so that she could reassemble it. But she did manage, with the same tech-nique, to put together all the pieces that we had found, essentially preserving what otherwise would have been a totally lost cause.

When Something Is Rotten In Denmark Or Elsewhere

Occasionally, moisture has caused a problem in furniture which simply does not leave a stain, but actually causes the wood to begin to rot. The water problem can be removed, but the moisture present can continue the rotting process. Once, I saw what appeared to be a perfectly good chest of drawers until the proprietor of the antique shop tried to move it. Just slight pressure with his finger near the base of one side was enough to rip the rotted wood into fragments. Although it did look a little discolored, it was not apparent that the rotting had taken place from the other side of the panel and had not quite progressed through to the visible side.

One material available is called Exide Cure-Rot that will strengthen rotted wood, so that this type of shattering will not happen. Basically, it is an epoxy that penetrates the wood and then cures in a form suitable to support substantially more weight than the delicate decomposed material. It cannot be applied over shellac or varnish, but must be applied directly to bare wood. Any paint or varnish residue will turn gummy. The epoxy will penetrate about one-half inch. If deeper penetration is necessary, holes must be drilled. I cannot assess how this substance will impair the finishing of a piece of furniture, since it was not really intended for this use. Check the appendix at the end of this chapter to find its source.

Droopy Drawers

Although it is wholly respectable for a doctor to ask a gentleman to drop his drawers in the examination room, it is embarrassing to pull forward on a drawer in a Victorian chest to find that it goes clunk and drops a fraction of an inch. This is a very common occurrence in old chests of drawers. The sides of the drawers are made from a wood that is softer than should have been used, although who was to predict that the piece of furniture would be in daily use for well over 100 years. Some drawer sides made from cherry or oak probably have lasted with minimal wear until today. Others made from pine or poplar have degenerated considerably. As the drawer is worked in and out daily, small amounts of a soft wood are abraded.

The front of the drawer is probably a suitable hardwood and is rubbed minimally over the wood on which it rests—and, therefore, may still be unworn. The drawer side immediately behind it, however, tapers back to an area of maximum wear and when the drawer is pulled out, sliding over this area produces the familiar clunk. As this happens, usually one edge of the drawer side will wear before the other edge, producing a point which then proceeds to wear a groove into the drawer runner on the inside of the chest.

There are varying opinions as to what can be done. First of all, with regard to the drawer sides themselves to prevent the clunk, the only mechanism is to either replace the entire side with a new dovetailed board (which destroys the authenticity of the piece) or alter the side by planing it flat and gluing another piece of wood to it. This piece of wood

The area above the dashed line shows where the wood on this drawer has been worn away after nearly 100 years of daily use.

120

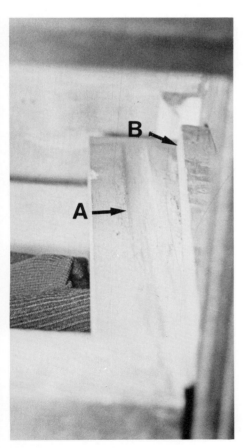

This drawer runner has been worn into a deep rut (A) from the friction of the drawer sliding over it. The guide rail (B) is out of place at the rear of the drawer, permitting the drawer also to move from side-to-side.

can then also be planed down to give the drawer side its original thickness. Of course, this thin strip of wood will wear, also, with time and should definitely not be nailed into the drawer side or the nails will cause even greater wear on the runners.

With regard to the runners, they can be recessed, using a router, or by a chisel held by a skilled craftsman, and a new piece of wood implanted which must be planed to the original runner thickness. Or, the runner can be removed and reversed to put its bottom side up for a new flat surface made from the original material. I would prefer this method myself, but experience would tell us that it can't last more than another 100 years of continuous daily use.

Sometimes a drawer will not pull out evenly, because the back of the drawer will move to one side or the other unless perfectly even pressure is applied to both drawer handles. Rails on the sides of the runners probably have fallen out of place and are allowing the drawer to move sideways when it is not supposed to.

If the drawer, when pushed back into place, moves an inch or more behind the front face of the chest, the blocks which originally were intended to stop the backward progress of the drawer have probably broken off. Although I definitely recommend replacing the stopping blocks and resecuring the guide rails, I will not advise restoring the runners or drawer sides. A trade-off must be made between the utilitarian value of a piece and its authenticity. This is a subjective decision that must

be made by each individual antique owner.

Keeping the drawers from sticking, however, requires very little innovation. Either soap or wax from a candle can be rubbed onto the runners and onto the bottoms of the drawer sides. This practice is probably something that should be prescribed at least once a year to reduce the friction and prevent any more wear than is necessary on those delicate drawers.

Accessories

There are all different types of accessories for Victorian furniture that may have been lost sometime during that furniture's lifetime. Some of these accessories can be fashioned in the home work shop, while others can be purchased from commercial firms that specialize in their reproduction. In 1870, for instance, a machine was made to turn wire into nails. These types of nails are available today, and are round with round heads. The first round nails had round heads that were probably not centered on the nail. Nails used before this time, during the Victorian era, were square. They had no sharp point, but were rather flat from the end that had to penetrate the wood and had four tapered sides going back toward the head of the nail. These were called cut nails and were also made by a machine in one operation. They are still available for replacement use in antique furniture from the source listed in the appendix.

Although certain drawer pulls, called teardrop pulls, were available in the 18th century, a certain modification in their

A common teardrop pull of the Victorian era made of brass and wood.

An unusual teardrop pull.

Although not exactly shaped like a shield, this fancy brass escutcheon of Eastlake vintage protects the wood around the keyhole from becoming marred.

A burl walnut escutcheon decorates this keyhole.

A simple walnut escutcheon decorates what would otherwise be a drab aperture.

A fruit and nut pull of carved walnut.

Both inlay and burl veneer decorate this walnut crib.

design and increase in bulk was made to utilize the teardrop design in Victorian furniture.

Escutcheon is a French word meaning shield. Originally, escutcheons were shield-shaped pieces of metal placed around keyholes to protect the wood as well as to decorate the drawer. During Victorian times, escutcheons were made in shapes not at all resembling a shield, and in fact were even made of wood.

Although not a shield in shape, they still provided the function of a shield as well as decoration.

Use of these accessories, in lieu of modern replacements, can add greatly to the appearance of originality for almost every example of Victorian furniture. Look at photographs of similar pieces of furniture to help you determine what served as those original details of ornament and function.

Even when folded, the distinctive lines of this walnut crib help show off its polished brass hardware.

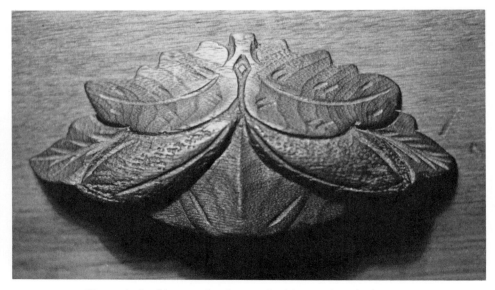

The grain in this carved walnut pull adds greatly to its beauty.

FURNITURE REPAIR APPENDIX

Cure-Rot and old-fashioned nails are available from:

Brookstone Company
Vose Farm Road
Peterborough, New Hampshire
03458

COLOR SECTION

This bust is made from pure white Carrara marble.

Before: A fancy Lincoln rocker in need of restoration.

After: Care should be taken with striped fabrics to see that the pattern in the seat meets properly with the pattern in the back.

Before: This small walnut sewing rocker requires refinishing as well as recaning.

After: The rocker has been transformed into a treasure.

127

Before: This ottoman needs to be structurally repaired as well as reupholstered.

After: It is nearly as good as new.

128

An 1864 bronze two-cent piece. Its natural shine has been preserved for over 100 years and should not be disturbed.

An 1855 U.S. half-cent. It has developed a rich toning over the years that cannot be replaced. Cleaning would decrease its value.

The reverse of the above coin.

A silver gravy boat. Tarnish can be removed from it in a manner similar to removing tarnish from silver coins.

The age-darkened varnish still remains, obscuring the colors on the left side of this Victor Mueller oil painting. Notice the change in every color on the right side where the varnish has been removed.

Before: This matchsafe was supposed to be silver plated, but it has been worn to such a degree that the brass from which it is cast is more visible than any of the silver.

After: The matchsafe has been resilvered.

131

Before: The left side of this oil painting has been cleaned. It is drab with little contrast. The right side of the oil painting still has discolored varnish which gives the painting an overall yellowish tone.

After: After varnishing, the painting takes on a high degree of contrast, but without the yellowing discoloration of the old varnish.

CHAPTER IX

SMART GUYS FINISH LAST (REFINISHING)

Very often, the first thing a person does when buying a piece of antique furniture that still has an old finish on it is to get it home, strip it and refinish it immediately. Such drastic procedure is not always necessary to make the appearance of an old treasure wholly adequate. Of course, sometimes there is no alternative. But understanding the various types of finishes used during the Victorian period and how to remedy certain problems will put one in a better position to make the decision on whether to refinish or repair.

The Big Three

Furniture from the Victorian period will most likely be finished with either shellac, lacquer or varnish. About 1840, the Rococo or French revival subset of the Victorian styles was beginning. A new wood for furniture manufacture was coming into vogue. For several generations preceding this time, the most popular woods for formal furniture were rosewood, satinwood and mahogany. But now walnut was coming into its own and, as we have seen since that time, a great majority of formal Victorian furniture was constructed from native walnut. At this time, the ideas that people had regarding finishes also changed somewhat. The popularity of the highly polished shine was giving way to a smooth satin or oiled finish, which allowed the viewer to observe more directly the beauty and grain of the wood beneath.

As time passes, however, the influence of sunlight, drying, dirt and interaction with environmental pollutants changes the character of these finishes. Of course, there are always the domestic disasters that result in additional marring or defacing of an otherwise perfect piece.

The most common finish on especially early Victorian pieces was pure shellac. Shellac is a hard and durable organic finish made by dissolving the exudation of the lac bug in alcohol. The lac bug is a type of aphid that makes its way through the twigs of certain trees in the Philippines and southeast Asia, leaving behind a gummy substance which we have learned to apply to wood. I would like to discuss in detail the process of exudation, but it would probably spoil your day.

Shellac is not impervious to water, it darkens when exposed to sunlight, and it hardens and becomes more opaque as the alcohol within it volatilizes over the years. Nevertheless, it was a good finish in the 1800's and it is still a good finish, provided that it is not abused. Great care should be exercised if the finish on a table is shellacked. Spilling a martini will most likely destroy the finish. Likewise, wet flower vases will cause white rings to appear.

Lacquer is made from the sap of the lac tree (Rhus verniciflua). The tree grows only in Malaya, China and Japan. Lacquer will dissolve in a number of solvents and primarily in what Americans term lacquer thinner.

Varnish is made from the resin of other types of trees, although the term varnish can also apply to a shellac or lacquer finish. Shellac and lacquer can be redissolved, using appropriate solvents, after they have fully cured. Varnish cannot be redissolved. It can be removed as a finish from a piece of furniture, but it cannot be reworked by using a solvent.

The seed of the flax plant can be pressed to produce a yellowish oil called linseed oil. Linseed oil, besides being an ingredient in a number of paints, stains and finishes, can also be a finish in itself.

And then, of course, we have paint. Paint is made by dissolving various pigments in oils or varnishes. Unfortunately, many of these pigments have been deposited on pieces of antique furniture that were not intended to be so pigmented. Paint always poses a special problem in the refinishing of antique furniture, because it tends to find its way deep into the grain of the wood and displays a remarkable reluctance to come out again.

Before discussing how to remove the above types of finishes, if necessary, it is appropriate to dwell on a few repair techniques that might make the refinishing process unnecessary, thereby saving the new antique owner a lot of time and, perhaps, money.

When You've Been Alligatored

Both shellac and lacquer after a period of time lose their solvents and shrink to form a crackled or alligator skin-type pattern in the finish. The alligatoring can go all the way from the surface down to the wood. It obscures the figure of the wood beneath to such an extent that the finish may even appear opaque. The novice would take a piece of furniture like this and immediately go about stripping off the old finish, getting ready

to apply a new one. This is not always necessary; in fact, hardly ever necessary, and the entire piece can be restored to a beautiful appearance in a matter of minutes by using the right technique.

First, you must determine what type of finish is on the furniture. Shellac will always dissolve in denatured alcohol and will sometimes dissolve in lacquer thinner. Lacquer will dissolve in lacquer thinner, but probably not in alcohol. Varnish will not dissolve in either of those solvents. Wind a small piece of soft cloth around your finger, dip it in alcohol and gently rub an inconspicuous spot on the back or underside of the piece of furniture. If the finish dissolves easily and rubs off onto the cloth, you have a shellac finish; if lacquer thinner does the job, you have lacquer; and if neither works, you have varnish. Most varnishes will not "alligator", and if they did for some unknown reason, then the following process will not be applicable. However, this process will work for shellac or lacquer finish.

Give the piece of furniture a thorough cleaning. Spray on synthetic detergent, like Formula 409, and scrub all the dirt and grime from the surface, including out of the cracks even if a brush is necessary. Many pieces of furniture were waxed during their lifetime and it is necessary to remove all wax residue; turpentine does this readily. Give a soft cloth pad a liberal soaking with turpentine, rub it over the entire wood surface and wipe with paper towels or clean rags. Wax will interfere with the reamalgamation of the finish unless it is totally removed.

Use denatured alcohol for a shellacked

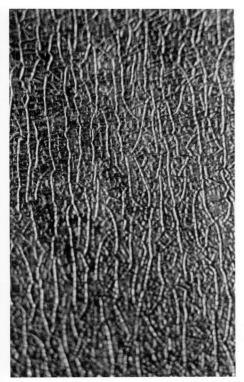

Alligatoring on this shellacked finish has ruined the appearance of the wood.

With one swipe of the brush, alcohol and a steady hand have reamalgamated the finish at the right.

piece of furniture and lacquer thinner for a lacquer finish as follows. Dip a new, wide, soft bristle brush, into the solvent and stroke it across the alligatored surface. Some experts recommend that this surface always be in a horizontal plane to let gravity help in the process of reamalgamation, but I have found that it is not absolutely necessary. Most of the work can be done with the brush with a little experience. Also, it is probably a good idea to try this technique on an unimportant place if one can be found before doing it on the most obvious portion of an important piece of furniture. If you mess it up, you have not ruined the furniture in any way, but you will have to strip it and completely refinish it.

The solvent is applied to liberally coat the surface against the grain of the wood. With very light strokes move the brush with the grain of the wood, stroking the finish in one spot and then moving over slightly with only a small overlap of the brushed area. Do not brush too long in one spot or apply too much pressure or the finish will peel off. The objective is to allow the solvent to penetrate through the entire finish and soften it. Once it has been softened, it will begin to flow like a new liquid and can again be brushed. The thicker the finish, the better the chances of success, because thin areas may lose their shellac or lacquer finish with just a little bit of brushing. The process works like magic, however, and will probably astound you.

With a little practice, it is easy to learn how to work even on a vertical surface by applying just the right amount of solvent and doing just the right amount of brushing with the appropriate minimal pressure. I have worked on pieces of furniture that would have taken several hours, at a minimum, to refinish properly, and have reamalgamated the finish in 20 minutes to make it look like new. If the finish shines too brightly when dry, it can be buffed lightly with 0000 steel wool to a satin finish.

Black Spots

Black spots or rings on wood are stains in the wood rather than in the finish. Water has soaked through the varnish or shellac, or whatever the finish is, and penetrated the wood itself. There is no alternative here except to remove the finish from the entire piece and bleach out the stain. The best bleach to use is oxalic acid. The local drugstore should be willing to sell you a small quantity of oxalic acid crystals, which are dissolved in a small quantity of water until they will no longer dissolve. The solution is then brushed liberally over the blackened area. The entire surface of the piece of furniture should also get one coat of this brushing, or the area being repaired will be obvious after the bleaching process. Additional oxalic acid should be brushed on the black spot until it has been bleached to match the surrounding area. Oxalic acid works quickly, and when the water has evaporated from the solution, it will form small white crystals on the surface of the wood that should be wiped away with a damp cloth. Be careful not to inhale these crystals or any dust from the oxalic acid. It will cause you to cough and sneeze. After the wood has

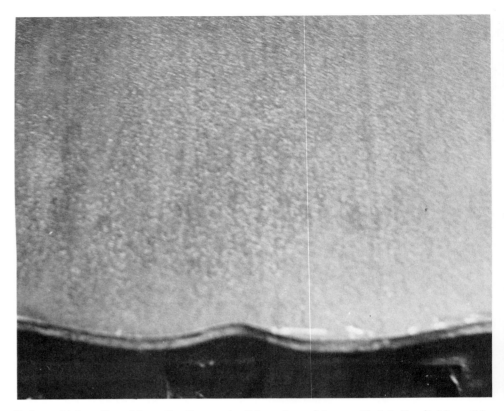

Before: Light reflected from the thousands of tiny edges of the crackled shellac finish on this old crank phonograph hides the wood grain.

After: Just 15 minutes of labor has reamalgamated the finish to reveal the beautiful mahogany grain beneath it.

dried, of course, a new finish must be applied.

White Spots

Pieces of furniture can take on an aura of whiteness if moisture has been absorbed by either a lacquer or shellac finish. This syndrome is known as hazing or blushing. It may look as though the piece of furniture has been attacked by some microscopic organism that has turned the finish opaque, or nearly so. Usually, the blushing has occurred at the surface and does not penetrate deeply into the finish, and therefore can be easily removed. Soak a pad of 0000 steel wool in linseed oil, squeeze out all excess oil and rub the blushed area gently. The clearness of the original finish should quickly return.

Of course, sometimes when water-filled containers are allowed to sit on a piece of furniture, moisture can trickle down and penetrate deeper into the surface. Here a soft cloth pad that will not lint should be dipped in lacquer thinner and excess thinner squeezed from the cloth. The cloth is then held with the fingers and gently rubbed over the white spots. Little by little, the lacquer thinner will penetrate the finish and when it gets through the portion that has been damaged by moisture, the clearness of the original finish should be reestablished. This process also results in shining the finish so that it may not match the surrounding area. Fine steel wool (0000) should be used to lightly buff the entire area, perhaps using a touch of linseed oil, until the surface is uniform in appearance. Use a clean cloth to wipe off any excess oil from either of the above techniques.

Cigarette Burns

Cigarette burns can be either serious or more serious. There is no way that you can burn a piece of furniture without somehow invoking some irreversible damage. Some cosmetic procedures can be followed to hide the cigarette burn, however.

If the burn is shallow, in other words has burned the finish but has not penetrated deeply into the wood, a small amount of paint mixed to exactly the same hue as the surrounding wood is applied to camouflage the burn. Your own adeptness at color matching will be the trick here. In fact, a fine brush with some black paint may also help by superimposing a simulated wood grain over the painted area.

For deeper burns, either a wax stick or shellac stick repair is necessary. If a wax stick is used, wax is melted into the burned area then scraped smooth to blend in flush with the surrounding surface. Wax sticks are available from a local lumber yard, but any colored wax, including crayons, will do if the color matches. If the color does not exactly match, different color wax sticks can be melted. The wax changes color, however, between its molten state and its solid state so a number of samples should be made and allowed to cool before being applied to the piece of furniture. In situations where a new finish is to be applied, a special caution is in order. Certain finishes applied over wax will cause an interaction with the wax which will not allow the finish to completely dry. Therefore, shellac must always be used over a wax area first—even if varnish is intended as the final finish.

The best way to fix a cigarette burn is by using a shellac stick. The burned area should be scraped to remove any loose pieces of charcoal. Using a shellac stick is a technique that must be acquired with experience, but basically you use a heated spatula or soldering iron to melt the material into the void. Shellac stick has the advantage that it is the same color whether in the liquid or solid state. It has the disadvantage that it must be worked while it is warm, because when it hardens it cannot be made to change shape. Shellac sticks are available from Albert Constantine and Son, Incorporated, listed in the appendix at the end of this chapter.

Chip Off The Old Block

Chips in a piece of furniture or the finish can be repaired by using a shellac stick in a manner similar to fixing cigarette burns as described above.

The Final Straw

If the above techniques are not satisfactory for repairing the finish on an old treasure, then it is likely that refinishing is the only alternative. All repairs, regluing, or anything else that is necessary to insure that the structure of the antique is sound can be done after the old finish is taken off. In fact, sometimes it is best to disassemble the piece entirely, scrape off the old glue and reglue it before the new finish is applied. And if this is going to be done, some of the solvent which will take off the old finish may also soften the glue in glue joints, facilitating the disassembly.

There are all kinds of techniques for removing finishes. Years ago, lye was the substance most often used, but I cannot emphasize enough how lye should not be used on Victorian furniture. It darkens the wood and, therefore, in the case of walnut, could be disastrous. It raises the grain and, therefore, creates the need for an excessive amount of sanding after the finish has been removed. And if left on too long, it can severely burn the wood. If you take the furniture to a commercial stripping business, they will dip the article in a chemical bath. Make sure that lye is not one of those chemicals. Of course, there is no reason for you to take the article to a commercial operation when you can do a wholly adequate job yourself.

The objective is to remove the finish with the greatest ease and with the least abrasion. If the furniture was finished properly initially (and it probably was), then most likely it was sanded sufficiently and will require very little, if any, sanding after the finish has been removed, provided care is taken not to scar the surface of the wood.

Take an old brush and cut the bristles so that they are only about one inch long. Dip the brush in a solvent and brush liberally over the finish. For a shellac finish, denatured alcohol with a small amount of lacquer thinner should be the appropriate solvent. For lacquer, lacquer thinner with a small amount of denatured alcohol added is the appropriate solvent. For varnish, a number of commercial paint and varnish removers are available that can be purchased

Before: This three-drawer walnut chest was commercially stripped of its painted finish. Traces of paint still remain in cracks and crevices.

After: After additional hand-stripping and refinishing, the chest becomes an acceptable piece of furniture.

from a paint or hardware store. My favorite happens to be Super Strip.

Commercial solvents have all kinds of varying characteristics that may make them good in one situation but not in others. Some produce inflammable fumes, while others do not. Some work quickly, while others work slowly. Usually, the most expensive ones work best. Following the instructions on the container will usually be the most suitable procedure. Examine the instructions on the container before beginning the job. In fact, it would be a good idea to make this examination before you purchase the stripper. Decide what is the best buy for you, depending on the job that must be done. Of course, it is somewhat difficult to tell how effective the stripper will be on the finish that you are trying to remove without first having had some experience with the brand and, secondly, having an intimate knowledge or experience with the finish that you are removing. Various varnishes and paints react differently to different solvents, and therefore it is not possible to give a complete treatise in this book to help you anticipate the pros and cons of those operations.

After the stripper has been applied with the stubby brush, hopefully you can let it sit for a few minutes while the finish actually raises up off the wood. A wide scraper is then moved along the wood, lifting the finish off and away. Scrape carefully so that the edges of the scraper do not gouge the wood. For carved or curved areas, use coarse (number 2) steel wool dipped in additional solvent to remove the finish. A minimal amount of pressure should be applied, because you do not want to scratch the smooth wooden surface underneath. Finish softens from the action of the solvent and is readily cut by the steel wool and absorbed. Periodically, return the steel wool to a canister of stripper, soak it and wring it out to remove the embedded resins or pigments.

Some strippers require washing after the application. Some require washing with water, while others require an alcohol washing. Avoid the strippers that require a water wash, because the water will raise the grain of the wood and require considerable sanding. Use an alcohol wash stripper. In fact, even if it is not required, it is a good idea to lightly rub some additional alcohol over the surface that has been stripped with coarse steel wool to remove all residue of the old finish. If necessary, use an old toothbrush with stripper to remove the finish from deeply recessed areas. Use of a cotton swab may also be appropriate. Do not skimp on alcohol during this process, because any residue that remains will cause an unsightly appearance in an otherwise finely refinished historical object.

After the wood has dried, it is appropriate to use 0000 steel wool or a very fine abrasive sandpaper to buff the area that has been stripped. This will remove any additional residue that may remain on the surface of the wood, as well as restore some of the smoothness that may have been lost during the stripping process. If a vacuum cleaner is not available, wipe all traces of dust from the piece of furniture with either a tack rag

Before: A brush with bristles cut short is used to apply stripper to a varnished finish.

Coarse steel wool is used to remove the old finish.

Additional stripper is applied with a toothbrush to remove obstinate finish from crevices and recesses.

A toothbrush is essential to remove the finish from any fine detail.

Alcohol is used to wash remaining residue away.

Fine steel wool is used to smooth the wood.

A vacuum cleaner removes sawdust and prepares the surface for its new finish.

After: The new finish is applied.

or a rag soaked in turpentine. A tack rag is a piece of cheesecloth that has been soaked in varnish, wrung out and allowed to partially dry. It is kept in a sealed container to protect it from drying entirely. Its tacky surface facilitates collecting loose dust and dirt.

Now any dents or gouges that are present in the piece should be removed using the technique described in the chapter on furniture repair. After this, all that is necessary is staining, if appropriate, and applying the new finish.

Before: The scratches in this Lincoln rocker arm should be removed before a new finish is applied.

After: The scratches are removed by sanding.

141

Before: A mixture of paint and shellac was used as the finish on this old frame.

Paint stripper is applied with a brush.

The finish is removed with light strokes of coarse steel wool.

Steel wool dipped in alcohol facilitates removing the paint from the grain.

The surface is wiped clean with paper towels.

After: The new finish is applied.

I Don't Want To Dye

My personal opinion is that wood should be finished for its own beauty and not disguised to look as though it is something else. The only exception that I ever follow to this rule in my own working is to apply some walnut-colored stain to pieces of oak furniture. I think I do this primarily because I treasure walnut more than oak, and perhaps also partially because the aged varnish on a lot of old oak furniture resembles the appearance of newly refinished oak with a tinge of walnut stain added.

The Victorians used walnut, oak, rosewood and mahogany primarily, especially for their formal furniture. These woods all have exceptional beauty, color and figure in the grain that deserve to be shown for what they are. Cottage furniture was made from walnut, oak and occasionally pine. Again, there is no reason to disguise the natural beauty that man cannot begin to effectively simulate.

But, some circumstances may require the application of stain. Therefore, an elementary knowledge of stain may be useful. If part of a piece of furniture is refinished and refinishing is not necessary for the rest of it, staining might be required to match colors. Stains come in various materials and are applied using different means. Varnish stains are aniline dyes dissolved in varnish. They are difficult to apply because even the slightest brush mark leaves a tell-tale sign. The trick is to put the varnish stain uniformly over the wood to avoid blotches and the like. Any sagging or running of the varnish will be immediately apparent because of the darker color of this thickened area.

Aniline dyes used as stains for wood can be dissolved either in water or in alcohol. They should not be used in water, however, because the water will raise the grain and require sanding before a finish can be applied. Therefore, the aniline dye should be dissolved only in alcohol for woodworking purposes. These dyes can be bought from most of the larger paint supply houses in powdered form. They have the advantage of ease of application without the worry of streaking and running as with the varnish stain. In addition, they dry in just a few minutes and allow you to continue with the refinishing process. If the color is not deep enough, another coat can readily be applied.

Oil stains are pigments dissolved in oil—usually linseed oil. The stain is rubbed onto the surface and the excess is rubbed off. These stains deeply penetrate soft porous woods, but hardly do the job on hard woods like oak. They are becoming harder to find because of the problems associated with their application—the most outstanding of which is the time required for them to dry before applying a finish over them. They usually require a minimum of 24 hours for appropriate drying.

Sealer dyes, of course, are usually made from some synthetic material, as are some new varnishes referred to as sealers. Most of these have a classic base and penetrate into the wood as well as covering the surface.

Before: A simple paint scraper removed most of the paint from this old kitchen cabinet.

After: The appearance of the cabinet is significantly improved by restoring it to its original finish.

Beware Of What Came Before You

I just thought it would be appropriate to make you aware of the fact that all of the preceding centers primarily around finishes that are to be found on antique artifacts when they come into your possession. However, we must remember that the original finish is not always on the original object. With 100 years or more of history separating the manufacture of the piece of furniture from your possible acquisition, it is highly possible and perhaps even probable in many instances, that the item has been refinished one or more times in the past. Because of the lack of knowledge years ago in many circles about refinishing, a common crime was simply to take an otherwise perfectly good piece of wood requiring refinishing and throw a coat of paint over it to hide scratches and discoloration. However, some enlightened individuals may have applied a new shellac, lacquer or varnish finish. As a matter of fact, it may even be possible that within the past decade or so, someone has refinished it using one of the new synthetic varnishes. If this is the case, special solvents may have to be sought to dissolve that finish. Manufacturers should be cognizant of the fact that at some time in the future it might be necessary to remove their finish from a piece of wood. Of course, a lot of them will proclaim that the finish will last indefinitely, but we know that accidents do happen, and the only appropriate way to remedy some of the effects of those accidents is to do a total refinishing job.

The point I am trying to make is that new solvents may have to be sought for dissolving plastic base finishes. I am confident that they will be found, if the need is pressing enough. In fact, plastic solvents may even be found by accident, as I discovered the first time I poured lacquer thinner into a styrofoam cup. You might try it just for the experience, but be sure that the cup is not over anything of significant value—the lacquer thinner will proceed through it as though the bottom of the cup was never there.

The New Finish

A lot has been written about how to apply the various conventional finishes and, therefore, I do not need to dwell on their detail here. Shellac is usually applied in a number of very thin coats, and allowed to dry thoroughly between each—which only takes a matter of minutes. It is steel wooled lightly between coats, and the finish can be built up to the desired thickness. Its gloss, or luster, can be reduced by gently rubbing with 0000 steel wool. A wax is usually applied over the shellacked finish to give it at least some protection from moisture.

An application of lacquer dries quickly and provides a smooth luster that can be free of brush marks if applied with a spray gun. Lacquer can be thinned so that spraying applications are almost always possible, and spraying is recommended.

Varnish is applied with a brush in a manner similar to shellac. Some varnishes are now available in aerosol spray cans that help to avoid the hassle of brush marks, cleaning brushes, or cleaning an individual spray gun. Some of the new nozzles on aerosol cans for spray finishes work well without dribbling. However, care must be taken with some of them, because instead of providing a fine mist with which to spray the finish, they emit a stream or large droplets after being used for awhile. Never use what is called spar varnish on a piece of furniture. It is primarily linseed oil designed in such a way that it may never dry. It is useful for waterproof-type applications on outdoor surfaces.

Linseed oil causes most woods to darken somewhat with its application. More linseed oil will be absorbed by a piece of wood if the oil was applied hot— and thus a hot linseed oil finish will be darker than a cold linseed oil finish. Walnut can be given a very deep, rich chocolate brown finish by applying linseed oil on a warm, sunny day. I did have one friend who applied linseed oil to an oak commode on a hot sunny day and the finish never dried. I still don't understand this one. Linseed oil does not dry in the same sense that other finishes cure. No volatile solvent is added to linseed oil that is intended to disappear and leave a hard residue behind. Linseed oil imparts beauty to wood furniture by being absorbed into the wood rather than being applied to its surface. Wood saturated with linseed oil will have good resistance to the effects of moisture. But furniture finished with linseed oil will dull with time and new oil application will be necessary. Usually four or five or more initial applications are rubbed in vigorously and allowed to sit for a period of time until the dullness becomes apparent, then a new coating is applied. Most furniture finished only with linseed oil will require an additional application about once a year.

New sealer finishes with plastic bases, such as Flecto verathane sealer, can be applied with considerable ease. They penetrate the wood as linseed oil does, but also set up a film on the surface which cures to a considerable hardness and offers a great degree of durability to a piece of wood. Because these finishes, however, have not been available for a long time, it is not clear what effects time will have on them nor what techniques may be used to remove them should that become necessary.

The Author's Finish

I personally prefer the durability of varnish and the deep-seated beauty of an oil finish. I also prefer to use a finish that will guarantee the absence of brush marks, sags and runs. My own formula is a concoction of one-third varnish, one-third linseed oil and one-third turpentine by volume. This finish is most appropriate for walnut. I prefer straight varnish for oak and lacquer for rosewood. I also still prefer shellac on pine. The slight color of shellac makes pine look richer. Oak does not absorb oil well and does not benefit, therefore, from oil in the finish. Rosewood already is oily in character so that lacquer, for my purposes, is most appropriate there, after the surface has been sealed. As a passing note, I might mention here that shellac is often used as a sealer before varnish is applied.

A mixture of varnish, linseed oil and turpentine is applied with a brush and allowed to stand for 10 minutes.

Excess finish is wiped off with a clean, lint-free rag.

Shellac is applied in one or two light coats to fill in the pores of the wood and then steel wooled before applying another finish over it. Other materials called wood fillers are brushed over wood with the idea that some of it will settle into the grain. The wood is then rubbed with a cloth across the grain to remove the filler from the surface, leaving only the clear or pigmented compound in the openings. The use of these fillers may be appropriate for surfaces that are to be absolutely smooth on older furnish-ings, such as federalist or empire. But the woodlike character of native walnut, in my opinion, should not be disguised by making the surface look synthetic instead of woodlike.

To apply my finish, the wood is strip-ped and prepared in a normal manner. The concoction of varnish, linseed oil and turpentine in equal quantities is then liberally brushed over an area of about five square feet. A clean rag is used after about 10 minutes to wipe all of the excess finish from the surface. The oil has been absorbed deep into the wood to afford it character and protection. The varnish remains mostly at the surface of the wood to give it all the smoothness that it needs. The turpentine thins the other two materials so that they flow smoothly.

Wiping the excess liquid away insures that no brush marks or running must be dealt with. You will not have to worry about removing bristles that have broken loose from the brush either, but this is only a net benefit if a cloth is chosen that will not leave straggling threads behind. An old cotton T-shirt will always do the job. Although one coat of this finish is normally enough, I enjoy putting on two and sometimes three coats. The only special care that must be taken is to make sure the excess is removed from cracks and crevices, because it will dry shiny while the rest of the surface is satin smooth. Varnishes can be bought that give a gloss, satin or flat finish upon drying. When using varnish alone, it really does not matter since a glossy surface can be made satiny smooth by rubbing it with fine steel wool and can be made flat by rubbing it with coarser steel wool. I prefer to use satin varnish in my mixture, because I don't like to do any more work than I have to.

Try this technique once on walnut and see if you don't agree with me.

REFINISHING APPENDIX

Although most of the finishes discussed in this chapter are available from local paint supply and hardware stores, some of the material, and especially shellac sticks, are difficult to find and can be found at Constantine, 2050 Eastchester Road, Bronx, New York, 10461.

CHAPTER X

ONLY SKIN DEEP, OR VENEERING IS A SUPERFICIAL ART (VENEER)

Veneering is the art of using one substance to cover another to add to its beauty or to hide its imperfections of one sort or another. Semiprecious stones, metals and other materials were used to veneer treasures found in the tombs of pharaohs dating back to more than a thousand years before Christ. Before the 18th century, veneering was not a common practice, but rather an art form used to decorate the treasures of the wealthy. During the 1700's, however, transportation and trade among distant points on the globe made it possible for rare woods and materials to be transported to places where furniture makers could use these rare woods to embellish their cabinet work.

One form of thinly-sliced wood was used to cover another type of wood to make it more pleasing. The veneering material was usually a rarer wood, or one with considerably more appeal because of its color or grain. However, there were also some practical reasons for using veneers. The end grain of oak might necessarily be displayed on certain parts of a cabinet. A piece of veneer laid over this end grain would make the entire piece of furniture appear more appealing, even though the veneer was of the same species of tree.

During the Victorian era, rosewood appealed to the most discerning cabinet-

Burl veneer is used extensively to accentuate this American walnut secretary.

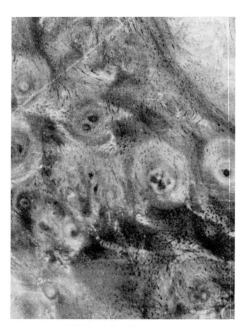

Walnut burl veneer.

Mahogany crotch veneer.

makers and buyers of fine furniture. For the most part, furniture made from rosewood is either rosewood veneer over some other type of wood or made of multiple laminations of rosewood with crosshatched grains to form a sort of plywood. Rosewood is very oily and heavy, as well as being brittle. Many pieces of furniture made during the 19th century out of solid rosewood have not lasted until today, because the furniture would often break of its own weight while being moved across a room, or lifted because of some other necessity. Although legs, carvings or reinforced curved pieces may be made of solid rosewood, large flat pieces are almost always rosewood veneer over walnut or some other wood.

During the middle part of the 19th century, the United States was growing at a rate disproportionate to the rate at which fine craftsmen and artisans could be trained and employed. Some woodcarvers brought their talents from Europe to America and carried on their trade of decorating pieces of furniture. But the demand for fine quality pieces of furniture outstripped the potential production of the limited number of these artists. As a result, furniture makers increasingly sought fancy-grained veneers to embellish furniture in place of intricate carvings. As an example, you need only to observe European cabinet work from the Victorian period which, in general, will have large, otherwise flat areas embellished with expansive carvings. In American Victorian furniture, however, burls, crotches and butt veneers were used to decorate cabinet work.

Wooden It Be Lovely

Nonhomogeneity is the aspect of fine woods that makes them appealing. Different colorings and grains make no two portions of the tree exactly the same. As a tree grows, it forms annual growth rings caused by the variations in moisture content and temperature over a seasonal cycle. An abundance of moisture and the presence of heat during certain parts of the year cause a tree to grow more quickly than it grows with lesser quantities of moisture, heat and sunlight. Various species of trees also inherently grow at different rates from other species. Softwoods, in general, grow faster than hardwoods. Hardwoods are denser and stronger than softwoods and, therefore, are used to make furniture. Since most hardwood trees have to grow for a significantly longer time to reach the same size as a softwood tree, the hardwood lumber has closer grain, with the potential of producing more figures than softwood grain.

Various parts of trees also produce different types of figures. The tremendous pressure caused by the weight of a large tree near its stump produces changes in the otherwise regular cell structure of the wood to form nonuniform patterns called butt or stump wood. Burls are nodules something like warts that form on a tree. They have abnormally dense cell structure, which produces round patterns in the grain of varying colors. Burls usually are thought of as the prettiest of all woods. A crotch grain is formed at the intersection of two limbs or a limb with the trunk. Mahogany crotch veneer, for example,

This oak log is cut in various directions to reveal its many patterns of grain.

The medullary rays on this piece of oak emanate from the bottom left of the photo.

was used extensively on furniture during the American Empire period immediately preceding the Victorian era.

The Pattern Is All In The Way You Slice It

Initially, veneers were made with a saw. The job was tedious and required a great deal of patience. Two men, one standing above the log and the other below, cut the length of a log with a saw as the log was supported on both ends. These forms of veneer were relatively thick compared with those that are produced using modern techniques. Eventually, with water power and steam power, band saws were developed that cut through logs much more easily and allowed men to guide the material, as opposed to having to use their energy to cut it at the same time. Cutting veneer with a saw, however, produces a void in the wood that means sawdust, as opposed to veneer, is being created from an appreciable proportion of a tree.

Thus, the technique of using a knife to slice the logs was developed to make the most of valuable wood. Depending upon the direction of the slicing action relative to the grain in the wood, various patterns can be produced. In general, five different techniques are used to slice logs into veneer.

Quarter slicing is done by cutting a log lengthwise in half and cutting each piece in half once again to get a quarter of a log. The knife is then used to slice through each piece at right angles to the annual growth rings. Varied grain is produced in some woods and a series of straight stripes in others.

In flat slicing, the log is cut in half and then the flat side of the half is moved along a guide plate so that the knife cuts parallel to the flat side.

Rotary cutting is done by placing the log between two centers and rotating it with the knife tangential to the outer edge of the log. The blade slices almost parallel to the annual growth rings and the veneer comes off the same as paper unwinding from a roll.

Half-round slicing produces characteristics that are somewhere between rotary and flat-sliced veneer. The log segment is mounted in a lathe off-center, and is then cut in fashion similar to rotary cutting.

Rift-cutting techniques cut a log section perpendicular to the medullary rays of certain types of wood to produce a distinct pattern. These rays present in oak, for example, are a certain type of cell formation that radiate from the center of the log toward the outside like spokes of a wheel.

The veneers are sliced in such a manner that consecutive sheets are produced from adjacent areas within the tree. The slices are stacked in piles called flitches. Consecutive pieces from the flitches can be rotated or inverted and put in various combinations on a flat surface to form a pattern, symmetrical or otherwise, used in decorating table tops and other panels.

Putting A Stick To It

When flat panels are to be veneered, the veneer is placed both on the front and back surface of that panel. The exterior veneer, the side to be seen by observers, is a figural or fancy veneer,

149

while the interior side may be of any simple, less expensive cut and kind of wood. Gluing a piece of veneer to the surface of only one side of a panel would allow moisture to penetrate from the opposite side and cause an imbalance in the moisture content through the thickness of the panel. Moisture causes the cells in wood to expand. Expansion of wood cells on one plane of a panel, with less expansion in the parallel plane somewhere else in the thickness of the piece, causes warping away from the moist side. Therefore, both sides of a panel must be veneered to protect against warping. This procedure, however, does not insure that moisture will not escape from the edges of the panel over a period of several decades. Occasionally, moisture does escape and the interior core, or "ground" as it is called, may fracture, thus putting a strain on the veneer and causing it to split.

At one time, hide glues were the popular adhesives used to fix sheets of veneer to the ground. Hide glues made from animal hides were used for various purposes through the 19th century. They had to be heated to make use of their adhesive properties.

Casein glue is made from the protein present in milk. The primary constituent of cheese is casein. Casein glues have the advantage that they can be worked for 15 to 20 minutes without setting up to the point that adhesion prevents the rearrangment of work. Casein glues were, therefore, much more popular for veneering work, because one did not have to worry about finishing the job before the glue hardened. The disadvantage of casein glue is that it stains woods like oak and mahogany, and great care must be taken when used so that it does not ruin the piece of furniture.

Other types of glues have been developed. Urea resin glues are probably the most popular for original veneer work at this time. Probably the best known brand is Weldwood. The advantage of urea resin glues is that they are not readily attacked by fungus and insects, nor are they affected after curing by such solvents as gasoline or lacquer thinner. Urea resin is a powder mixed with a catalyst that will stay usable for several hours at room temperature, allowing the workman from one-fourth to one-half hour to complete his assembly before the glue begins to cure.

Other types of synthetic glues, such as polyvinyl resins, resorcin resins and epoxies, have also been developed that have some, but not widespread, applications in veneering.

In the past few years, another type of rubber-based glue has been developed for use in veneering work. It is especially valuable for restoration when repairs involve small areas, as opposed to large flat areas. Most arts and crafts enthusiasts are familiar with the common rubber cement that is used to glue papers together. Veneering contact adhesive is similar in consistency and odor, but is a much stronger bonding agent. It is applied to the two surfaces to be bonded in one or two coats that are allowed to dry thoroughly so that they are not even sticky to the touch. Then both surfaces are put in contact and an instant bond is achieved. Pressure, or tapping with a rubber mallet, is used to make sure that all of the area on both surfaces is in contact. The disadvantage of this type of glue is that the work cannot be rearranged after contact. The first time it touches, it holds firmly and will not release. The work must, therefore, be aligned properly and brought into contact only when all edges of the work are fitted as intended.

When contact adhesives are not used, the veneering process normally consists of coating the layer of veneer with a urea resin adhesive, and securing the sheets on a flat table adapted for the use of clamps and braces. This device is called a veneer press. The work is held tightly and firmly at all points uniformly across the surface until the glue has cured.

Blisters

From time to time, blisters appear in veneered work that can absolutely ruin the appearance of an otherwise fine piece of furniture. Blisters can occur if the piece was not originally fabricated correctly, and glue did not adhere to all portions of the veneer and its ground. Absorbing a small amount of moisture can cause the veneer to expand and blister where it is not held fast by some adhesive. Moisture can also seep through veneer and dissolve the glue underneath until it no longer holds fast. Years ago, I purchased a square grand piano made from Brazilian rosewood veneered over some lesser wood. The former owner had set flowerpots and vases along the surface of the piano and was not careful to prevent excessive water from dripping onto the surface. In several places on the piano top, the moisture

had caused the veneer to buckle, creating blisters that ranged from one inch to about six inches in diameter.

If you are lucky, the blisters can be fixed by applying heat and pressure directly over the blistered area. Waxed paper is put over the surface of the veneer to protect it from direct contact with a clothes iron. The iron is heated so that it is too warm to be touched, yet not so warm as to scorch the waxed paper. The wax will melt, but will not harm the wood. The iron is held on top of the waxed paper over the blistered area and pressure applied for several minutes, if necessary, until the surface of the wood feels very warm or even hot to the touch. The heat should evaporate excessive moisture from the blistered surface and cause it to shrink slightly. The heat being applied also will soften the glue underneath, if enough pressure has been applied to afford direct contact between the glue and the warm veneer. Pressure is continually applied as the heat is turned off. When the surface has thoroughly cooled, the iron is removed, and hopefully the blister will have shrunk and the veneer will have been reattached to the ground underneath.

Sometimes this method does not work, because either the glue has deteriorated to the point where it cannot be useful for the process of readhesion or the blister cannot be shrunk so that the veneer is once again flat over its substrate.

In the first case, two small holes can be drilled in the surface of the blister about one-sixteenth inch in diameter. Glue is then injected into one of the

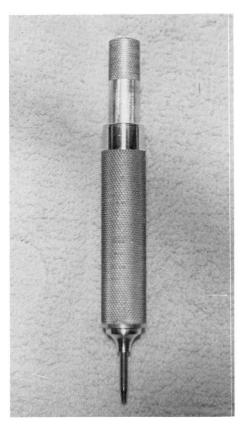

A glue injector.

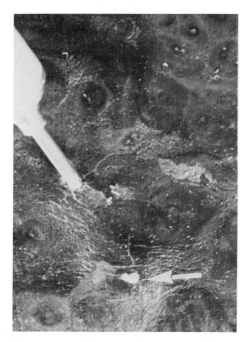

Using a glue injector to innoculate a blister through a $1/16$-inch hole. Excess glue oozes out of a second hole (see arrow).

holes using either a hypodermic syringe with a large needle or a device especially designed for this type of glue injection. White glue or Elmer's glue is suitable for this purpose, but it may have to be thinned with a little water so that it flows from the syringe into the blister. The second hole is to allow both air and excess glue to escape. Press the blister and wipe away excess glue before you place bricks or books or other items on top of a sheet of waxed paper over the blister to hold it firmly in place for one to two hours while the glue dries. Don't skimp on the weight—a full 20 pounds of books may be necessary to get the veneer firmly in contact with the surface beneath it.

If the wood has swelled to the point where the blister cannot be pushed down so that the veneer will lie flat, the blister must be slit with a razor blade and straight-edged along its grain. Half of the blister can be glued into place and the other half slowly pushed into place with pressure applied. There will be a slight amount of overlap from the second half of the blister over the first. This overlap must be trimmed very carefully with a sharp single-edged razor blade. When done correctly, the cut along the grain of the wood will not be noticeable and the repair will not be visible even to an expert observer.

Loose Veneer

Moisture may loosen the adhesive or cause the veneer to swell, so that it rises at a seam or edge. The procedure for solving this problem is similar to solving the problem of blisters. If the raised veneer is a recent problem, you can apply the waxed paper and heat

Veneer glue has the consistency of rubber cement, if it has a rubber base. It is applied to both the veneer and the piece to which it will be attached. The two surfaces are pressed firmly into contact only after the glue has dried.

treatment as a solution. However, if the raised portion has been in this state for some time, it is likely that dirt and grime has gotten into the area between the veneer and its ground. This dirt will contaminate the adhesive and make a good bond impossible. In these cases, it is necessary to use a sharp knife, toothpick or other type of probe to scrape out as much of the dirt and loose glue as possible. Be careful not to needlessly break the veneer, but do not be afraid of lifting it further off its substrate if the adhesive near the edge of the lifted area is not strong enough to hold it. It will probably eventually come up anyhow. After scraping as much of the loose glue and dirt as possible, use a portable vacuum cleaner or a brush to further clean where possible. Then use white glue and pressure to put the veneer back into place. If the sheet of veneer overlaps an adjacent sheet at a seam, a razor blade is once again used to trim the overlap so that the two sheets fit flush together at their edges. When veneer is appropriately fixed on a panel, it has a solid sound when tapped with a finger. Improperly glued veneer will produce a hollow sound that indicates a gap between the veneer and the panel.

Grafting

In some cases, veneer will be missing from certain areas of a piece of furniture. If the missing piece is a border or an edge, it may be possible to replace the entire piece with a sheet of new veneer without the repair being especially noticeable. But in other cases, it may be very difficult to find a veneer that matches adjacent areas so that the repair does

A rubber mallet or roller is used to attach veneer to a curved surface.

not stand out as an obvious recent alteration. For missing pieces in swirled grains like burls or crotch, it is easy to make the repair if a relatively close matching color of burl or crotch veneer can be found. The objective is to cut out the area needing the repair into an irregular shape, using curves similar to the curves in the grain, and to make an identical cut in the new piece of veneer that is going to be used to make the patch. Sometimes the original work can be cut with a razor blade or an Exacto knife into the pattern desired. But the easiest way to make the repair is to use a veneer punch. Veneer punches are difficult to find but are devices that are tapped on the handle to cause an irregularly shaped cutter to penetrate through the surface of the veneer. Using a chisel or knife, any veneer still adhering inside the incision on the piece of furniture can then be removed. The punch is then used on the sheet of replacement veneer and that patch glued into the appropriate spot on the piece of furniture.

Sometimes the veneer has been broken on a plain-grained flat area of a piece of furniture. Repairs here usually are difficult to make, because modern veneers do not have the same color as a piece of veneer more than 100 years old. Attempts should be made to salvage veneer from other pieces of furniture that cannot otherwise be salvaged. Sometimes veneer can be removed from the back of a panel from the same piece of furniture to assure an appropriate vintage of the veneer. Although this should be done only as a last resort, it can be effective in matching both the grain and color of the veneer to be used. Care must be taken to reveneer the panel where any veneer has been removed, so that moisture will not cause warping. Individual judgment must be used to decide whether an entire sheet of veneer should be removed for replacement, or whether appropriate cuts can be made and a patch affixed without causing the repair to be unduly noticeable. Occasionally, a stain or ammonia can be used to darken a patch where the surrounding veneer has a naturally deeper tone.

Getting Around Those Curves

If the surface of the work to be veneered is curved, it is impractical to place a stack of books on the surface hoping that it will cause enough pressure to form a firm bond between the veneer and the panel. For most applications, the use of the contact adhesive is the best approach. Any old portions of veneer or remaining old glue must be carefully chiseled or shaved from the work surface and then the work surface sanded smooth. The contact adhesive is applied in two coats to the piece of furniture and then in two coats to the piece of veneer. The veneer is carefully fitted to the curved area and then rolled with a rolling pin type roller and/or pounded with a rubber mallet to insure that the bond is complete. Sanding and finishing is then appropriate. If the piece is surrounded by already finished areas of a section of the furniture which does not need to be refinished, the veneer should be sanded and finished before it is applied.

153

It is sometimes useful to take advantage of another glue that does not form the immediate bond of the contact adhesives. In these applications, the veneer is glued to a curved panel which is then placed face down in a box of fine sand deep enough to make contact with all of the curved surface. Weights are then applied to the back of the panel to hold the entire surface under pressure until the glue is cured. For curves that are not this extreme, a hard rubber block can be used in place of the sand. If the sandbox approach is used, care must be taken to remove all traces of the sand from the edge of the work or it may have become affixed to oozing glue. It should be removed either by sanding or scraping with a scraper, as opposed to using power tools or chisels which will be ruined by trying to cut through the hard grains of sand. Occasionally, it is also possible to use sand bags to form the veneer around the curve and hold it tightly. I have used this technique successfully in shaping the veneer around a slight curve at the edge of a picture frame by applying the glue and using a 70-pound sand bag on top of the veneer until the glue was dry.

Getting Rid Of That Greasy Kid Stuff

Occasionally, some veneers contain so much natural oil that it is difficult to get a glue to stick to the wood. This problem is most commonly found in teak and rosewood. If experience shows that the glue will not do the job that it was intended to do, the veneer can be soaked overnight in lacquer thinner. The veneer must be submerged so that the lacquer thinner will have a chance to penetrate through the wood and dissolve some of the oil. Lacquer thinner will not harm the wood in any way. The veneer can then be removed from the lacquer thinner, placed between 20 or so sheets of newspaper on either side and held firmly with weights to insure that the veneer will be flat after drying. Sometimes one or two days of drying time will be necessary. Be careful not to use this practice near a furnace or hot water heater. Even a pilot light could ignite the volatilizing lacquer thinner and cause a fire or explosion. Use blotters if the wood is not dark, so that the newsprint does not leave an impression on the wood.

Reducing Those Unwieldy Lumps And Bumps

Because of the uneven grains in burl, crotch and butt veneers, it is highly likely that these veneers when purchased will be unsuitable for veneering any smooth surface. Absorbing even small amounts of moisture will cause these veneers to swell unevenly, giving a piece of what was once a flat veneer a completely distorted and lumpy appearance. These veneers are likely also to be brittle, and any straightforward attempt to put them back into their original flat shape will cause them to crack and break, rendering them less useful for furniture repair. On smaller lumps and bumps, I have found it possible to apply a contact adhesive on one side and then use a wet cloth on the face side of the veneer. Use just enough moisture to make the veneer flexible. Apply the veneer with a rolling pin to the piece of furniture being repaired. The veneer will not crack, but great care must be taken to insure that no bumps are being forced into the finished surface.

A more intelligent approach, however, is absolutely necessary when the veneer has been extremely distorted.

To make the veneer flexible enough to work with, immerse it in a solution of one part wood alcohol, two parts glycerin and four parts water. Immerse the veneer in this solution until it is thoroughly soaked. Then remove and hold on edge until all excess liquid has drained from it. Place the veneer between two sheets of metal, and then between sheets of newspaper and weight it until the veneer has dried. Since the glycerin is too thick to be used as the flexibilizing agent in itself, it has to be extended by adding water, and the alcohol is used to speed evaporation of the water. Ex-

tremely brittle veneer can be strengthened by adding powdered Weldwood glue to the solution in the same proportion as the glycerin.

The Missing Link

Marquetry is the historic art of using woods of different grains and colors to veneer another surface to form a design or picture. If a piece of the puzzle, so to speak, is missing, repair will be difficult, because a strip of the picture cannot be removed and replaced by a single sheet of veneer. Veneer punches also cannot be used. The piece must be fit exactly into the puzzle, and considerable care is necessary to insure that it fits properly.

Plate a sheet of thin paper over the area of the missing piece. Rub a crayon or pencil over the paper to provide an impression of the void left by the missing piece. Glue this section of the paper to

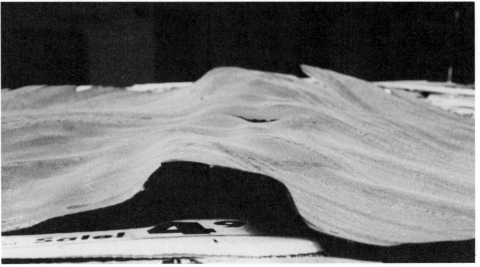
Some bumpy and brittle veneers require treatment before applying.

155

the piece of veneer you will use to make the repair. The color should be as close as possible to the other pieces of wood in similar locations within the pattern. Make sure that the grain is running in the appropriate direction under the piece of paper. Next, cut the piece of veneer along the lines on the paper showing the outline of the missing link. File the edges of the piece carefully to provide a slight taper toward the bottom of the piece, away from the face, which is the side with the paper glued in place. The taper around the edge will provide a place for the glue to move when the veneer is forced into position. Place glue in the void in the pattern, put the piece of veneer in place and pound it in to be flush with the surface.

Sometimes veneer cannot be found of the right thickness. Veneers have been made throughout history in just about every thickness imaginable, and modern veneers can be found in 1-100th, 1-64th, 1-40th, 1-36th, 1-28th, and 1-20th of an inch in thickness. For this, or any other application where small pieces are necessary and surrounding veneer thickness does not match, sheets of paper or other veneer can be glued beneath the veneer before it is put into place and sanded flush. Of course, if it is thicker than the surrounding veneer, there is no special concern because it can be sanded until it is flush with surrounding surfaces.

If the veneer can be found in the appropriate thickness and the entire surface of the wood being repaired does not require refinishing, then the missing link should be sanded and finished before placing it into the void in the puzzle.

Splits

After some people become aged and dehydrated, doing the splits can become an irreversible phenomenon. So, it is too, with splits in many wood panels. If the ground has split completely through, causing the veneer to split on its surface, there is no way that the veneer can be repaired without first repairing the ground beneath it. Splits are less likely to occur when veneer has been affixed to the surface of the panel with the grains running perpendicular to each other. However, sometimes this is not what was done out of necessity. Drying over the years of the ground can cause it to shrink nonuniformly and result in a serious split.

The panel may be cut with a saw and a piece sectioned into the split area like a piece of pie fitting into the puzzle, with veneer added to the top and bottom by performing a marquetry repair. If the split is not very large, appropriate-colored wood filler, such as Plastic Wood, can be used between a sandwich of veneer and allowed to cure before the veneer is applied. Your own judgment must be used in these cases. Remember that simply pulling the piece together and clamping it to reglue it will probably not solve the problems that caused the split in the first place, and the crack will likely reappear either near the same area or someplace else.

Metal And Pearly Inlays

Veneering is not always done with wood—it is sometimes done with metal or mother-of-pearl. Mother-of-pearl is the shiny, irridescent material that lines the shells of oysters and other mollusks.

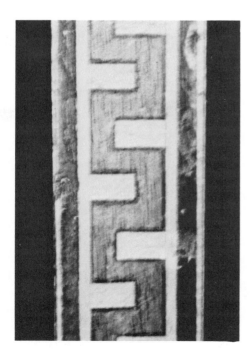

Marquetry is the art of inlaying intricate patterns of different veneers.

Metal and mother-of-pearl do not expand or contract with the application of moisture. Wood, however, expands when absorbing moisture and shrinks when drying. Objects that have a combination of woods and inlays of other materials very often will need repair, because the wood has shrunk so that the spaces for the inlay of other materials no longer fit.

To repair a section with lost mother-of-pearl, use a procedure similar to that to repair voids left by missing links in a marquetry design. Care must be taken to insure that the mother-of-pearl is the appropriate thickness to fit flush with the surface, because it cannot be sanded later without ruining that surface. With metal, care must be taken not to bend or crease the metal pieces necessary for inlaying.

If the metal inlay has not been lost but is simply pushed out of place in the pattern, it should be carefully removed without bending or damaging it. The piece of metal can then be filed to fit snugly back into a pattern that has changed shape or size over the years. Before it is put back into position, be sure that all old glue has been cleaned from its surface as well as from the surface of the void into which it will be placed. New glue should be used and pressure applied until the glue has set.

This rosewood lap desk has inlays of both metal and mother of pearl.

157

VENEERING APPENDIX

Veneers and other assorted equipment, such as rollers and adhesives useful in veneering, can be obtained from the following companies:

Albert Constantine and Son
2050 Eastchester Road
Bronx, New York 10461

Craftsman Wood Service Company
2727 South Mary Street
Chicago, Illinois 60608

Homecraft Veneer
Box 3
Latrobe, Pennsylvania 15650

Real Woods
107 Trumble Street
Elizabeth, New Jersey 07206

Woodcraft Supply Corporation
313 Montvale Avenue
Woburn, Massachusetts 01801

The above companies will supply catalogs upon request.

Veneer punches are available from:
H. L. Wild
510 East 11th Street
New York, New York 10009

CHAPTER XI

UNDER-COVER OPERATIONS (REUPHOLSTERING)

Have you ever stopped to wonder what magic and what materials have been maneuvered under the covers of upholstered furniture? As time progresses, material wears, webbing tears and springs have sprung. It is then time to disrobe the upholstered antique, examine it and restore it. Occasionally, the furniture simply needs to have a new cover to make it look like new or rather, old but not worn. Other times it needs to be completely redone.

This chapter will describe the basics of reupholstering antique furniture. Although the basics are enough to begin experimentation with upholstering and, indeed, to produce a reasonable quality of finished item, it is also useful to spend the time in an adult education upholstering course to learn about upholstering techniques that cannot be experienced by reading. Only through actual experience can you learn the feel of appropriate tension on webbing or material. Only through feeling the firmness of cotton padding can you really understand the relationship between the looks of the final upholstered product and how it will feel when used.

Before embarking upon any complicated upholstering challenge, try several easy upholstering jobs. The experience will facilitate graduation toward coping with the problems of more involved projects. The first item upholstered should be something small to experiment with the basics without risking significant funds on a large volume of expensive upholstery material. Straight lines and square corners with no curves or tufting would be appropriate. Reup-

holstering an ottoman would be ideal for the first project.

Some pieces of antique furniture have slip seats and backs. That is, the seat can be removed in one piece simply by removing some screws, or by exerting moderate force against the friction of perhaps dowels that may hold the seat in place. Similarly, some chairs have backs that can be removed in one piece without having to remove material from the frame of the chair. These are the simplest projects that sometimes require nothing more than replacing a little padding and covering with a new section of upholstery material. Sometimes, not even webbing or springs are involved. Other times, slip seats and backs are constructed more like conventional furniture, which employs the use of springs. These must be reconstructed in a manner similar to a complete reupholstering project. If springs are not part of the furniture, the reupholstering project is almost self-explanatory. If springs are present, and they usually are, then this entire chapter should be read through at least once before taking on the challenge.

Tools

The most conventional upholstering technique employs a hammer and steel tacks with broad heads. The tacks are used both to hold twine in place as well as burlap and upholstery material. Although these tools can be used for inexpensive modern furniture, they should not be used for antiques. Unfortunately, many reupholsterers will use them nonetheless. Tacks leave large holes in wood when they are removed. Any antique worthy of restoration will prob-

159

ably be even more worthy of restoration by future generations. Many items have been reupholstered three or four times in the past 100 years. Not many fabrics can withstand more than 25 years of daily use without wearing considerably and requiring replacement. As old wood has more tacks driven into it after removal of old tacks, it begins to splinter and become spongy. It will no longer hold tacks, and reupholstering becomes impossible. Occasionally, old wood may be hidden from view and can be replaced with new hardwood to make reupholstering possible. This job is very tedious and can be postponed for several hundred years if the reupholsterer uses staples instead of tacks.

The stapler used is not the type used for stapling papers on the desk in the office. It is a heavy duty instrument powered either by compressed air or electricity. Just a few years ago, the pneumatic stapler was the only alternative, but now the electric stapler can eliminate much of the expense. The pneumatic staple gun generally costs upwards of $80. In addition, a compressor with pressure regulating valves is needed to power it. This item probably will cost more than $200—still less than the cost of having a major piece of furniture reupholstered commercially.

Electric staplers will vary in price according to manufacturer and degree of sophistication. Either tool is suitable and will allow using staples of varying length in different parts of the reupholstering project. Be sure that the tool uses round wire staples and not large flat staples. Although each staple will make two holes in the supporting piece of hardwood, these holes will be

small in comparison to the shattering effect of driving a wedge-shaped tack into the same piece of wood. An additional benefit of a stapler is the ease with which it is handled—requiring the movement of only one finger to drive the fastener into place with 80 pounds of force. Using a stapler will allow the novice to upholster two or three times as fast as he could with a hammer and tacks.

Webbing stretchers must be used to apply appropriate tension to the webbing before it is tacked or stapled. Canvas stretching pliers, which are used to pull the canvas over stretchers to produce oil paintings, can be used instead of the conventional webbing stretcher. The conventional tool can easily be made at home by cutting a piece of three-quarter inch thick hardwood into a handle about three inches across and six inches long. Drive nails into one end, about one-half inch apart and to a depth of about one and one-quarter inches. Then snip off the heads about one-half inch above the surface of the wood. File the snipped ends of the nails to sharp points. Use of this stretcher tool will be described later in this chapter.

A staple puller is useful for removing staples that are either put in the wrong place, do not penetrate the material appropriately, or that require removal because they were intended to be only temporary. A staple puller can be made by cutting or filing the end of a one-quarter inch screwdriver such that a notch in its nose provides two points on the end. The end is also ground so that the points are wedge shaped to be inserted under a staple so that it can be pried loose.

Tacks act like little wedges to split the wood apart. After several reupholsterings, the wood may no longer function to hold the upholstery in place and must be reinforced. The best way to do this is to cut away the splintered sections, glue and screw a good piece of wood to this section, and trim it to the original contour of the frame.

160

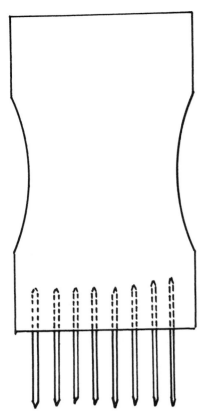

A webbing stretcher made from hardwood and nails.

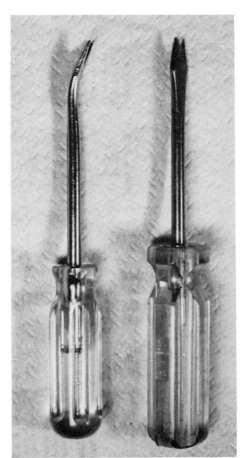

A staple puller left and a tack puller right. Note the curved end of the tack puller is similar to that of a pry bar.

A staple puller is inserted under a staple and rotated about the point that is free of the staple.

A tack puller is forced under the head of a tack and pressed downward to pull the tack up.

A tack puller can be purchased at most hardware stores similar to the staple puller, except its end is curved. The tack puller is pushed under the head of a tack and then pushed down like a pry bar to lift the tack from its mooring. Occasionally, a mallet will be useful to force the tack puller into position.

Good quality sharp sheers are absolutely necessary to cut upholstery fabric.

Various needles, both straight and curved, are used to sew layers together in the stratified upholstering process.

A regulator is used to move padding under the upholstering fabric from one place to another to eliminate voids and bumps. An awl or an ice pick can suitably serve as a regulator.

Some, but not all upholstering projects require sewing the material. A good heavy-duty sewing machine is necessary for these projects. The skills of sewing with this machine cannot be adequately covered in this publication.

Therefore, we will consider these techniques to be left unaddressed.

Occasionally, it is necessary to manufacture buttons for use in tufted upholstery. Tufting is somewhat of an advanced technique that will only be touched upon in this book. A button machine is a simple device that takes a portion of fabric and fastens it over a metal cap that is then inserted into a button back. This makes a button with the head covered by upholstery material. This simple machine resembles an arbor press. Unless extensive upholstering is to be done, the most economical way to make buttons is to purchase the service from a professional upholsterer.

Materials

It is a good idea to familiarize yourself with the materials that are used in the upholstering process. Most projects begin with weaving the webbing. Webbing is a woven band of coarse jute fibers that supports the springs or pads when springs are not used. Springs can be purchased from local upholstery supply houses, but hopefully the old springs will be usable in a restoration project.

Burlap is a cloth woven from jute yarn and used to prevent other upholstering layers from falling into the springs. "Hair" is the curled hair of hogs, cattle or horses that is used as a stuffing. The modern replacement for this hair is rubberized hair (the same product processed with rubber), which is stronger and more form-retaining than the old-time hair. It is more expensive than the other variety, but well worth the expense because of its durability.

Spring twine is simply twine used to tie springs into place. Stitching twine is a thread used to tie together various elements in the upholstery process.

Muslin is used as a temporary cover, and also, basically, as a general utility fabric.

Cotton batting, or cotton felt as it is sometimes called, is a thickness of about one inch or so of cotton linters spun into sheets or rolls. It is used to pad the areas between the covers and coarser stuffing.

Gimp is a fancy braid used to cover the edge of upholstery fabric where that fabric stops and the wood starts. Occasionally, welting is used for this purpose. Welting consists of a long cord over which upholstery fabric has been sewed.

Major Or Minor Surgery

Either the piece of furniture needs to be entirely redone or it doesn't. That is the simple form of logic that never fails.

However, sometimes deciding in which category the artifact belongs can be troublesome. If the item has a simple slip seat, then probably all that is required, if the fabric is torn or worn, is to remove the cover. Be careful to note where the folds lie and where the tacks have been placed, and then simply reverse the process to put on a new cover. No special knowledge is needed for this procedure. However, if the item has a more complex construction, where webbing may have been torn or springs may have been broken or are coming through the fabric, a major operation is required.

The first procedure is to remove the existing covering. Use a tack puller to reach under the head of each tack and with a prying motion pull it loose from the wood beneath. Care should be taken not to allow the base of the tack puller to come in contact with bare wood. The pressure will hurt the finish, and perhaps even the underlying wood. If the area being worked on is of such construction that it is absolutely necessary to put the tack puller onto bare wood, a piece of burlap should be used to shield the furniture from damage. Sometimes access to the head of the tack can be made easier by using one sharp edge of the puller to get under the tack. With a rotating motion of the wrist lift the head enough to insert the puller so that the shaft of the tack slides up the "V" of the puller. Occasionally, a mallet needs to be used to hammer on the tack puller and loosen a particularly obstinate tack. Save the fabric after it has been removed to use as a pattern from which to cut the material that will replace it.

After the covering is free, carefully examine what lies underneath. If the springs are not emerging through the padding—good. Feel around the item carefully to see whether or not the springs have become untied and are free to wander. If the object has held its shape and no clashing of metal is heard when pressure is put to bear (one spring banging upon another), so much the better. Maybe a little additional padding can bolster stuffing that has become flattened and matted over the years. If this is the case, add the stuffing, then cut a new cover and apply it as described later in this chapter. If greater problems are apparent, continue with the tack puller.

Remove any muslin covering if one exists. Remove old horsehair. Remove all cotton stuffing, but do not discard it. The cotton used in most old upholstery is of better quality than the cotton available today at reasonable cost for upholstering. Some of the old cotton can be used as fill-in material, or as a supplement to new cotton felt. Remove the old burlap that covers the springs, being careful to take out the tacks that hold the burlap but not the tacks that hold the springs together.

When all coverings have been removed and all that remains is the webbing, the springs and the frame, carefully examine the placement of the springs. The old twine is probably suffering from the fatigue caused by age and years of wear, but even so the springs will probably be fairly close to their original placement within the frame. Carefully note the height of the springs in various areas. It is likely that the springs near the border have been compressed somewhat or turned on a slight angle and tied into place. The springs in the center of the item are more likely to be nearer full extension.

Springs are not sewn to webbing, but rather are fastened to a solid plank of wood that underlies the upholstered piece. In this case, webbing should not be substituted for the original planks. Fasten the springs to the wood from the top by folding a small section of webbing, about two and a half inches long, in half lengthwise, looping it around the bottom coil of the spring, and then driving two staples through it near the spring to hold it in place on the plank. Two or three of these fasteners are used on the bottom spiral of each spring to keep them in place.

In some upholstered pieces, a wire support is used to keep the springs adjacent to each other along one boundary at the same height. Each spring is fastened to this heavy gauge wire. In some cases, metal rings are used as fasteners. In other cases, simply tying them with stitching twine will work.

Cut the strands of twine that hold the springs to the frame. Also cut the thread that sews the springs to the webbing underneath. Leave the twine between springs. The entire spring assembly can then be removed in one piece with the springs still held by twine in their positions relative to each other. The tack puller is then used to remove the tacks remaining in the frame. The webbing is also removed from the underside of the seat. Of course, a similar process is used to strip upholstering material from items like chair backs,

Refinishing and regluing should be done, if necessary, before reupholstery begins.

remembering that we do not expect to find springs there.

You'll need to decide at this point whether any refinishing or regluing are required. This is the time to do it. Any loose joints should be reglued, and all sanding and refinishing should take place before continuing with the reupholstering.

Weaving The Web

Start replacing seat webbing by stapling one end of the roll of webbing at one end of the underside. Place the staples about one-half inch apart and continue across the width of the webbing. Leave about one inch of overlap extending past the stapling. Fold this back over the staples that have just been inserted and staple this flap with another row of staples close to and parallel to the first row. Then, across the long dimension of the underside of the seat, use either a webbing stretcher or a canvas stretcher (with burlap if necessary to keep from marring the wood), to stretch the webbing so that it twangs when it is plucked. Hold this end of the webbing strip in place with a row of staples. Trim the webbing from the roll with about one inch of overlap, which is folded back over the staples and fastened similar to the other end. Parallel rows of webbing are then added adjacent to the one preceding until the bottom is covered by webbing. If one strip of webbing would overlap and show near the edge, it should not be cut with the sheers, but rather folded back over itself and tacked into place.

Now it is time to apply webbing at right angles to the webbing just placed. It is tacked in a similar manner but woven through the first set of strips. Over the first strip, under the second, over the third, under the fourth, et cetera, until it reaches the other side. After it is stapled into place, another strip of webbing is placed next to it and woven in the opposite fashion. When the job has been completed, striking the woven pattern soundly with the hand should produce a rumble which resembles a drum. If you are not familiar with the appropriate tension that should have been applied to each strip of the web, examine a piece of furniture in good condition by placing a hand underneath and checking the tension before beginning the above process.

A webbing stretcher is used to pull the webbing tight across the bottom of this ottoman. After strips of webbing have been placed in one direction, they are placed in a perpendicular direction and woven through alternate strips of already attached webbing.

Staples are placed across each strip of webbing along the length of the frame.

The slight overlap of webbing is folded over the first row of staples, and additional staples are used to fasten the webbing even more securely.

Springs are placed on top of the webbing in the original pattern found in the piece of furniture. Each spring is sewn in four places with needle and thread to the webbing (see the arrows)

165

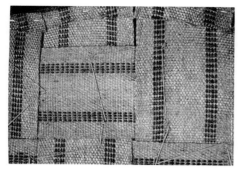

From the underside, the spring sewing thread can be seen to make a continuous pattern across the bottom.

A clove hitch is the knot used to tie springs.

Burlap is tacked to the frame to cover the springs and prevent padding from falling down into them.

Rubberized horsehair is sewn to the burlap so that it does not shift after reupholstering is complete.

Each spring is tied in at least six places and usually eight. Spring twine crosses at right angles and diagonals across each spring. Knots are also tied at the intersection of lengths of twine.

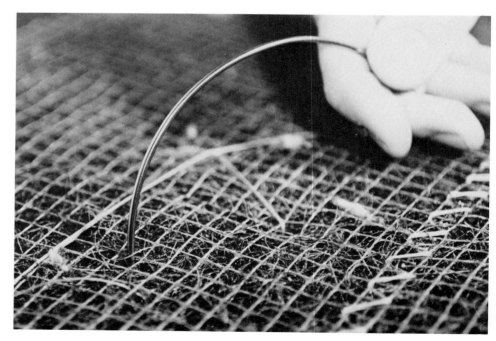

A large curved needle is used, so that the thread can be inserted through the top of the horsehair and come out at the top when the needle has been pushed through its arc.

166

Cotton padding is torn and fitted over the rubberized horsehair.

The upholstery material is pulled tight over the cotton and stapled to the frame. After all staples are in place, excess material is trimmed away with shears or a razor blade.

A thin strip of glue applied over the end of the fabric near the staples glues gimp to the material to cover the staples.

The reupholstered ottoman.

Springing Into Action

After the webbing has been put into place, the item of furniture can be placed back in its upright position. The spring assembly, which has been kept roughly in its original order, is then placed back into the frame on top of the webbing. If you remember the original pattern of the springs, they need not be kept tied together with the old twine but can be placed into the frame singly. But it is often helpful simply to place the entire assembly back into place at one time. A double-pointed needle is threaded with stitching twine. Starting with an end spring of the back row, the needle is inserted adjacent to the base of a spring which has been put in its final position. The needle is pushed through the underside of the webbing next to the spring wire, crossed over the wire and pushed back down through the webbing. A knot in the end of the stitching twine keeps it from pulling through. The twine thus forms a loop around the coil. Secure the first loop around the frame with a slip knot. In this way tie the spring to the webbing at four different points. The first and last loops on each spring are knotted to provide additional security. Move to an adjacent spring and sew loops in the same manner until an entire row is sewn into place. Then sew an adjacent row into place, and so on until all of the springs have been sewn to the webbing. From the underside, the twine should have a "U" shaped pattern, so that the last sewing forms the corner of a square closest to the place where the next spring will be sewn first.

Now, use new spring twine to tie the springs into place relative to each other, and also to the furniture frame. Carefully examine the way the springs were formerly tied in place and then remove the old twine. Leaving it in place will interfere with tying the new twine. The objective is to tie each spring into place with a strand of twine reaching from left to right across the piece of furniture. Another row of twine is then tied at right angles to this one. Two diagonals are then also tied across each spring. The twine is tied around each side of the spring as it crosses it. The second diagonal, in addition, also is tied around the intersection of all previously applied lengths of twine at the center of each spring. The tying should begin with the spring in the center of the pattern, working out. A clove hitch is the knot used to tie the twine around the spring, as well as around the other twine in the final diagonal.

When all the springs have been tied together in this fashion, it is time to fasten the end springs to the frame. At first, the diagonal lengths of twine are ignored. The lengths of twine that have been placed at the original right angles are fastened securely around the frame, being careful to provide just the right amount of tension on the springs around the border so that these springs are depressed, or shaped, according to the way they were originally placed when the item was first manufactured. One staple is put across the twine to hold it in place in the frame, then the twine is folded back over itself and a second staple is placed over both the overlap and the first length of twine. If the

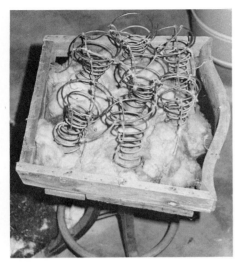

Before: A slip seat with springs after it has been stripped. The spring twine has been broken, and the cotton has fallen through the springs.

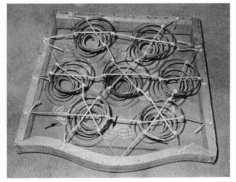

The springs are being retied as they were originally in the slip seat. Notice that instead of webbing across the bottom of this seat, it was constructed with plank boards. Since the springs cannot be tied to the boards, they are fastened with small pieces of webbing stapled into place (see the arrows).

After covering the seat with burlap, cotton is rolled to form the front section of the seat as was done in the original upholstering.

fastening takes place near the outer edge of the frame, the twine can be further tightened by placing an additional staple closer to the interior edge of the frame.

After all of the lengths of twine from the original two tying operations have been fastened in place, the diagonals are similarly fastened. Most times, it is advisable, however, not to bring the diagonals across the top of the boundary springs, but rather to bring them through the second or third spiral down from the top, tie it to the boundary spring there and then fasten the twine to the frame. If there are more than four springs across one dimension of a seat, then it is advisable to bring down an additional length of twine from the inside edge of the top spiral of the second spring and tie it through the first spiral on that same spring beneath it, through the third spiral and fourth spiral down on a border spring. This section of twine is then tacked into place. Carefully observing the way in which the springs were originally tied into position before the twine is removed will greatly aid the restorer to tie the springs in a similar manner to help shape and secure these sometimes uncooperative steel devices.

Burlap

After the springs have been tied into place, a sheet of burlap is placed over the top of all the springs. The burlap is pulled tightly over the springs, but not so tight as to take tension off the spring twine underneath. It is stapled into place on the frame and excess trimmed away. Sometimes it is advisable to roll the edge of the burlap back on the frame before it is stapled to pre-

vent it from unraveling. In some cases, some stuffing has been sewed into a roll at the front or side of the piece to give it more shape. Try to duplicate this by adding stuffing and sewing it in a similar fashion. The burlap must then be sewed to each individual spring to prevent it from wandering. Use a curved needle and stitching twine to sew through the burlap and up around the coil spring underneath. The same technique is used in this tying process as was used to sew the spring to the webbing, except that the burlap needs to be sewed to each spring in three places instead of four. The first and last stitch of each spring should be knotted to prevent the entire matrix from unraveling should one section of twine break.

Hair

Save any hair stuffing taken out of the furniture to facilitate trimming the new rubberized horsehair to similar shape and size. Rubberized horsehair will probably be thicker than the old hair, since the old hair has been sat upon and matted down for a period of years. The rubberized horsehair is put into place on the seat and sewed to the burlap, much in the same manner that the burlap was sewed to the springs. A large curved needle facilitates this stitching. Rubberized hair is also cut into the necessary shape to serve as the base stuffing in arms, if appropriate, as well as the back of the upholstered furniture. In some cases, more than one thickness of hair stuffing is required, even though it may only be for certain sections of the artifact.

Burlap rolled over the cotton at the front of the seat holds its serpentine shape. The burlap over the roll is sewn into place on top of the other burlap and stapled at the front.

Rubberized horsehair is sewn to the burlap.

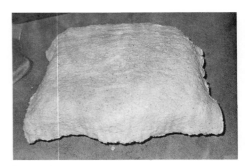

Cotton is torn and placed over the rubberized horsehair.

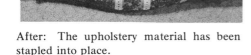

After: The upholstery material has been stapled into place.

Cotton

The last layer of stuffing is composed of cotton which can be purchased either in 100-pound bales or in 15-pound rolls. The cotton is **pulled apart** and **never cut** to size. Cutting with shears leaves an abrupt edge that would produce an unsightly lump somewhere in the overstuffed furniture. Pulling the cotton apart with the hands serves to feather the edge and allow it to blend in with adjacent pieces of cotton. Cotton should be laid in thicknesses similar to the original cotton within the upholstered piece, except that the new cotton should be about 50 percent thicker. The reason for this is that over time, the cotton will mat into a thinner cross section and some compensation for this must be allowed.

There are different types and grades of cotton. Virginia cotton is the softest and fluffiest and feels very smooth. But the fibers of Virginia cotton are short and do not stay together very well. Egyptian cotton has long fibers, and when used in a blend with Virginia cotton helps to hold the mat together.

Other materials such as feathers are used for stuffing in pillows or cushions, if appropriate. The technique used is probably better referred to as stuffing, rather than upholstering.

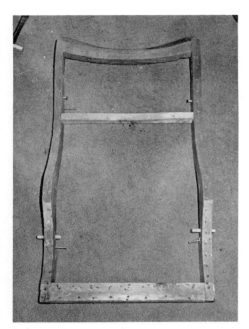

Before: The back of a rocker which slips out of position. The screws and dowels hold it in the right place in the chair frame.

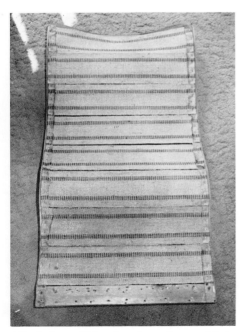

All of the webbing has been fastened into position. It should be tight enough that it rings when snapped with the fingers.

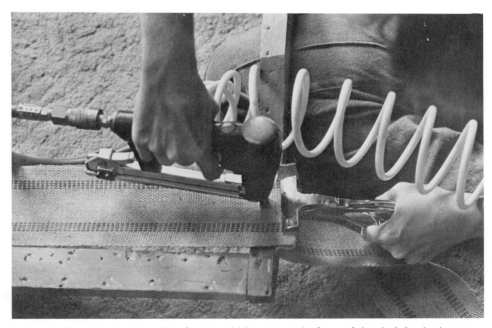

A pneumatic staple gun is used to fasten webbing across the front of the chair back. A canvas stretcher instead of a webbing stretcher is used to hold the webbing tight while it is being fastened.

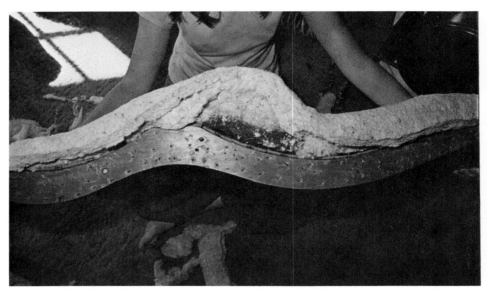

The edge of the chair back shows the ends of the webbing covered by horsehair, with cotton being placed as the upper layer.

Horsehair is sewn directly to the webbing. Since there are no springs in the back there is no need for burlap. Scissors are used to trim the horsehair after it has been fitted and fastened.

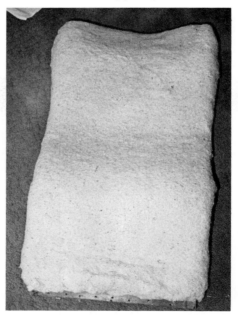

Cotton is torn and shaped to the contour of the back.

After: If tufting were going to be done on this chair back, muslin would be the next layer over the cotton. Since no tufting was to be done, the upholstery material was placed directly over the cotton.

Covering Material

On better pieces of furniture, a muslin covering should be used to upholster first. Hopefully, the springs and internal works will remain in good condition until sometime after the outer covering has worn. The outer cover can then simply be removed, and there will be no need for redoing the webbing or retieing the springs. Laying out the muslin sheet for the reupholstering gives practice for making the plan to cut the final covering. Final upholstery material will range in cost from about $10 per yard to $75 or so per yard. Because of this high cost, it is important that no material be wasted. There will usually be more waste with patterns than with a plain-colored material. Different sections of cut patterns must be made to match from piece to piece, thus introducing a certain amount of unusable material to be trimmed here and there. The old material that has been saved can be pieced together as adjacent sections of a puzzle to make most efficient use of the new material. Practice using the muslin first by stretching it out on the floor and placing the various sections of old material over it. Rearrange them until maximum use has been made of the smallest piece of muslin. This will give some clue as to the amount of final material needed, but be careful to allow for added waste if you choose a complicated large pattern as the final covering.

Material is cut carefully using sharp shears. The following procedure is used to place both the muslin and the final covering in place. The material is placed over the stuffing and temporary staples are placed in the center of all four sides. The temporary staples are put in position by not holding the stapler hard and fast against the piece of furniture. Instead, it is held about one-quarter inch away so that the staple head stays some distance above the fabric. This holds the material in place, but the use of pliers or a staple remover later can easily remove the temporary staples. Pull the material in both directions until it conforms to the desired shape. Use considerable tension, because after a little wear the cotton inside will mat substantially, and sags and creases may result in the upholstered product. This is a good thumb and index finger exercise, because with a piece of any size, the old thumb and index finger will end up being nearly worn out by the time the project has been completed.

After the temporary staples have been put in position and tension applied across the cover, begin working toward the corners from the center by placing a little additional tension on the material and putting a final staple into position. Work toward the corners first on two sides and then the other two, from the middle outward, to give the fabric a nice smooth look. Be careful to remove all wrinkles as the staples are put into place. Any wrinkles that develop may require removing staples and refixing the fabric.

Once all the staples are in place except for the corners, it will be necessary to pleat and fold the material. Folds should always be toward the outside of the furniture, or downward, so that they do not trap dust or dirt. Usually several small folds will look neater than one massive fold.

Before: This rosewood chair should have a tufted back.

After: It has been reupholstered appropriately.

Sometimes in order to complete a corner properly, cuts must be made into the fabric so that part of it can be pulled over an adjacent area, overlaying it, and then stapled into position. Unsightly lumps or bumps can be removed by pounding them with a mallet or with the side of the hand. Stubborn bumps can be removed only by inserting the regulator through the material and moving the cotton stuffing underneath from areas of excess to areas of not enough. Although the regulator can be used with most finishing fabrics, it cannot be used with velvet because it will leave holes that will not disappear. Most other fabrics will allow penetration of the regulator between threads, but the threads of velvet and silk are too fine and will be damaged if the regulator is forced through. When these types of fabrics are used, it is even more important to use muslin first. All the bumps can be taken out with the regulator to give a good finished appearance before the final covering is applied. The muslin, by absorbing some of the tension, also allows for a longer life of the outer cover.

After all staples are in place and the fabric has its final finished look, cut the excess fabric away from the stapled edge with a single-edge razor blade. Occasionally, a second row of staples may be applied parallel to the first row before the excess material is trimmed away.

Welts And Gimp

If welting is to be used to finish the boundary between the fabric and the wood, you will have to make an additional allowance for sewing the welting by laying it out first on the exterior fabric. Muslin is never used to cover welting.

Welting is made by sewing fabric folded over a long cord, and joining additional pieces of fabric to the end if necessary to complete a length. Double welting is made from two cords attached like Siamese twins along their lengths. Two sewings must take place, one at the outer boundary of one of the cords and one in between the two cords. This sewing is very tricky and time-consuming, and will tax the patience of all but the most experienced of sewing machine users.

The other type of finishing material is called gimp. It is a braided fabric that is pliable and can be bent easily around the corners. Either gimp or welting is glued along the edge between the fabric and the wood by using a thin coating of Elmer's glue. When moving around corners or turning at right angles, the gimp or welting is held in place by a temporary staple. After the glue has dried, the temporary staples are removed.

Foam Rubber

Some upholsterers use foam rubber in their reupholstering techniques. Foam rubber was not available 100 years ago and takes away from the authenticity of any piece of upholstered furniture. For the most part, foam rubber has been used when the furniture has been tufted. The use of foam rubber creates a pseudo tuft. Real tufting is accomplished by folding the material and shaping the

174

cotton stuffing underneath. Tufting with foam rubber is done simply by applying pressure in certain areas and pulling a button through, thus compressing the foam rubber at those points while allowing other areas to stay at full extension away from the frame.

Tufting

There are basically three different types of tufting: diamond tufting, biscuit tufting and bun tufting. Diamond tufting is the technique used most often in fancy pieces of Victorian furniture. It is almost always necessary to use a muslin cover before a final covering when doing tufting, because of the complexity of the shaping process and the often required rearrangement of cotton under the fabric with the regulator. An additional 50 percent of fabric is also needed for a tufted cover.

Appropriate instruction in tufting would require a book in itself. Proper tufting requires the patience of art as well as science. The first love seat that I ever tufted required about seven days to reupholster. Practice will help cut down considerably on the time, and once you have done it you can understand why the cost of tufting in reupholstered furniture is so high. One way to practice tufting is by upholstering a simple scrap lumber frame about two feet by two feet in size.

If tufting is essential to your reuphol-stering needs, you'll have to uncover a number of secrets first. These secrets are revealed in a book called *Tufting Secrets*, printed and published by John K. Burch Company, with sales branches in San Franciso, Detroit and Chicago. The book is a small green paperback, and hopefully would be available from many upholstery supply houses or adult education classes dealing with upholstering.

The Finishing Touch

After the seat and back have been upholstered, any other panels of material that require attachment have been stapled into place and gimp or welt has been applied, the project only appears to be completed. With all the time and effort that has been used to make something old look like a new something old, an additional touch is appropriate. If the fabric does not have a protective coating to keep it from being stained by accidental spills, a coating of a product called Scotchguard should be applied. Scotchguard comes in a spray can and is applied much like spraying lacquer on wood. The coating, however, is not nearly as thick and when dry is hardly noticeable to the touch on the fabric. Yet this thin coating will significantly repel liquids, and is well worth its cost to insure that the entire reupholstering procedure does not have to be repeated prematurely.

Before: This loveseat needs to be completely restored.

After: It has been tufted with the same technique used more than 100 years ago.

CHAPTER XII

USING YOUR CANE (CANING)

Reeds from various types of palms and swamp grass have been used throughout history to fabricate various forms of furniture. The Egyptians as long ago as 4000 B.C. initiated the art of basketweaving made from these materials. Some boxes and chairs they made have survived until modern times preserved in ancient tombs. The Romans and Greeks similarly fashioned wicker furniture using the techniques learned from earlier civilizations.

During the 1850's, furniture was first made from the outer bark of the rattan palm which grows wild in the East Indies. Thorny leaves are removed from the wild palm after it is cut, leaving lengths of glossy water-resistant and flexible cane.

Rattan cane was used extensively to weave seats for dining room chairs, as well as seats and backs for Lincoln-type Victorian rockers. Most of this furniture was fashioned from either walnut or maple drilled with holes equally spaced around the perimeter of an open area to be covered by the woven cane. There are actually two types of caning used to complete a chair or other pieces of furniture. They are both made from the same material, but one is hand woven and the other is machine woven. Most older pieces of Victorian furniture were undoubtedly hand woven. Eventually, as the furniture needed to be refinished, repaired, and thus recaned, it was sometimes modified to accept machine-made caning. Furniture incorporating the use of machine-made cane was very popular for several decades following the end of the Victorian era. To redo a

chair seat with machine-made cane takes about one-half hour of casual work. The same size seat redone by hand weaving will require many hours of skillful work with intense concentration.

Machine Woven Cane

We will concentrate on chair seats, because chairs get more abuse than most other types of furniture and, therefore, will require restoration more often than other forms of furniture. But the techniques discussed in this chapter are fully applicable to items other than chairs. Basically, machine woven cane is a sheet composed of thin rattan strips woven into an octagonal pattern. A groove is cut some distance away from the edge of a hole in the seat frame, the sheet is glued into this groove and then finally secured with a spline.

The first step in the restoration process is to remove all of the old spline from the damaged chair. A chisel no wider than the groove into which the cane has been glued is used to fully dislodge the spline and to dig out the remaining strands of caning which are then discarded. The chair is then reglued, if necessary, and refinished.

Machine woven cane can be purchased from local as well as mail order supply houses. Check the appendix at the end of this chapter for a list of some of these sources. The cane is soaked in warm water for two or three hours to thoroughly saturate it. It is removed from the water five or ten minutes before it is to be used and excess water is allowed to drip free. The spline that is to be used should fit snugly into the groove, allowing only

First step in replacing machine woven caning is to remove all old cane and spline from the groove in the chair with a chisel.

The machine woven cane is soaked in warm water for three or four hours, then trimmed to overlap the grooves by about one inch in each dimension. It is first forced into the front and rear grooves with a small wooden wedge, and then into the side grooves.

Before: The clean groove is ready to be fitted with machine woven cane.

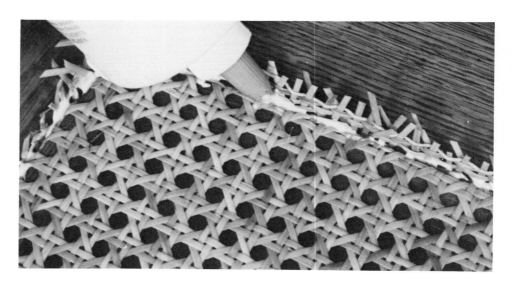

Ample glue is applied to the entire groove.

178

Tap the spline into place with a mallet in the groove over the cane sheet. The spline can be applied dry, or soaked first if it is too brittle. Where fit is difficult as in turning a sharp corner, shave the spline with a knife for a better fit.

The spline is forced in further with a mallet and a block of wood.

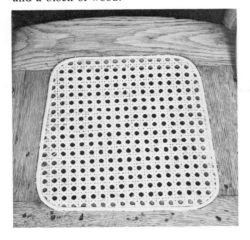

After: When the seat has been finished, keep it in a shady place to dry at least over night. If the cane dries too quickly, it will pull loose from the glue joints as it shrinks. After drying, a properly caned seat should ring when plucked with the fingers.

Excess cane is trimmed from around the outer edge of the spline.

enough extra space for a layer of cane on either side. Spline that is too thick can be trimmed with a knife or plane so that it is the appropriate thickness. It is soaked in warm water for only about 15 minutes prior to its use.

The sheet of prewoven cane is removed from the water and trimmed with scissors to be no more than one inch larger in each dimension than the opening that is to be covered, plus the additional dimensions needed to reach the grooves. The cane is aligned over the opening, glossy side up, so that the strands running from the back toward the front of the chair make a right angle with the back and front of the chair. It is laid over the groove and a one or two inch piece of spline is tapped in at the back of the chair to hold the sheet of cane fixed in position. The sheet is then held taut while another small wedge of spline is tapped into place at the front of the chair.

A small wooden wedge with dimensions allowing it to be inserted into the groove is used to force the overlapping sections of the cane sheet into the groove around the perimeter of the seat opening. A hammer or mallet will most likely be necessary to shape the cane in this groove. The objective is to have the sheet of cane extend across the opening down one side of the groove, across its bottom, up the other side of the groove, and out on that side. As long as the cane is sufficiently wet, it should be pliable enough to accomplish this scenario. Be careful not to break or damage the cane when you use the wedge to force the cane into the groove.

The small sections of spline placed at the front and back are now removed. Then, either Elmer's glue or Weldwood glue freshly mixed is applied evenly around the groove. Both the bottom and each side of the groove should have a generous coating of glue. The narrow bottom edge of one end of this somewhat wedge-shaped reed spline is now pressed into the groove at the back of the chair. The spline is then tapped with a mallet or with a wooden wedge and hammer to securely fit into the groove all the way around the chair seat. If it is necessary to force the spline to bend at the corners of the chair seat, the spline can be notched with a knife to make the bending easier. The spline should meet exactly at the back of the seat, and therefore should be cut just before the last section is tapped into place so that this meeting is as exact as possible. Wipe away any excess glue that may ooze out of the groove when the spline is forced into it with a wet cloth or sponge.

A knife or other sharp tool is used to trim any cane away from the chair seat that extends beyond the spline. Force the spline into the groove level with the rest of the seat by tapping with a hammer and blunt wooden wedge. Then pour a little additional glue over the top of the spline to seal it into the groove. Remove excess glue and let the chair dry at normal temperatures out of the sun for about two days.

If the chair is placed in direct sunlight, the cane may dry and shrink before the glue has cured and the seat will not be as tight as desired. If the cane has been properly applied, it should offer a slight ring when snapped with the fingers. Any small strands of frayed reed can be singed with a quick motion of a torch to remove them. Be careful not to hold the torch in one place too long, because the reed can easily be scorched. It might be advisable to slightly dampen it with a wet cloth prior to attempting the singeing. The thoroughly dried cane seat should then be spray varnished both top and bottom to protect it from moisture that would allow it to stretch. Of course, if desired, a water-based stain can be used to color it prior to varnishing.

Hand Weaving

In order to facilitate the hand weaving of cane, a number of tools must first be fashioned. Required will be a number of quarter-inch dowel rods about two inches long with one end tapered somewhat in a pencil sharpener, although not necessarily to a sharp point. A caning needle should also be made from a one-eighth inch dowel rod flattened at one end, with a hole through this flattened end large enough for a strand of cane to be inserted through this "eye". A caning needle should be about six inches longer than the largest dimension of the opening to be caned. If the object being caned is a Lincoln-type rocker, several caning needles should be fashioned to use, depending upon the dimensions of the opening. The end of the rod opposite the flattened end can be inserted into a wooden handle (which may be a three-quarter inch dowel rod) and fastened so that pulling on the handle will not strip it from the rod if the rod is held fixed. The caning needle is not absolutely needed, but it will make the work go faster. From the description of the cane weaving process below, it will be obvious that a thick piece of wire can also be used, but will take more time than using a caning needle.

Five different sizes of cane are available. The size you use depends on the size of the hole in the furniture through which the cane is to be woven and the spacing between those holes. The cane sizes are superfine, fine fine, fine, medium and common. Superfine is used when the size of the hole is $1/8$ inch and the distance between holes is $3/8$ inch. Fine fine is used when the hole size is $3/16$ inch and the distance between the holes is $1/2$ inch. Fine is used when the size of the hole is $3/16$ inch and the distance between the holes is $5/8$ inch. Medium is used when the hole size is $1/4$ inch and the distance between holes is $3/4$ inch. Common is used when the hole size is $5/16$ inch and the distance between the holes is $7/8$ inch.

An additional material called a "binder" is used to finish the edge of a caned seat and somewhat hide the holes. A binder is not necessary, but binding cane is always the same size regardless of the cane size used in weaving.

A few words of advice to beginners are in order here to minimize the labor as well as the possible frustration of having to redo a part of the weaving done incorrectly. If the chair has to be restored other than simply recaned, it may be a good idea to leave the arms off so that they do not interfere with caning the seat. Gluing the refinished arms into place after the seat has been caned may save a lot of work that otherwise would have to be censored. Next, when recaning a seat that is not perfectly rectangular, beginning caners will want to put the cane through every hole. The experienced cane weaver knows that the cane should be woven so that as many strands as possible in each step of weaving are parallel to each other, and this sometimes means skipping holes. Although there are essentially six steps in the caning process, it is not likely that any hole will have more than three or four strands woven through it. For a perfectly rectangular pattern, each hole except the corner hole will have four strands passing through it. The corner holes will have only two strands passing through them.

The cane needs to be soaked in warm water for several hours, but soaking it overnight will not hurt. The weaving does not have to be accomplished in one sitting, but can be done over a period of several days provided that the cane which has already been woven is sufficiently wet before addtional weaving is attempted. Because the cane contracts and becomes less flexible as it dries, the weaving process becomes more cumbersome and it is more difficult to pull each strand of cane through the already woven lines. Therefore, it is best to cane an entire opening at one sitting provided that time allows. Using a sponge to keep the already woven cane wet will facilitate the weaving process.

The first thing to do is locate the center hole along the front of the chair seat and the back of the chair seat. Count the number of holes along the front and divide by two. Do the same with the holes in the back of the seat and thus locate the middle hole. One strand of cane is inserted through this center hole at the front and the center hole at the rear. The shiny side of the cane should be facing up—it is intended that one eventually sit only on the shiny side of the cane. Run the strand down through the hole at the front, bring it up through the adjacent hole on one side or the other and fasten it with a caning peg to hold the cane in place while weaving half of the chair. The cane should not be pulled too tightly, because the weaving process itself will tighten it somewhat and drying will tighten it further. The first step in caning is completed by continuing to weave the strand through holes at the front and back of the chair, always placing the cane down through the top of the hole and up through the next hole from the underside of the chair seat. Try to keep the cane strips running parallel to the first strand placed through the seat even if you have to skip a hole either at the front or the back. As you near the end of a strand of cane, it must be tied underneath the seat to hold it in place. It is tied simply by looping it back across the bottom of the chair to the nearest hole where a strand of cane passes between two holes. The end is looped under that strand, then back between itself and that strand and pulled tight. If the remaining end is too long and obstructs the work, it should be trimmed. Otherwise, it can be left dangling until the entire seat has been caned and all the ends trimmed at once.

A new strand is inserted to continue the pattern where the old one left off, tying the new end in the same way that the old end was tied. Proceeding in this manner will result in parallel strands running from front to back across one-half of the chair seat—either the left or the right. If necessary during the process, additional caning pegs can be inserted into the holes to keep the cane from drooping excessively. The other half of the seat is then similarly woven with the strand that passed through the center hole of the back of the seat.

The second step consists of following the same procedure, only rotating 90 degrees so that the first strand of cane is passed through the center holes on either side of the chair. The resulting pattern should be a grid of small squares. The cane which moves from left to right across the seat top simply lies across the cane that runs from the front to the rear.

The third layer of cane is placed identically to the first layer, except over the first two layers that have already been applied. When the fourth step in the caning process is begun, this third layer will be pulled slightly aside of the first layer so that it runs parallel and adjacent to the edges of the first layer.

The caning needle is now used to begin weaving with the fourth step. The caning needle is placed parallel to the direction in which the second layer of cane was applied. It is pushed down over each strand of cane laid in the third step and under each strand of cane laid in the first step. It is woven across the seat in this manner or from the center if the seat is large. It should only go through as many strands as it can and still be pulled out without having to do any unweaving. Then the process is repeated going across the seat.

The fourth step in the caning process then consists of inserting the end of a strand of cane into the eye of the caning needle. The caning needle is then pulled through the strands through which it has been woven, thus weaving the fourth strand into place. This strand of cane is pulled completely through across the chair leaving only its other end tied underneath the seat in the fashion described earlier. It is inserted into the hole, passed underneath and brought up through an adjacent hole and back across the seat, woven through the appropriate strands again. The caning needle need not be used and a thick wire can be placed through the strands to separate them as the caning needle did. The fourth layer of cane can then be "snaked" through by making sure that it passes over each strand laid in the first step of caning.

A peg should be used to pair off all of the strands woven thus far to form hollow squares created by woven strands of cane on either side. Each side of the square should be composed of two adjacent cane strands that emerge from the same hole. Care should be taken to do a good job of making the strands parallel and equally spaced throughout the pattern, or the following step will prove difficult.

The fifth strand of cane is started in one corner and woven through the pattern to form a diagonal across the squares. Be sure that the cane is not twisted either in the pattern being woven or underneath while it is carried from one hole to the next. One hand should be kept above the seat and the other below the seat. The cane probably will

Before: This walnut rocker has been refinished and made ready for caning. However, the arms have been left off so as not to interfere with the process.

The first step in caning is to thread the strands from front to back across the seat, using pegs in appropriate holes to maintain tension.

When the end of a strand of cane has been placed through a hole and a new strand must be started, a knot is made as pictured above by tying the end of the strand through an already woven strand.

The second step in caning is to thread strands from left to right across the seat on top of the first layer. Note that not all of the holes have been used for the first layer. The objective is not to use all of the holes, but rather to insure that strands are parallel and equally spaced.

The third step in caning is to thread another layer from front to back over the first layer and perpendicular to the second layer.

This is a close-up of the completed third step.

A caning needle is woven through the strands going from front to back so that it is placed over the strips from the third step and under the strips from the first step. A strand of cane is then put through the eye of the caning needle and pulled through to pair up with every strand placed in the second step.

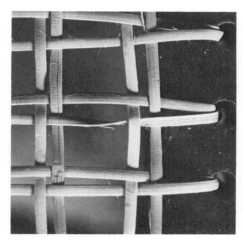

This is a close-up of an improperly woven strand. It is twisted and will bind and probably break after a little use. Be careful to avoid such twisting of the cane.

After the fourth step is completed; a caning peg is used to pair off the vertical and horizontal strands into nearly equal-sized squares.

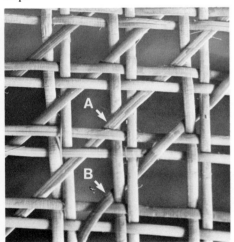

The fifth step in caning is to weave a diagonal. These diagonals go from the front left to the back right of the seat. Each square has two of these diagonals woven through it. Diagonal A is properly woven so that the corner will not bind. Corner B is improperly woven so that each corner binds along its length.

A close-up of the first diagonal completed.

The second diagonal is placed from the left rear to the right front. It is shown here after weaving. Small fibers remaining after this process can be singed by quickly moving a flame across them.

After: An optional seventh step is to place a binder over all of the holes and fasten it by weaving a strand of cane through each hole from underneath.

have to be pulled through its entire length after only going through several squares, because binding will make it difficult to pull it through more than this number. A strand of cane is brought out of one corner of the chair seat and woven diagonally across the chair so that it passes under all of the double strands running from front to back and over all of the double strands running from side to side. Although holes may be skipped because of the shape of the chair, each square in the pattern should have two diagonals running through it. One diagonal will emerge from a corner of the square, while the other diagonally woven strand will go down through the opposite corner.

There are two ways in which this diagonal can be woven, depending upon the choice of paths after the strand emerges from the corner hole. One choice is wrong because it will cause the diagonal to bind at the corners and be difficult to pull through the woven pattern. The other choice allows the diagonal to be pulled much more easily. The right choice is that which will not further tighten the already woven pattern.

Study the two alternative routes for weaving the diagonal from a given hole. If the diagonal strand is to move from the left front of the chair to the back right of the chair when it is pulled out of its hole, it can be brought under the double strand which emerges from the hole to its right and passes from the front to the back of the chair. Or, alternatively, it can be brought under the first set of double strands which it must cross which move from left to right across the chair. The first choice is the correct one because when pulled through along the diagonal, it will not have a tendency to further tighten the corners. The second choice will bring the strands that meet at 90 degrees at the corner of the square into closer contact, thus tightening the pattern.

Another diagonal is then run starting from the front right-hand corner of the chair and going to the back left-hand corner. Of course, once again, if the chair seat is not square, the diagonal emerging from one corner will not terminate at the other corner but somewhere else along the back. It is woven in similar manner to the other diagonals,

186

thus completing the entire woven chair seat.

Additionally, a binder sometimes is used to hide the holes and provide a more finished look. The binder is simply placed across the holes going all the way around the chair seat, while thin strands of cane are looped through each hole over the binder and down through the same hole again to hold it in place.

While the seat is still damp, a torch can be passed quickly over the caning to singe away any small hair-like fibers that are projecting.

The seat is allowed to dry for about two days, then is either stained with a water based stain if desired or left natural and then varnished both top and bottom to prevent the absorption of moisture and loosening of the pattern. If the weaving was done properly, the caning will ring when snapped sharply with the fingers.

As a final note, it might be necessary to take some additional precautions to prevent scratching the finish on the wooden frame when using the caning needle. A small piece of burlap or felt placed between the needle and the frame should suffice to prevent any abrasion.

Before: This small walnut rocker was removed from a chicken coop in poor shape.

After: The rocker has been excellently restored to near original condition.

CANING APPENDIX

Caning supplies can be purchased from:

Albert Constantine and Son
2050 Eastchester Road
Bronx, New York 10461

Craftsman Wood Service Company
2727 South Mary Street
Chicago, Illinois 60608

Dick Blick Company
P.O. Box 1267
Galesburg, Illinois 61401

Local American Handicraft Retail Outlet

CHAPTER XIII

SKIN (LEATHER)

Animal skins have been used throughout history to fashion various products from wine containers to bookbindings. Materials made from skins found in the tombs of Egyptian pharoahs had given up all of their moisture through the ages. It is not easy to determine whether or not they were treated to promote their preservation, although it is highly likely considering the other preservation techniques known to the Egyptians. The ancients probably used various oils to help preserve their products derived from animal parts.

Biblical accounts tell of the use of goatskins to hold wine. It is noted that the goatskin should not be used more than once, because there was no technique to preserve its strength and it was likely to burst upon refilling with wine.

As time progressed, various techniques have been developed to preserve the chemical and physical integrity of skins. The first was through curing to prevent putrefaction when the skin is initially removed from a dead animal, and then through tanning to indefinitely preserve it from physical and chemical attack. Because of the mechanisms used in tanning, however, the process is not really effective indefinitely, and various problems will most likely arise that will require treatment.

Food For Thought

An elementary knowledge of skin products is necessary to understand some of the problems that will develop and require restoration. For the most part, skin products contain water, protein, carbohydrates, fats and minerals.

Proportions of these materials vary, depending upon the species of the animal from which the skin was obtained, as well as that animal's age, sex, diet and environment. The organic constituents of skins should make it readily apparent that they are ideal foodstuffs. The physical features of some skins such as horse and cow skins, commonly known as hides, do not make them easily chewable, and they therefore have not been used as human foodstuff. Certain bacteria, molds and insects are not quite so fussy, and will readily dine on these hides whenever and wherever available; that is, unless the hides are treated to make them unappetizing to those little creatures.

Basically, there are three layers of skin: the epidermis, the derma and the flesh. The epidermis is the outer layer that contains the hair of the animal. Hair emanates from follicles that penetrate the epidermis into the derma. After the flesh and the epidermis is removed, the derma is treated to remove the hair follicles and then tanned to make leather.

Derma consists of connective tissue and cells of fat. Where large groups of fat cells are interspersed between the collagen fibers, the leather will be soft and spongy because of the spaces left between the fibers when the fat cells are removed in the leather preparation process. Collagen is a form of protein that composes about 95 percent of the protein in cowhide.

The Cure

Curing animal skins primarily means removing the fats, blood vessels and

189

muscles that provide nutrients to the microscopic critters that wish to make pigs of themselves. Eliminating moisture from the skin by drying it further impedes the action of bacteria on the remaining protein.

However, drying renders the skin hard and brittle, leaving it not very useful for most purposes. The skin can be made supple once again through applying lubricants or through repeated conditioning by mechanical manipulation. In some parts of the world, skins were trampled in tubs to make them supple. The Eskimos have chosen to chew on skin to soften it. Neat's-foot oil, castor oil and lanolin (from sheep) have been applied as lubricants. These oils partially replace the moisture lost in the curing process, but they also dry and must be replaced from time-to-time.

Getting A Good Tan

The purpose of tanning is to infuse the protein fibers remaining in the derma with a chemical or chemicals that replace the water lost in the curing process. The chemicals used can be either organic or inorganic. When organic in nature, the process is referred to as "vegetable tanning", while the alternative is referred to as "mineral tanning". Tannins, as the organic chemicals are referred to, originally were derived in Europe from oak trees. In fact, the old English word for oak is "tann". Similarly, many people are familiar with the brown compound present in oak leaves, tea leaves, and the like, known as tannic acid.

In mineral tanning, chrome salts replace the water that was bound to the protein fiber in the leather, producing a superior product that does not readily absorb moisture. Chrome leather is not very pliable, and therefore cannot be molded easily into a desired shape—nor is it easily tooled. It is used in modern times primarily in shoe manufacture. Vegetable tanned leather is more easily molded and tooled when damp, but is more susceptible to attack by molds and chemicals. Vegetable tanned leathers are susceptible to attack by sulfuric acid.

Insect Bites

Various insects, primarily moths, have been known to attack leather objects. The objects can be fumigated with various insecticides to provide some relief. However, carefully washing the leather with carbon disulfide, or another insecticide that will not stain the leather, will be good enough, although repeated applications probably will be required periodically. Fur skins can be rubbed with boric acid to prevent insect infestations.

Insects occasionally bore through leather bookbindings and infest the book itself. An infested book can be placed in a small airtight container into which dichlorobenzene crystals (mothballs) are added. The container is sealed with tape around the seams to prevent the fumes from escaping. The book should be opened to allow the vapors to penetrate through the pages, but they should be kept separated from the chemicals so that they do not become stained.

The process may have to be repeated periodically, because the insecticide will kill the insects but not necessarily the eggs or larvae left behind.

Acid has attacked this leather book binding to produce red rot. The fibrous protein in the leather has been irreversibly destroyed.

Although the faces of book covers may be protected because of the way they are stored on a shelf, the exposed backs and edges are most susceptible to deterioration.

Removing Dirt

The use of many commercially available detergents can cause leather to deteriorate. Therefore, only saddle soap, which is available from most supermarkets, can be used with the comfortable knowledge that the leather will be hurt in no way. In fact, besides its cleansing action, saddle soap also contains lubricants that will somewhat lubricate the leather.

Of course, suede cannot be cleaned with saddle soap. Fine wire brushes can be used to readily remove dirt and raise the nap to restore the suede's texture. Light dirt deposited on the suede can be removed by rubbing it with a soft art gum eraser, or by the use of art gum powder described in the chapter on cleaning paper. Grease spots can be removed by lightly rubbing the soiled area with a cotton swab moistened with a cleaning solvent. Suede that has been compressed smooth through excessive wear can be given back its original texture by sanding very lightly with a fine sandpaper.

Preservation From Chemical Deterioration

Acid is used in the tanning process; namely, tannic acid. Although tannic acid is relatively mild and necessary for the tanning process, unwanted residual acid deposits left in the leather will eventually cause its chemical deterioration. The biggest enemy of leather bookbindings is sulfuric acid. Sulfur dioxide, resulting from the burning of sulfur-laden coal and by other means in modern-day society, combines with oxygen to form sulfur trioxide. This gas can seep into leather bookbindings where it combines with moisture to form sulfuric acid. This process normally takes some time, but is speeded up considerably by the presence of iron which acts as a catalyst. Leather bookbindings undoubtedly contain traces of iron compounds and that is all that is needed to cause problems.

Sulfuric acid attack on leather alters the molecular structure to produce, instead of protein fibers, a simple red dust. The reaction is irreversible, and leather that has turned to red dust cannot be restructured into fibrous protein. This chemical deterioration is referred to as "red rot". Red rot can be prevented to a great extent; but if it has already occurred, the leather is lost.

Red rot usually is most apparent on exposed edges of books where air pollution and moisture find the books accessible. Books stored side-by-side on a shelf normally can protect each other along their cover surfaces, but exposed backs, tops and edges of the covers are most likely to suffer from this chemical malady. In fact, many modern books may be found to have deteriorated to a greater degree than many older books. Dyes used to color leather a long time ago were applied primarily to the surface of the leather. Modern techniques involve soaking the dye through the leather. This soaking process removes many of the water-soluble salts throughout the leather, thus freeing the way for it to absorb moisture and sulfuric acid throughout its thickness.

It has been found that replacing the water-soluble salts before red rot starts can prevent it from occurring. The

An application of potassium lactate with a brush or cotton ball will prevent red rot, but will not cure it.

A brush is used to apply a heated mixture of lanolin and neat's-foot oil to act as a lubricant and prevent physical deterioration of leather.

chemical most often used for this is pure syrupy potassium lactate, but potassium lactate is susceptible to attack by fungus. A fungicide added to the potassium lactate makes an ideal solution. An appropriate fungicide is paranitrophenol. A water solution of 7 percent potassium lactate and 0.25 percent paranitrophenol mixed especially for to treat bookbindings is available from the source listed in the appendix at the end of this chapter. It should be noted that potassium lactate will stain many materials slightly yellow. Therefore, it is important not to use it on leathers that cannot afford this yellow stain, and it should not be allowed to be absorbed by the paper in the book.

Preservation From Physical Deterioration

Physical deterioration results from abrading and plying leathers after they have become dry. Rubbing books on a bookshelf will eventually wear away the leather on the bottom edge of leaves and hinges. Opening and closing a book after the leather has dried out will break the bindings and may even result in the unintentional amputation of a book cover. A solution of appropriate oils must be applied to soak into the leather and prevent the dried-out fibers in the leather from damaging each other when moved. The best solution for doing this is a mixture of 60 percent neat's-foot oil and 40 percent anhydrous lanolin. Neat's-foot oil is used to lubricate leather baseball gloves and can be purchased in sporting goods stores. Lanolin is available from most pharmacies, but it

is often hydrated for ease of application; that means it contains water and is not usable for book leathers. Ask the pharmacist to check his stock for anhydrous lanolin. Anhydrous lanolin, though, is thick and not easily workable at room temperature; it must be slightly heated so that it can mix with the neat's-foot oil. To save all this trouble, however, the solution can be purchased from the source named in the appendix at the end of this chapter.

The best treatment for leather bookbindings, then, is to wash the binding carefully, using a moist cloth and saddle soap. The potassium lactate solution is applied with cotton balls to soak into the surface of the bookbinding. Rubber gloves should be used because the fungicide mixed with the potassium lactate is somewhat toxic. The book is allowed to stand for about 24 hours before the neat's-foot oil and lanolin is applied. A paint brush is used to apply the warmed liquid liberally to all exposed surfaces of the book. The book should be allowed to stand for about 48 hours, and then a Turkish towel is used to buff away any excess solution. The result is a chemically preserved, well-lubricated volume which has been deepened in color by the presence of the lubricant.

An additional caution for the conservator is in order. Dried leather under gold tooling may result in the loss of the gold leaf if excessive pressure is applied during any of the above procedures. Due caution should be taken. After the application of the lubricant, there should be less danger of dislodging the gilding.

The lubricant is allowed to soak into the leather for 48 hours and the excess is removed by rubbing with a turkish towel.

The three books on the left are richer in color and more supple than the three books on the right which have not been given the treatment described in this chapter.

LEATHER APPENDIX

The potassium lactate chemical preparation and the neat's-font oil and lanolin preparation are available in kit form from:

Newberry Library
60 West Walton Street
Chicago, Illinois 60610

The solutions may be purchased from:

Talas
Technical Library Service
104 Fifth Avenue
New York, New York 10011

CHAPTER XIV

REPLACING THE UPPER PLATE (METAL PLATING)

Since Benjamin Franklin made his "shocking" discovery nearly two centuries ago while flying a kite, electricity has been employed for a number of purposes—not the least of which is electroplating. Electroplating utilizes a direct current, an anode, a cathode, and a solution which removes metal from the anode and deposits it on the cathode. This method is used to put silver and gold plate on copper objects, to put a black or nickel plating on guns, and to deposit various other metals either for decorative or protective purposes.

The principle of electroplating is simple. Either batteries or a transformer, such as an electric train transformer, is used to provide a D.C. voltage of two to six volts. The positive terminal is connected to the anode, which is a chunk of the metal that is to be deposited on the surface of some object. The cathode, or the negative terminal, is the object to be plated. A plating bath is a solution containing a compound that includes the metal to be deposited and is also present in the anode. When the electricity is allowed to flow and both electrodes are immersed into the plating bath, metal deposition occurs according to the following description. Metal ions of the metal salt in the plating solution are positively charged and migrate to the cathode surface where they are transformed into the metallic state and attach themselves to the cathode surface. As this action occurs, the metal in the anode is dissolved and replaces the metal ions that are pulled out of the plating solution. Thus, the net effect is to transfer particles of metal from the anode to the cathode.

Theoretically, the thickness of the plated coating is determined by the amount of time allowed in the plating process and the density of the current used. However, some practical problems are involved in some of the plating operation. Therefore, the time needed for plating is usually only a few seconds, unless the object being plated is removed from the plating bath and treated in some manner before replating. Normally, silver can be plated directly on copper, brass, bronze, nickel, tin, pewter, gold and most while metal alloys. Gold can be plated directly on tin, copper, brass, steel, nickel, stainless steel, pewter and silver. Gold can also be plated on white metal objects if those objects are first plated with copper. Copper can be directly electroplated on all common metals and alloys except aluminum, stainless steel and chromium.

Clean Is The Thing

Although plating a metal object may take only a few seconds, it does take considerable time to prepare the surface for such plating. Either physical or chemical processes must be used to bring the surface of the object to be plated to nearly the luster desired before plating. Plating will not transform a dull object into a bright object, but merely takes one color and type of metal and deposits it on the surface of another metal object. Therefore, an antique that is rusted and pitted will not be restored simply through electroplating without first removing the rust and pits.

Many chemical polishing compounds use an abrasive to remove easily any

A stiff bristle brush and polishing compound are used to remove any traces of dirt and thin coatings of oxide from this worn match safe.

A detergent is used to wash the polishing compound away. The object is then rinsed with water.

surface coating of oxides, dirt and grime from the object to be plated. Often you can use a stiff toothbrush with the polishing compound on objects that have a considerable amount of detail or relief. Areas that are not thoroughly cleaned will not be plated. You can use a muslin buffing wheel with jeweler's rouge to bring a luster to otherwise dull surfaces. The use of this wheel is an absolute necessity for such hard metal objects as a steel gun. Bottled metal polishing compound is usually good enough to clean brass, copper, silver or gold objects. In the case of copper, however, one hour of sitting in the atmosphere after cleaning is long enough to form a thin oxide on the surface of the object that will prevent plating.

After the object is polished and cleaned with either polishing compound or the muslin wheel, it should be washed in warm or hot water with a detergent. Soap that leaves a film should definitely not be used, because it also will have to be cleaned off. Using an organic solvent after the detergent will insure that no deposits of wax or grease remain. These solvents include trichloroethylene, acetone and methyl alcohol. After cleaning, be sure not to touch the object, or the fluids left from your fingerprints will interfere with the plating process.

Preparing The Bath

Although only one chemical theoretically need be used in the bath to attain the movement of ions for the electroplating process, other chemicals are used that facilitate ion movement and de-position on the cathode. These chemicals are usually organic compounds, colloidal in nature, that add to the smoothness or brightness of the metal deposits. Theories of why these chemicals work to improve the plating process are not fully explanatory, and their use is based essentially on empirical information. In the past, many different items, such as gelatin, glue and albumen, have been used as additives in the plating bath. To date, the best explanation for their importance seems to be that they somehow interfere with the crystal growth of the plating metal, and therefore the plating develops with a smaller grain size and a smoother finish.

Aside from the additives, the plating bath most commonly used for copper consists of cuprous cyanide, sodium cyanide, sodium carbonate and sodium thiosulphate kept at 40 degrees centigrade.

The chemicals are added respectively in the proportions of 31 percent, 46 percent, 20 percent and 3 percent by weight per liter of solution.

To plate bright nickel, a liter of solution is composed of 240 grams nickel sulfate, 45 grams of nickel chloride and 30 grams of boric acid.

Silver and gold are plated exclusively from cyanide baths. In the case of silver, sodium argento-cyanide is used.

Use of the word cyanide in these baths should be alarming but not distressing. In other words, the solutions are poisonous and should not be swallowed and their vapors should not be inhaled for prolonged periods of time, but simple exposure to them should not result in serious illness. Always heed the cautions on the label of any chemicals.

Taking A Dip

When dip plating, be sure you use a clean china, glass or plastic container to hold the plating bath. A metallic container will undoubtedly interfere somehow with the plating process. The negative terminal of the transformer should be connected to the object to be plated. If a transformer and volt meter are not available for your use, simply use a number of dry cell batteries connected in series. Small dry cell or flashlight batteries are 1.5 volts each. Connecting the pointed end to the flat end of each battery puts them in series. The pointed end is usually positive and is marked in that fashion, and the flat side is negative. Putting two batteries in series will give 3 volts. Putting three batteries in series will give 4.5 volts, and putting four batteries in series will give 6 volts. Higher voltages are not needed. The larger the battery, the greater the current, and therefore the greater the thickness of metal deposition per time unit. The positive terminal is connected to the anode, which is always placed into the plating solution first (except in the case of black metal plating when both the cathode and anode are immersed simultaneously). Copper wire (with the insulation removed, of course) can be used as the anode for copper plating. Old silver coins are probably the cheapest source of silver for a silver anode. Gold can be purchased from a jewelry supply house.

After the anode has been placed in the solution, the cathode is dipped into the solution for 5 to 20 seconds. The efficiency of the plating is considerably reduced at this time, and both the cathode and the anode should be removed from the plating bath and washed before dipping them once again. The article and the anode should both be wiped with a clean cloth. If additional plating is desirable, the process of plating and cleaning is repeated. It is difficult to replate the worn areas of a steel knife directly with silver. In general, they have to be copper plated first and the silver plated over the copper. Occasionally, silver plating does not result in a brilliant finish. The problem is a minor one, however, because the surface can be buffed to a high luster after plating. Hold the object near the anode and rotate it to assure even plating.

When A Bath Is Not Necessary

Occasionally, the object being restored does not have to be completely replated and only small areas require a touch-up plating. The J. M. T. Manufacturing Company of Stormville, New York, has developed an ingenious little device to accomplish this task with great facility. It looks like a fountain pen into which two penlight batteries are inserted. Out of the back of the pen is a wire with an alligator clip to attach the cathode. The other end of the pen consists of the small loop of plating metal to serve as the anode with a brush surrounding it. No dipping is required to use this device. Simply fasten the alligator clip to the object to be plated, dip the brush into the plating solution, and then wipe the wet brush with the anode several times over the area to be plated. Repeat the process as often as necessary.

The alligator clip is attached to the match safe making it the cathode and the silver wire anode appears in the pen holder. The anode is placed in the solution first and then the cathode. To insure a uniform plating, the anode is moved around the surface to be plated without touching it for five to 20 seconds. (The solution in the photograph above is water used for demonstration purposes only. The actual plating solution is nearly opaque.)

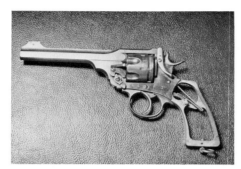

Before: This is a worn .45-caliber Webly revolver used by the British in World War I.

Cleaning solution is applied with a cotton swab to remove any traces of wax or oil. The item is then rinsed in hot water and immediately dried. The item should be oiled and lubricated after plating.

The gun becomes the cathode when the alligator clip is attached to it. The anode is a small wire hidden inside the brush. The brush is dipped in plating solution and stroked along the surface to be plated.

A buffing wheel and an abrasive are used to remove small scratches and polish the metal to make it ready for plating.

After: The old .45 has been replated.

198

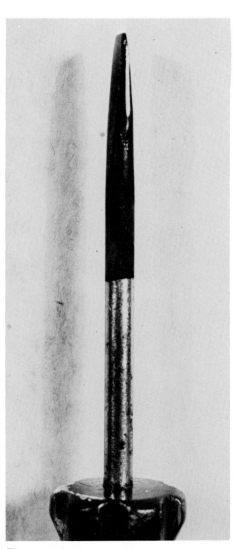

The end of this screwdriver was blackened by dipping for five seconds in the chemical solutions.

Everything needed to do small plating jobs, whether using the dipping or brushing technique, can be obtained from J. M. T. or Edmund Scientific Company. Their addresses can be found in the appendix at the end of this chapter.

Chemical Treatment

Although electroplating can be used to restore the black finish to an old gun, it also can be done chemically. The process is sometimes called "bluing", but actually results in a black finish. This application is useful only for iron and steel, and consists of treating the surface with a solution of selenium dioxide, nitric acid and nickel sulfate. The object to be blued is cleaned and buffed to as great a luster as desired, and then a cleaner-degreaser such as methyl alcohol is applied to completely remove any waxy or greasy deposits.

The solution will not act on rust, so all traces of rust first must be removed. The solution may be applied with a brush, cotton swabs or sponge, and rubbed-in thoroughly to insure complete coverage. The item is then wiped dry with a clean cloth. Steel wool, a cloth or fiber brush can be used to polish the object. Then a coat of oil, wax or lacquer can be used to preserve the blackened finish. Use a cloth to rub on the solution if the object is too small to be immersed in the available amount of chemicals.

Results obtained can be utterly amazing. Only a few seconds are necessary to do the blackening. All of the solutions necessary to blacken steel are manufactured by Birchwood Casey of Eden Prairie, Minnesota, and can be obtained from the source listed in the appendix to this chapter.

PLATING APPENDIX

Electroplating kits can be obtained from:

Edmund Scientific Company
7782 Edscorp Building
Barrington, New Jersey 08007

Edmund Scientific Company also has a vast supply of other interesting and often useful items. It might be advisable to write for their catalog.

The manufacturer of the plating kits is:

J.N.T. Manufacturing Co. Inc.
Stormville, New York
12582

The blackening solution, called Presto Black PC6, can be obtained from:

Brookstone Company
Vose Farm Road
Peterborough, New Hampshire
03458

CHAPTER XV

TAKING CARE OF THE OLD TICKER (CLOCK REPAIR)

Time pieces are devices used to keep track of the hours of the day. A clock, in general, at least according to all definitions, includes a separate mechanism for notifying the hour by sounding either a gong or a bell.

Basically, a clock is a machine that records the passing of time. A device that performs regular movements in equal intervals of time is linked to a counting mechanism that records the number of these movements. Most mechanical clocks of the 19th century were made by using a weight or spring to drive a series of toothed wheels that were linked by an escapement to a pendulum. The escapement allows the regular movements of the pendulum to control the rotation of the wheelwork so that it rotates at a constant rate. Simultaneously, the escapement transmits to the pendulum enough energy to maintain its swing by replacing the energy lost due to friction.

The first clocks were used in religious rites in Europe to mark the time of religious services. Many of these were recorded in the 13th century.

In 1581, Galileo discovered the principle of the pendulum. A weight is suspended on the lower end of a rod that oscillates freely about the upper end fixed on a pivot. The period of time it takes the pendulum to move back and forth through one complete oscillatory motion is governed by the influence of gravity and the length of the pendulum. It is not affected by the mass of the pendulum. An arch of oscillation about three inches in length will have its rate of oscillation increased about one second per day if the length of the pendulum is increased $^1/_{10}$ inch. The time of one swing in seconds can be calculated by multiplying pi, which is 3.1416, times the square root of the quotient of the length of the pendulum divided by the acceleration caused by gravity in feet per second per second.

Like Clockwork

Most clocks made in the 19th century employ a brass mechanism powered either by weights or by springs. Both mechanisms are similar, and only the spring mechanism will be treated in this chapter. Brass is a valuable material for making time pieces. It does not easily corrode and it offers a sort of natural lubrication that can last for years. Most spring-wound 19th century clocks were used either as a mantle piece or as the well-known kitchen clock. Some had alarms and some did not, but almost all had two separate mechanisms—one to keep time and one to produce an audible signal to notify people of the time.

Looking at a clock mechanism for the first time can be somewhat of a scarey experience. There are a lot of wheels with a lot of teeth, a lot of things moving, some noises emanating, and without further study it's not apparent how all the magic is put together to make some sort of sense. Roughly, the time train works as follows. A bob, or pendulum weight, is connected to a pendulum rod. This rod can be followed up to a thin piece of metal that appears flat, and actually is a flat spring that goes through the slot in a brass pillar. This spring in the slot acts as the pivot point with a minimal amount of friction to interfere

Flat pendulum spring (A), slotted pillar (B).

A key fits over a post (A) to wind the spring for the timing mechanism (B) that provides the energy for turning a series of sprockets up to the escapement wheel (C). The key also winds another post (D) which is used to wind the gong spring (E).

An old oak kitchen clock to be cleaned is biding its time.

with the motion of the pendulum. Whenever a clock is moved from place-to-place, the first course of business should be to remove the pendulum bob. A heavy, free-swinging bob not only can become detached and damage either the clock case or the works upon transport, but also can force itself against some of the delicate mechanism and cause it to break.

Looking carefully around the pendulum rod, you can see a loop of wire that is called the verge lever. It bends and passes into the clock mechanism, and is attached by means of a pivot to the verge, which looks somewhat like a staple with curved ends. Each of these ends is fixed in the opening of a sprocket on the escapement wheel. The purpose of the mechanism thus far is to count the oscillations of the pendulum by allowing the pendulum to move the verge in such a way that one sprocket progresses for each oscillation or half-oscillation of the pendulum.

The motion of the escapement wheel is forced by the tension built into a spring and connected through a mechanism to be described shortly. The escapement wheel would turn freely if it were not for the verge connected to it. Time is actually kept by the swinging of the pendulum. The verge mech-

The pendulum (A), the alarm winding mechanism (B), the alarm bell (C), and the gong (D).

anism fixes each oscillation over a specific time interval. Of course, no machine is perfect, and there is some loss of energy due to the mechanical movement of the pendulum (friction caused by the pendulum moving through the air as well as about its pivot point). Therefore, the spring provides enough energy through the escapement wheel to the pendulum to compensate for this slight loss.

Starting at the spring side of the mechanism, you can see that turning a key tightens the spiral spring. Energy from your hand working against the tension of the spring is stored as potential energy in that spring, which tries to unravel the spring and cause it to move into a larger spiral. However, a ratchet on the ratchet wheel prevents the spring, which has both ends attached to the clock mechanism, from unraveling freely. The spring does, however, apply tension to turn a large wheel, which is a thin brass gear with a large number of teeth. As this wheel turns, it rotates a pinion affixed to another arbor. The pinion is a small device made of two disks of metal with small parallel steel rods between the two disks. The teeth from the first wheel intermesh with these rods and cause another arbor to rotate. In addition to the pinion on that

The counting wheel has shallow slots and deep slots.

The counting wheel rotates in the direction of the curved arrow. The pencil points to the counting lever. The small arrow points to the slot which represents 10:30. The counting lever will bounce off the shallow slots and stop when it penetrates into a deep slot. The counting lever therefore rests in the slot designating 11:00.

arbor is another thin brass gear with a number of teeth on it. In a similar manner, this gear turns a pinion affixed to another arbor attached to another gear. There can be varying numbers of these gears according to the design of the clock, but five is a common number. The last one is the escapement wheel.

Somewhere along the line, one of the wheels interacting with the pinion attached to another arbor also interacts with a gear attached to the minute arbor. This mechanism is designed so that the speed of rotation of that wheel causes the minute arbor to rotate once in one hour. A similar mechanism is set up so that the hour arbor rotates once every 12 hours. The minute arbor is the solid shaft that comes out the center of the clock face to which the minute hand is attached. The hour arbor is a hollow arbor concentrically placed over the minute arbor emerging from the center of the clock face.

The Gong Show

Unlike the time-keeping half of the clock, the striking mechanism is not in continual motion. It moves only a few times during an hour. The clock may be designed so that the number of the hours strike at the appropriate time, and some in addition provide for a single tone to strike on the half-hour. Other variations of this scheme also provide for striking the quarter-hours, et cetera. Basically, another spring mechanism with a ratchet provides energy for the striking train. The minute arbor is connected to a cam that engages a mechanism called the lifting

lever, which is attached to the same arbor of another mechanism called the locking lever. When the lifting lever is raised by the center arbor cam, a mechanism called the drop lever is also raised by the unlocking lever and sets free the striking train. At that instant, the unlocking lever engages the warning pin and stops all the gears in the striking train. This particular action takes place several minutes before the time at which the striking train again goes into motion and rings a gong or bell.

You can easily find the counting wheel by looking carefully at the striking mechanism. It is a thin, brass sprocket with deep and shallow slots. The counting lever is the steel device, looking like a wire, with a flat end bent to fit into the slots in the counting wheel. When the counting lever is positioned in a deep slot, its connection with the locking lever provides that the mechanism is not in a striking mode. As the mechanism prepares to strike, it lifts the counting lever out of its deep-seated slot and the action makes itself ready for working against a spring to push on the gong hammer. As a cam rotates, the gong hammer is released and strikes the gong. Watch the counting wheel. It rotates just enough so that the counting lever can return to the next slot in the counting wheel. If the counting lever returns to a deep slot, the striking train motion is stopped. If it returns to a shallow slot, it bounces back into position and the striking train once again goes into action.

Let us try to understand, by looking at the counting wheel, what time the striking train thinks it is. Of course, unless the striking train is synchronized with the time-keeping mechanism, it will ring out the number of hour it is set for regardless of the time showing on the clock face. The two mechanisms must be synchronized, and it is easier to do this if you understand what time the counting wheel thinks it is. If the clock strikes on the half-hour, a number of deep slots in the counting wheel will be immediately followed by another deep slot. When the counting lever is raised from the first slot and the gong sounds, the counting lever returns to a deep slot and the striking mechanism is halted. This is also what happens at one o'clock. Therefore, there will be one deep slot to stop the striking mechanism after the clock strikes twelve, immediately followed by another deep slot which stops the striking mechanism after a single gong at twelve-thirty. Another deep slot follows to stop the mechanism after the striking of one o'clock, and yet another deep slot which stops the striking mechanism after the sounding at one-thirty. Therefore, four deep slots found successively on the counting wheel signify the time between twelve and one-thirty, where the first slot is the end of the twelve o'clock striking and the last slot, in that series of four consecutive deep slots, is the slot that stops the strike train at one-thirty.

Immediately following that fourth deep slot will be a shallow slot followed by a deep slot. At two o'clock, the counting lever will be raised from its position in the fourth consecutive deep slot. When the gong rings once at two o'clock, the counting lever returns to a shallow slot position where it cannot engate the locking lever, bounces back up

into position to allow the clock to strike again, and then returns to a deep slot that engages the locking lever and stops the action. You can continue with this description of the counting wheel and counting lever mechanism until you find the 11 shallow slots that separate eleven-thirty from twelve o'clock and cause the mechanism to strike twelve times.

If the clock works fine except for the synchronization of the striking train with the time train, the matter is easy to correct. Simply wait until the hour and lift the counting lever out of its stable position in the deep slot in which it rests. This will engage the unlocking lever and cause the clock to strike whatever number of times is dictated by the counting wheel. Sometimes an additional wire is included to directly link with the the unlocking lever and provide this service, but it is not found in all clocks. Continue to lift the counting lever and let the clock gong its heart out until the number of gongs matches the hour showing on the clock face. The clock is now synchronized and will serve adequately. Be sure that the spring is wound enough to give all the gongs that you require.

If lifting the counting lever does not result in movement of the striking train and the gong hammer, but rather results in freezing the striking train, do not fret. Occasionally, lifting the counting lever will lock the striking train in position to prepare for its next striking. This will be the case until the time train has advanced about five minutes. The counting lever should then be moved as described above to synchronize the two mechanisms. If the counting lever is

204

The pencil points to the wire connecting the alarm winding mechanism to the lever that trips the alarm.

If there is no wire through this hole in the alarm arm, the alarm cannot work. Very often this wire is lost and must be replaced.

lifted out of a deep slot and remains there without activating the striking train, simply wait until it moves on its own and then repeat the procedure.

A Sick Gong

Occasionally, everything works okay in an old clock except that the gong sounds more like a sick cow than a musical note. The gong can be either a cast bell or a piece of spiral steel suspended from a single screw. The other end of this spiral gong vibrates freely and produces the musical tone when struck. Sick tones result when something interferes with the vibration of a gong. The most common form of interference occurs when the gong hammer in its fully extended position remains in contact with the gong instead of dropping clear after striking it and thereby absorbs energy and mutes the tone. This malady can be corrected in one of two ways. The first treatment would be to rotate the spiral gong slightly about its fixed point, in such a way that it rotates away from the gong hammer. It should be moved just enough so that the gong can still strike it, and yet the tone will ring freely because the gong hammer does not remain in contact with the gong. This procedure should always prove successful, but another treatment may be necessary because of other confines within the clock case.

This second type of first aid is to slightly bend the gong hammer shaft, so that the hammer will clear the gong immediately after striking it. If you must bend the gong hammer shaft, be careful to insure that undue pressure or leverage is not applied to hurt the rest of the

mechanism. It should be bent only with the fingers, ever so slightly, with a firm pressure about two inches away from the gong hammer.

If the tone produced is musical but very weak, often the opposite of the above described effect is the cause. Since the gong hammer has only so much forward motion, the gong is too far away, the hammer makes only minimal contact with it and does not hit hard enough to ring the gong with the desirable amplitude. To remedy this problem, the opposite procedure is used to bring the gong and gong hammer into a more solid contact upon striking.

Don't Be Alarmed

Many kitchen clocks have an alarm that simply rings at a predetermined time until it is turned off. A separate key winding mechanism is provided for the alarm. The alarm mechanism, in general, will be completely separate from the clock and striking mechanism, and will be found elsewhere in the clock case. It is connected to the rest of the clockworks by means of a single wire attached to the alarm mechanism at a lever. In one position, the lever starts the alarm ringing, and in another position stops it. The wire leaves this lever and is attached to an arm on the clockworks that rests on an alarm arbor. This alarm arbor is another concentric device that slips over the hour arbor and rotates at the same speed. A slot is provided in this arbor so that when it is aligned straight up, the alarm lever falls and pushes down on a stiff wire attached to the alarm lever, thereby engaging the alarm mechanism.

205

The small arrow points to the alarm arm resting on the alarm arbor. The time at which the alarm is to sound is set by the wheel in the center of the picture.

To increase the period of oscillation and therefore slow down the clock, the nut on the pendulum is rotated to allow the pendulum bob to come further down on the pendulum rod. The reverse makes the clock run faster.

If the alarm spring is intact and working, it is likely that nothing else is wrong with the alarm mechanism (that is, if no one has stolen the alarm bell). If there is no apparent link between the alarm and the time-keeping mechanism, look carefully for a small lever that rests on the alarm arbor. A small hole drilled through this lever indicates that there should be a stiff steel wire connecting this lever to the alarm lever. Oftentimes, moving a kitchen clock will result in loss of this steel wire and it will need to be replaced. Any stiff steel wire will do. It should be slipped through its attachment points on both ends, bent over so that it does not slide free, and trimmed so that it does not interfere with any of the mechanism.

Keeping A Good Beat

A clock that is keeping appropriate time should have equal "ticks" and "tocks". That is, the ticktock of a clock should be a rhythmic symmetrical sound and not an uneven sound. Clocks were meant to be placed on level surfaces or leveled if they are wall clocks. If the "ticks" and "tocks" are not equal, a clock will probably not run very well or keep very good time. Use a level to make sure that the surface on which the clock rests is level. Wall clocks also should be mounted level on a wall so that the "ticks" and "tocks" are rhythmic. For a mantel or kitchen clock, small pieces of cardboard or paper can be placed under opposite sides of the clock to level it, if necessary.

Occasionally, the beat is uneven not because the clock is not level, but rather because the verge lever has been bent.

Use your fingers very delicately to bend the verge lever one way, either left or right a trifle amount, about two and a half inches away from where the verge lever meets the pendulum rod. Note the rhythm of the ticking once again. If the rhythm is worse, you bent the verge lever the wrong way, and so bend it back the other way. Carefully following this procedure will result in the appropriate ticking of the clock. Many clocks will run for a few days with uneven beats, but most likely will eventually stop. Unless the "ticks" and "tocks" are balanced, the amount of energy imparted to the pendulum rod through the verge by the escapement will not be equal on both ends of the pendulum oscillation, thereby eventually losing the small increments of energy necessary to keep the pendulum swinging.

Improving The Pace

The clock may run fast or slow after being moved to a new location or not being operated for some time, because the pendulum may have fallen out of adjustment. As mentioned earlier, the time oscillation of the pendulum eventually will determine whether the clock runs fast or slow. Because the attraction of gravity is slightly less at 20,000 feet than at sea level, a pendulum clock will run slower on a mountain top than in the depths of a valley. The time it takes the pendulum to complete one oscillation is longer when the attraction due to gravity is less. Similarly, lengthening the pendulum arm increases the time of oscillation and makes the clock run slower. Think of it this way: the longer it takes the pendulum to swing back and forth, the longer the time between "ticks" and "tocks" in a clock that is functioning to keep appropriate time. Most pendulums come with a thread on the rod and a knurled nut on the pendulum bob to adjust the weight. Simply turning the knurled knob one way or the other will increase or decrease the pendulum length. Make the pendulum longer to slow the clock down and make the pendulum shorter to speed the clock up. Some experimentation might be necessary, but you should be able to zero in on synchronizing this clock with other clocks in just a few days.

Giving The Clock A Face Lift

Sometimes all is well with the clockworks, but the face has suffered from undue exposure to sun or household elements so that it has faded or otherwise been "defaced". Some clock faces are made of porcelain. If chipped, the porcelain can be repaired according to the procedures described in the chapter dealing with china repair. Most often, the clock faces are of paper. The techniques described under paper restoration should be used. I did have one instance, however, of an Ansonia clock face that had so deteriorated that it was no longer usable. Someone apparently had tried unsuccessfully to clean the face and had abraded most of the visible numerals out of existence.

When you remove a clock face, it is always necessary to remove the hands first. Note the position that they are in

This clock face is actually the cutout photograph of another clock face.

as well as bushings which might separate the hands from each other and the clock face. Remove any pins or other devices used to hold the hands in position and carefully remove them with your fingers if possible. Be very careful not to bend the hands; it may be difficult to flatten them once again. The clock face should then come off easily by removing screws from its circumference. Once the face is off, it can be examined carefully for appropriate restoration techniques. With the face that I mentioned above, it was impossible to provide any adequate restoration so it had to be replaced. New clock faces can be bought from sources specified in the appendix at the end of this chapter. Clock hands can also be bought from the same sources, if necessary. New clock faces can be made by using an appropriate paper and numerals that are available for this purpose either from a clock supply house or from an art supply store. Plastic press-on numerals are handsome, if they can be found in a style similar to those that were originally on the clock face.

My solution was a little more involved, but wholly adequate for my purposes. I had a friend who owned nearly an exact duplicate of the clock on which I was attempting to restore the face. With his permission, we removed the face of his clock and laid it on a piece of black craft paper. I then used a good camera with good film to take a black and white photograph of his clock face. A color photograph would have done just as well, except that there were no colors on that particular clock face. Going into my dark room, I then developed

A bearing.

The screwdriver points to one of the four screws that hold the clockworks in its case.

the film and printed a clock face exactly the size necessary for my replacement. I carefully cut the face from the print and glued it into place on the bezel which supported the old clock face. It looks as good as the untouched original on my friend's clock, and because of its gloss can even be mistaken for porcelain.

When The Ticker Won't Tick—Or Tock Even

A clock that will not run is either broken or dirty. Most often, it is dirty. If it is broken, the problem can be quite involved. If the spring is broken, I would suggest that the clock be taken to an expert clock repairer. Replacing a spring is a tedious and dangerous job. A spring can unravel with tremendous force and any sharp edge will act as a knife to cut you. If the spring needs to be replaced, the clock maker must take appropriate measurements to find a suitable replacement part. I have, at times, shortened broken springs and reattached them to a clock, shortening the eight-day movement to five or six days. But the danger involved with removing a broken spring and replacing it with another should warrant someone who has had experience with these risks.

Replacing broken sprockets that are either bent, cracked or have suffered a loss of teeth is best done by a clock repairman who knows where to order the replacement parts. Of course, they can be manufactured, and I would discuss with you how to go about machining these pieces, but they require equipment that is rather expensive and cannot normally be found in the average residence.

However, we are somewhat lucky that almost all clock problems are related to cleanliness and not broken parts. People with diets that are too rich in fats eventually gum up their arteries, which brings about heart disease that either slows them down or stops their ticker from working. Similarly, a clock mechanism can be slowed down by buildups of grease or oil. Clock bearings are lubricated with a very small amount of oil, and over the years this oil can become more viscous by collecting dirt or being chemically altered through interaction with its environment. Cooking fumes is one such source of interaction, as well as environmental pollution. The oil turns almost to a varnish, which not only impedes the normal action of the clock, but also essentially glues it into a frozen state. A technique I have devised for cleaning the works is simple and never has failed. The clockworks need to be removed from the clock case. For mantel clocks, this means removal from the back, and for kitchen clocks, it usually means removal from the front. There are usually only about four wood screws, one in each corner of the works, which go through a brass loop on the clock chassis to hold the works in place. Remove the pendulum, take the hands off the face and, if necessary, remove the face to facilitate your work.

With the screws removed, it's a simple matter to lift the works out of the clock case. Then, you must decide what to do with it. A simple board, nailed perpendicular to a two-by-four, will make a stand adequate to fasten the clockworks to so that it can be observed easily

A simple support can be constructed from a 2 x 4 and other scrap lumber to support the clockworks for cleaning.

The works is attached to the support and suspended above a plastic dish that will collect wasted cleaning solution.

Cleaning solvent is sprayed into the clockworks after the works has been wound and started ticking. Note that the pendulum bob is not attached.

and both hands will be free to operate on it. If necessary, a weight should be placed on the horizontal two-by-four to keep the stand from falling forward. Two screws through the loops on the clock chassis should be enough to screw the works firmly on the upright supporting board. If the clock is wound, it should be ticking madly without the weighted pendulum to slow down the energy transfer through the escapement. If it is not wound, this would be a good time to wind it. Do not overwind it; that is, when a certain degree of resistance is found to the winding motion, do not force it any further. If the clock is not ticking at all, it is really gummed up. Normally, a clock that might not run with the pendulum bob attached will run with the pendulum bob removed. Of course, that's no consolation since it cannot keep time without the pendulum bob. But it is a consolation in another sense, because if it runs without the bob in place, you have an indication that the bearings are not frozen.

Some solvent must be used to dissolve the varnish and oil that has caked up and is preventing the mechanism from functioning properly. A sure-cure solvent comes in a spray can called "Gumout" or "Gunk". These solvents clean grease and varnish off carburetors and automotive engines and will readily dissolve grease and grime without harming the clockworks. When sprayed under pressure, they provide the slight amount of force necessary to clean areas that would be inaccessible to swabs or other aids without completely disassembling the works.

Place a plastic or glass pail under the clockworks, and while it is ticking away spray the degreaser over the works until it is saturated. You should immediately see dirty solvent dripping into your tray. If the clock has not been ticking and does not start ticking soon after this treatment begins, try to spray additional solvent into the ends of each of the bearings. If the works still do not begin to move, loosen the nuts that hold the chassis together by about one-half turn, BUT NO MORE! This loosening should be enough to break the sealed area at the end of the bearings, so that solvent can get in without loosening the works enough to fall apart. Give the works another spray of Gumout. This process should be done in a well-ventilated area, because the substance is flammable and prolonged breathing does not have a positive effect on one's health.

If after completing the steps above, the clock still does not begin ticking, it is very obstinate. Move the verge back-and-forth with your finger to force some movement in the escapement. If it still does not start ticking, put the key over the shaft that winds the spring and apply pressure to rotate it in the direction that would cause the spring to unwind—DO NOT WIND MORE TIGHTLY! Moderate pressure in the direction of unwinding effectively gives the spring more power without having to wind it tighter. Many springs can lose up to half of their energy-producing potential through physical changes that occur with age, just as with many of us.

The pencil in this picture points to one of four nuts that can be loosened to take pressure off the bearings. If it is loosened even a little too much, the entire works may come apart.

Look carefully at the clockworks for a stamped patent date that will give an idea of the clock's vintage.

The clock most certainly has begun ticking away by now, but if it hasn't, one last effort can be attempted. Remove the clock from its support and place it in a tray or container deep enough to fully immerse it in liquid. Use enough degreaser, which can be thinned if necessary with other solvents like alcohol, and place the mechanism on its back in the tray. The verge wire should be up so that its movement is not impeded. The entire mechanism should be drowned in the solvent and allowed to soak overnight. The next morning, it should be ticking away, even in the liquid. If it is not, remove it, put it vertically on its wooden support and allow it to drain. Then repeat the other process described earlier by pushing on the verge movement with your finger and moderately unwinding the spring with a reverse rotation of the clock key. I have never found a dirty clock mechanism that wasn't completely cleaned and working by this time. If the four nuts on the clock chassis have been loosened, they should be tightened now.

When the mechanism has thoroughly dried, it is ready for lubrication and placement back into the clock cabinet.

To lubricate the clock properly, dip a toothpick or needle into clock oil bought from a clock repair shop, or other appropriate outlet, and place one drop, and only one drop, on each of the bearings. Normally, no other lubrication is required, and any additional lubrication may interfere with the workings of the clock. However, if the clock is required to perform in very humid conditions, I have found that it may be desirable to take a precaution against the steel parts rusting. A simple spray with WD-40, so as not to soak the works but simply mist it, will be enough. Repeat spray the clockworks about once a month. This will have the desirable effect of preventing rust, but eventually may cause the type of buildup that interferes with the bearings and requires that the works be cleaned every few years. The works are then replaced in the clock cabinet after the cabinet has been refinished, if necessary. The face is attached, the hands are reapplied, and the striking mechanism is synchronized with the timekeeping mechanism after the appropriate time is set on the clock. The pendulum bob must be placed back into position, and the clock should be running as good as new.

CLOCK REPAIR APPENDIX

Some clock faces and hands are available from:

Craftsman Wood Service Company
2727 South Mary Street
Chicago, Illinois 60608

CHAPTER XVI

HOW TO REED MUSIC AND PUT A STOP TO A HEALTHY ORGAN (ORGANS)

The instrument that we call an organ has a diverse and varied history that can be traced back into ancient times. Study of ancient manuscripts, sculpture, mosaics and coinage figures shows evidence of the use of an instrument that we might call a pipe organ during ancient Greek and Roman times. Most inventions of any complexity resulted from evolutionary development by several generations of learned minds. However, tracing the history of the organ does not indicate that any such device existed before about the 3rd century B.C.

Alexander the Great founded the city of Alexandria in 332 B.C. About 50 years later, Ptolemy Philadelphus became the King of Egypt. He was part of a family of Ptolemys who commissioned the purchase of vast numbers of original works, as well as copies and translations of books that were put into a magnificent library of about 500,000 manuscripts. Many great scholars of the period were attracted to Alexandria because of the resources provided by Ptolemy. In Alexandria at about this time, first records indicate the invention of the pipe organ.

A man named Ktesibios, the son of a hairdresser in Alexandria, was known for his mechanical aptitude and inventiveness. Indeed, he was considered to be one of the outstanding engineers of the time. He is credited with the single-handed and single-minded invention of a new instrument. Although common illustrations of Pan playing his pipes might lead one to believe that the first pipe organ was merely a mechanism to blow wind through pipes, the original pipe organ was a more complex device nearly approximating the pipe organs of the present. Both the Greek text of *Hero of Alexandria* and the Latin text of *Vitrubius* point to Ktesibios as the engineer of the pipe organ and describe his invention. A hydraulic pump forced air into a wind box and from there through a series of pipes operated by a keyboard.

The organ today is a familiar instrument that captures our attention between innings of baseball games and slow periods in ice hockey and basketball arenas. It will probably surprise many to note that pipe organs were also used in amphitheaters of ancient Rome to entertain spectators at athletic events. Although 2,000 years have passed since those Roman games, the spectators at the events then and now probably understand very little about pipe organ operation. Later in this chapter, we will attempt to understand the mechanism of the organ so that you will know enough to repair it if broken. Needless to say, early organs were not mass produced, but rather made as individual instruments to be used for specific purposes. Although it is hard today to fathom a church in either Europe or the United States without organ music to accompany religious services, such was not the case in the Middle Ages. The organ had pagan beginnings and was used at the athletic events of pagans. For a considerable period of time, Christians resisted musical accompaniment to their worship. Eventually, however, thinking changed and the most magnificent of organs were built for use in cathedrals.

Parelleling the evolution of the pipe organ were reed instruments developed along similar lines. Although they are more rightly called harmoniums, they have been referred to in this country for well over 100 years as reed organs. It is the reed organ of the 19th century in America that we will concentrate on in this book. Its popularity during Victorian times took it from the choir loft of town churches into the parlors of wealthy and middle-class homes.

More than 200 manufacturers of reed organs in the United States and Canada were identified as operating in the third quarter of the 19th century. One of the better known organ companies, the Estey Organ Company, proclaimed that they manufactured one organ every 10 minutes. Reed organs were produced at a cost ranging, in general, from $200 to $500, and were significantly able to underprice pipe organs. The reed organ became so popular in American homes that Europeans commonly referred to them as American organs.

A. M. Peasely patented the first organ in the United States in Boston, Massachusetts, on November 11, 1818. From this time on through 1856, various modifications, improvements and attachments were patented to improve the quality and versatility of the reed organ. Various names as "Seraphime", "Aelodeon", and the most common name, "Melodeon", were all used to denote musical instruments which produced sound by pumping air into or out of a ballast that forced air movement through reeds.

It is striking to note the rate at which the popularity of reed organs in America increased. During a patent hearing in 1860, Elias P. Needham and Emmons Hamlin estimated that the total number of reed organs built in America before 1846 was less than 300. Barely 50 years later, however, the Estey Organ Company (only one of many organ companies) estimated its sales at over 100,000. The reed organ's popularity continued to increase throughout the 19th century, until it dropped to almost nothing with the advent of the phonograph and the player piano.

If You've See One, You Haven't Seen Them All

In the first half of the 19th century, various instruments were all classified as reed organs but having their own specific generic names. For instance, lap organs were devices designed to be played on a person's lap. Both hands played the keyboard, while one elbow worked the bellows.

The harmonium was originally a copyrighted name, but eventually came to be a generic term referring to keyboard reed organs that had a foot-pump forced bellows. A forced bellows provided the pressure that pushed air through the reeds to make music.

The term melodeon became the generic term that applied to keyboard reed organs with horizontal cases and a single foot-pumped vacuum bellows. The vacuum bellows, or exhaust bellows as they are sometimes referred to, are deflated and thus draw air through the reeds into the bellows to produce the musical tones. Some melodeons are built like miniature square grand pianos with octagonal or cabriole legs. Other

This is a melodeon vacuum bellows with a single exhauster. A foot pedal activates a rod that moves the top section up and down to pump air out of the vacuum bellows beneath it. Most reed organs would have two smaller exhausters instead of the large one shown in this picture.

models are lyre-legged that sometimes can be folded and easily transported to a new location.

The above instruments had few stops (controls which changed the tonal quality of the instrument), if any. The instrument became more sophisticated, however, after the Civil War. With its rise in popularity, marketing managers devised all sorts of reed organs with different names and titles to suit all types of purposes. The flat top looked similar to a melodeon, except that its base was enclosed. In general, it had additional controls to vary the volume and tonal quality of the sound produced.

The most popular of the reed organs were referred to as parlor organs. They were made out of oak, walnut, mahogany or rosewood, and generally had elaborately carved high backs adorned with shelves or mirrors. Most of these organs had two pedals to pump the bellows. A cottage organ was the same as a parlor organ, except not quite so elaborately made. It may have had fewer stops, less carving and a lower back.

Another category, called salon organs, referred to elaborately built instruments made for use in public places. Emphasis in organ design was placed on their beautiful, elaborately worked cases, most of which were not made on a production line, but rather individually crafted according to the purchaser's specifications. Artists' organs referred to a class of instrument designed especially for the professional musician. They had additional sets of reeds and exceptional quality actions to facilitate playing complicated musical pieces.

School organs were made of unelaborated materials fashioned into rugged cases. They were intended for use by pipe organ students to become familiar with organ technique.

Church organs were crafted as fine instruments, as were the artists' organs, except that most had elaborately fashioned cases to complement the church decor.

Chapel organs were developed to use in churches where the back of the organ had to face the congregation. These organ backs were finely crafted, in contrast to the plain or even coarse organ backs on most other types of reed organs.

Some organs were made to be used by traveling entertainers, armies and missionaries. These portable organs folded into compact cases that were easily moved by wagon.

Piano organs were reed instruments built into cases that resembled upright pianos. Near the turn of the century, some of these were made into player organs that were the forerunners of the soon to come player pianos.

Many organ dealers and manufacturers knew that they had a "good thing" going during the last quarter of the 19th century. Much competition among the various organ manufacturers gave rise to features and tactics that typify other fast money ventures throughout American history. For example, the quality of the first radios manufactured for household use often depended upon their sophistication. In general, the more tubes a radio had the more sophisticated it was, and therefore, the

215

Reach through the opening just above the pedals to turn the latch that allows the fancy walnut panel to be removed from the organ case.

This old catalog advertises an organ selling for $33.50.

Straps attached to the pedals run over pulleys to the exhausters. The face of each exhauster appears above the pedal it serves. The white strip across each exhauster is the leather that covers the openings. The leather acts as a valve that allows air to escape, but not to be pulled into the exhauster.

more expensive it was. However, some radio marketers advertised 12-tube radios that really had only a few functional tubes; the others were kept in sockets inside as spares for those that burned out.

Similarly, an unscrupulous organ manufacturer could place a set of non-functional reeds in an organ and advertise this product as having more reeds than his competitor's. A 16-stop organ was thought to be more sophisticated than a 4-stop organ. However, sometimes these more sophisticated organs had a number of stops that did nothing more than modify the volume of the music coming from inside. During this time in our history, America's literacy rate was not expecially impressive. People without much formal education saw the organ as a mysterious box they could purchase to make music. Lacking understanding of the real simplicity of these devices, it was hard for many to place a monetary value on organs they had a chance to buy. For example, Daniel F. Beatty sold direct to the organ user. He would advertise an organ as worth $1,200, claim that his normal price was $550 and that he would give a special deal on it for only $150. Some of his models listed for as low as $27. He also would sell an attractive model for $30, provided that he would get advance payment. After the payment was received, he would reply to the mail-order purchaser that the model was sold out, but another model was available for additional money. He also offered to subsidize transportation and meals for those who wished to visit his place of business and purchase an organ.

At the turn of the century, Sears, Roebuck and Company prided itself upon being the cheapest supply house on earth. Full-page advertisements in their catalogs showed reed organs selling for around $35.

Working Anatomy

The reed organ is a very simple instrument that can be easily understood with a little bit of inspection. It is a totally mechanical device that does not rely upon any of the magic or wizardry of electronics or any other sophisticated science. Most organs use an exhaust bellows for the wind supply. Pushing down on a pedal pulls an attached strap that goes over a pulley and is connected to a device called an exhauster. A spring pulls on the exhauster and raises the pedal when pressure is released. Pushing down the pedal expands the exhauster, which is a kind of bellows. The exhauster is hinged on one side even with the bellows, and has material or fabric extending around it on the other three sides to make it airtight. A number of holes on top of the exhauster board are covered by a tight strip of leather that forms a valve. Extending the exhauster volume pulls the leather strap into the holes and prevents any outside air from entering into the exhauster directly. However, another series of holes on the inside of the exhauster goes into the bellows. These holes are also covered by a leather strap, and when a partial vacuum is created, air is drawn from the bellows into the exhauster. When pressure is taken off the pedal, the spring causes the exhauster to contract because air cannot go through the inside valve, and there is no place for the air to go except to leak out through the holes covered by the leather strap on the outside. This strap does not prevent such air movement.

The exhauster, therefore, draws air from the bellows to create a vacuum and allows that air to be exhausted outside of the organ. The bellows is a large cavity formed by boards connected by skins or cloth and sealed to be airtight except for certain designed openings. At one time, bellows were made from goatskins or other types of leather. Some were even made from pieces of cardboard bent to be flexible and sealed at their seams with cloth or skin. Most bellows material nowadays is laminated cloth with alternating layers of fabric and rubber, made especially to be both airtight and flexible, and not deteriorate over time. As the exhauster pumps air out of the bellows, its volume decreases and tries to draw air inside.

When one of the organ keys is depressed, pressure is put on a small rod, called a pallet rod, which extends vertically inside the organ works. The pallet rod presses upon the pallet valve, which is a small strip of wood covered with soft leather underneath a reed.

The "forte" stop lifts this muffler from the board on which it usually rests to permit an increased volume of sound from the reeds inside.

The knee swell opens the forte muffler considerably more, allowing a greater volume of sound to emanate.

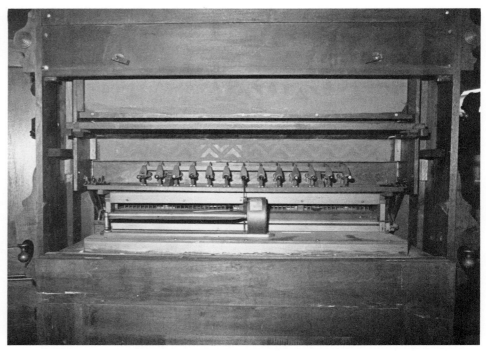

The opened back of a reed organ. The bellows lie enclosed in the cabinet beneath and are not visible.

A spring attached to the pallet valve closes the valve when pressure is taken off the key, and seals the hole through which air would otherwise pass. Depressing the key opens the valve and allows air to pass through a slot in the sounding board to the reed and through an opening into the bellows. The reed vibrates to produce the musical tone. Properly sealed bellows can be deflated for 15 seconds or so after the pumping has ceased. Air will always leak in, even though none of the keys is depressed.

Stops on an organ are also very simple mechanical devices. You can observe their function simply by watching the parts move as the stops are alternately pulled out and depressed. In general, stops remove mufflers from the sounding mechanism to allow more volume from certain acting reeds. Usually, one large muffler across the back of the mechanism is partially removed through the use of the stop called "forte". The "knee swell", a lever activated under the keyboard by the use of the right knee, lifts this muffler considerably further and thereby allows a greater volume of sound to emanate from the back of the organ. The other mutes are either partial or entire strips that go across openings at the front of the organ immediately under the keys. Some stops activate only mutes on the treble side, while other stops activate mutes only on the bass side. A muffler simply dampens the sound before it has a chance to reach your ear. On the other hand, a mute prevents air from passing through certain reeds, and thereby, prevents their vibration. The mutes are additional valves, in a sense, that are covered with soft leather to form a reasonably airtight seal within the organ. A spring normally holds the mutes in the closed position, so that pulling a stop forward applies additional tension on the spring and pulls the mute up and away from its seal.

The stops are connected to bent rods that pivot at the back of the stop through a channel that holds them in place. They rotate a series of levers on either side of the organ and move the mutes or mufflers.

Other stops called "bass" or "treble couplers" activate a key one octave above or below the key being depressed. This feature is sometimes called "harmonique".

A full organ swell is activated by the left knee. It lifts all mufflers and mutes, as well as puts on the couplers to provide the organ with full power and volume.

The names on most of the stops affecting the tone of the organ refer to functions that are supposed to give the reed organ a tone quality similar to the pipe organ stops bearing a similar name or to the instrument that bears the name of a stop. Therefore, names like diapason, dulcet, echo, bourdon or cremona refer to tones produced by a pipe organ with those stops activated. However, the bassoon, flute, clarinet, French horn or oboe stops are all supposed to copy the tone of those respective instruments.

Physical Fitness

Since organ operation is relatively easy to understand and it is a totally physical device, there should be no magic in learn-

The stops are connected to rods that pivot in various channels. Here all of the stops have been pulled forward except the one connected to the vox humana.

ing how to repair or restore the instrument. The extent of an organ's problem can be assessed in short order. First of all, a pedal lying flat indicates either a broken strap or exhauster spring. The strap should be easy to either reconnect or replace. The nylon material used for webbing in lawn chairs or for seat belts in automobiles is an appropriate material to replace old broken straps. Other material, such as canvas, can be used, but most materials other than synthetic fibers are affected to some degree by temperature and humidity and may expand or contract due to exposure to the environment or use so that adjustments must be periodically made. A broken exhauster spring is not very common, and a new one will have to be purchased from an organ supply house or fabricated from spring steel.

If the pedals appear to be in good working condition and can be pushed down and returned relatively quickly to their original position, check the organ for other problems. Pumping at a reasonable pace should produce tone when various keys are depressed. If no tones are produced, either a massive hole exists in the bellows or none of the stops have been pulled out to allow air to pass through the reeds. Try pulling out all of the stops except, perhaps, the couplers and the vox humana or tremolo to make sure that all the keys are working. Then depress each key singly from left to right across the keyboard to be sure that each key produces a tone. If no tone is apparent, then either a reed is missing or is clogged in some way to prevent air from moving through and vibrating it. If a note sings without a

key being depressed, then some foreign material is obstructing a pallet valve from closing properly. The bass and/or treble coupler stops can now be tried to make sure that keys one octave away from the key depressed on either end of the keyboard likewise depress a key exactly one octave away. If any of these stops do not work, then most likely there is a broken connection between the rod that the stop activates and the various levers that move the mutes or swells into and out of position.

Very often, another stop is called the "vox humana", which was not described above. The vox humana is essentially a fan at the rear of the treble side of the organ. Pulling out the vox humana stop pulls a small leather square away from a hole in the top of an otherwise airtight box. Air then moves through the hole to turn a fan inside the box. This fan is connected to a shaft that extends across the entire treble side of the organ back. A thin wooden blade on the shaft as it rotates alternately expands and contracts available reflective volume within the organ to produce a vibrato effect. A malfunction of this stop would be easy to detect and remedy by observing the action of the fan when hypothetically engaged.

If a key stays down when depressed, it is probably because of a broken pallet valve spring or a spring displaced from its normal position. This condition can also be caused by a broken pallet rod that may have to be replaced. A key can stick because dirt or grime on the pallet rod prevents it from sliding freely. Graphite can be placed on this rod so that it slides without binding. It is also

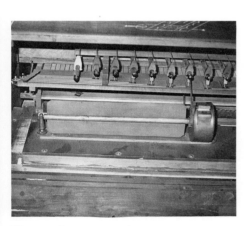

The vox humana provides a tremolo effect by allowing air to pass through a cylindrical chamber and cause a thin fan blade to turn, which expands and contracts the sound reflecting surfaces inside the organ case.

The keyboard and stop assembly removed from the organ.

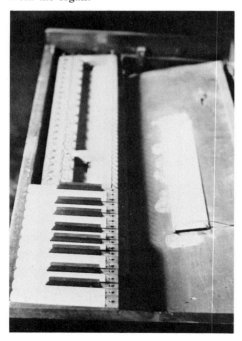

The keys from this melodeon have been individually removed, marked and set aside for later re-assembly.

possible that the board on the organ case in front of the organ keys is either too tight or has warped. If keys in the center of the keyboard stick, additional space must be provided between the board and the keys. If a screw holds this board in place, it can be loosened. If not, then the board needs to be removed and small, perhaps cardboard, spacers added on either side of the organ to provide greater clearance for all the keys. In general, keys sticking near either the bass or treble side can be allowed to move more freely simply by loosening the screws on the appropriate side of the keyboard.

Cleaning Out The Works

Humans who are getting on in age or who have not been particularly active often find it necessary to clean out the works in order to return to a more normal life. Similarly, organs that have aged or have been inactive for some time may find themselves impaired from their full working potential due to the presence of foreign material or just plain dirt. The back should be taken off the organ to reveal the action which consists of all the keys, stops, reeds and associated amenities. The top or part of the front of the organ may also have to be removed to get easier access to the works. If the only problem is a disconnected stop, it should be apparent by moving the stop in and out at the front of the organ and looking for unattached levers. If the stop sticks, an appropriate lubricant or cleaning around the stop rods can be used to al-

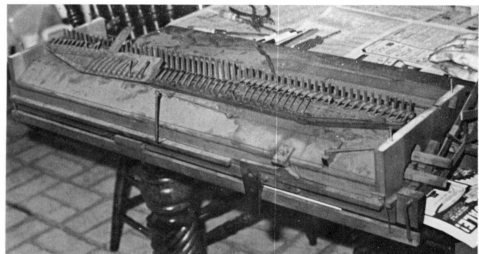

With the keys removed, the rest of the works show many years accumulation of dirt and grime. The rods sticking up along the works are pallet rods that are depressed with the action of the key.

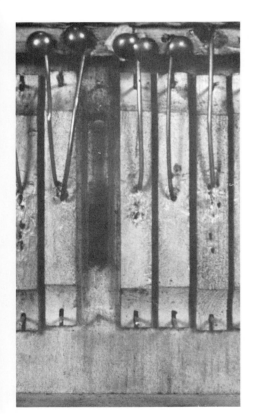

With a pallet valve removed, a reed is visible through the opening. Notice the thumbtacks used to hold the pallet valve springs in place by an earlier amateurish repairman.

leviate the problem. If the problem is with one of the tones or one of the keys, it may be necessary to go deeper into the action to perform some minor cleaning-out surgery. The stop assembly will have to be removed temporarily. A photograph should be taken of the stop assembly before its removal to facilitate reconnecting the stop rods and appropriate sequence of levers. The stop assembly should be removed as a whole by removing the rods on both the left and right sides of the organ from the appropriate lever assemblies. Do not remove individual stops from the stop assembly unless it is absolutely necessary to repair or replace some of the stop parts.

After the assembly has been removed, it is appropriate to use a vacuum cleaner and damp cloth to remove all dirt, dust, grime and any little critters lurking about in the organ action. Any dirt or dust that remains can potentially work its way into the reeds, making necessary another premature repair. Look for the appropriate screws to remove to take out the rest of the action, including the keyboard. So many organs are different that it might require a bit of searching to find all the screws.

After the action is taken out, it sometimes is convenient to number all of the keys so that they can be put back easily in their appropriate positions without pretending they were meant to be part of a jigsaw puzzle. Individual keys can now be removed so that they can be shaved to move more easily, or expose the pallet rods underneath to examine them for breakage or sticking. Turning the action upside down will reveal all of the pallet valves. These valves should also be numbered on their wooden part with a pencil, so that they can easily be put back into place. Each can be removed simply by lifting the wire spring from one end and pulling the entire valve free. It probably sits in place snuggled against one end of the spring with a little slit in the wooden portion of the valve and held tightly in place against the action by the other end of the spring. Undoubtedly, a silhouette of dirt will define the leather outline of the opening that goes to the reed. Remove and clean all the pallet valves before putting them back in place.

None of the above steps is necessary to remove the reeds. But if they are dirty, the above steps are most likely necessary to insure that a dirty reed problem does not immediately recur. A reed can be pulled out of its cell by using a small hook or a reed puller which is simply a rod with a hook or 90-degree tab on its end. Only friction of the body of the reed against the wooden sides of slots cut along the bottom edge of each cell holds the reeds in place. Each reed is a piece of solid brass with a center opening in which is placed a thin brass strip fastened at one end to the large solid piece of brass. The back end of the solid metal frame has an indentation into which the reed puller can be placed and pulled back with even pressure to remove the reed.

Individual reeds can be removed to address specific problems, but if the organ has not been cleaned in some time, it is probably appropriate to remove them all for cleaning. Besides ordinary dirt, I have found unusual pieces

Each pallet valve can be removed simply by lifting the spring and pulling the valve out of position. The valve is a flat piece of wood with a strip of leather attached. Notice the accumulation of dirt on the leather strips in the outline of the reed opening.

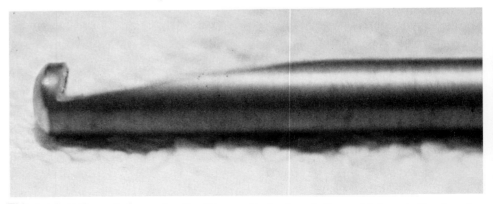

This notch at the end of a reed puller fits over the back end of a reed into a shallow trough. Pulling it backwards forces the reed out of its wooden chamber.

of foreign matter stuck in the reeds that prevent vibration. I have found moth wings stuck in reeds. I have also found a centipede that was apparently making its way across a reed opening when someone decided to play the organ. The vibrating reed beat him to death and then held his carcass in the reed to prevent playing taps at his funeral. Since the reeds are brass, they can be washed in water with a little mild detergent without great worry about their corrosion. They should not be washed in acid or polished with Brasso or any other type of metal cleaner. The rest of the organ action can be similarly cleaned with generous quantities of water, but be sure **not** to saturate any of the leather or wood. The result would be warping or cracking of the wood and

shrinking of the leather padding on the valve or mute. Use common sense at all times to insure that none of the parts of the action are damaged or destroyed.

After thoroughly cleaning the action, look for felt or leather pads that have deteriorated with time or are too dirty to be easily cleaned. These pieces of material should now be replaced before the action is reassembled and put back into the organ. All leather replacements should be from a similar type of material of similar thickness and texture to insure a continued harmonious working relationship among the action's various parts.

While the action is removed is a good chance to do any cosmetic repairs to the organ case that might be appropriate.

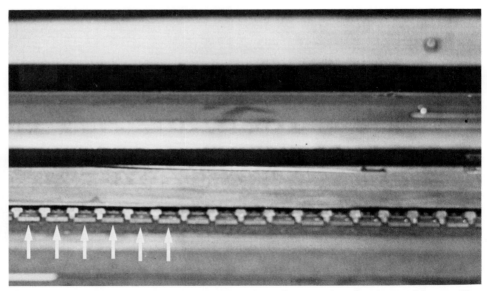

Several reeds have been removed from the organ and placed side by side to be cleaned. A moth's wing is shown lodged in a reed.

Remnants of a centipede are visible. He apparently was making his way through the reed when someone began to play and clobbered him to death. He got his revenge by preventing the reed from vibrating properly, thereby causing the organ to malfunction.

The rear ends of a number of reeds are visible in their respective chambers, with a muffler lifted and another slat moved out of place.

Refinishing may be necessary or replacing the labels on stops. Some of these labels can be purchased from an organ supply house. If the stop label is missing, it might be difficult to determine what label is proper for that stop. After the organ is reassembled, the function of the stop can be documented, then searching through a stop dictionary at your local library should help in finding the correct name for the stop. These dictionaries can be found in many texts dealing with reed and pipe organs.

The cloth that covers the openings leading to the interior of the organ sometimes needs to be replaced. Many people mistakenly use felt for replacing this cloth which is essential to keep the inside of the organ clean. However, acoustic cloth, which can be purchased from organ supply houses, is the most appropriate material. It prevents dirt and grime from reaching the inside of the organ, while at the same time not unduly muffling the tones that are supposed to come from the interior.

Jackie Stanek stands guard over an almost completely disassembled organ case.

This is an organ case with the entire bellows and action removed. Other removable panels have also been taken off.

Here is the melodeon bellows with the exhauster collapsed and the reservoir inflated.

Exhausters and reservoir are both collapsed. The holes in the board on the right are the passages through which the air moves from the reed into the evacuated reservoir.

It will be surprising how many parts in the organ case can be removed to facilitate refinishing. It may be appropriate while in the refinishing process to take out the bellows and reglue the joints on the organ cabinet. One organ that found its way into my household required four husky men to carry it into the house. My 120-pound wife managed to take it into the basement herself, after completely disassembling the works and exterior cabinet into its many component parts.

Loss Of Wind

If the problem with the organ happens to be its breathing apparatus, it is probably necessary to repair a hole in the bellows. The use of an inner tube-type bicycle or automobile patch kit can be used to cover a hole or cut in the bellows material. If the exterior surface of the bellows cloth is not made from rubber, some other suitable flexible material along with a flexible cement can be used to repair the wound. If the material is totally deteriorated, it may be necessary to replace it. The material on exhausters is usually heavier than the material on the bellows. The exhausters take considerably more flexing and pounding than the bellows material, and therefore must be made of a more substantial substance. A similar material should be sought, and probably can only be found at an organ supply house.

Carefully examine the way that the material is glued or otherwise fastened to the bellows or exhauster assemblies. Then remove the old material and use a sander to completely sand away the old glue from all wooden surfaces. The new material then should be glued and tacked or stapled to the same surfaces as the original material was. You might have to use thin boards and clamps to hold the material fast while the glue is drying to the flat surfaces where the material makes a 90-degree bend for a joint. Actually, what we have been referring to as the exhausters in this chapter are rightfully bellows in themselves, and what we have called the bellows could more appropriately be referred to as the reservoir bellows. But since most organs hold a vacuum instead of an air supply in the reservoir, it seems inappropriate to refer to it as a reservoir.

After the organ is mostly reassembled with the action in place on top of the bellows, the organ can be checked for other leaks in the wooden structure of the sounding board or other areas of the organ where a crack or split may have developed. Gluing a piece of rubber or bellows cloth over a crack will work fine, and sometimes the simple use of a rubber cement or glue will do. It is also possible that the cork or rubber gasket between the action and the bellows may have developed a leak, and it may be necessary to either replace the gasket or otherwise repair the leak with rubber cement.

Buzzing In The Ear

Buzzing can come from the organ when a vibrating reed causes some other part of the organ to vibrate. First, all material within the organ should be checked to make sure that it is fastened securely and free from vibration when a reed is set into motion. Sometimes the buzzing is caused by a vibration that cannot be easily detected. A buzz can result from a reed vibrating loosely in the reed chamber. To remedy this problem, a piece of paper can be placed under the butt end of the reed to hold it fixed while the tongue produces the wanted tone.

Buzzing also can result from a reed being placed too tightly into a reed chamber, causing the tongue to vibrate against the side of the brass body. Sometimes this problem is caused by the tongue not being riveted firmly into place. The end of the tongue can be tapped lightly on its rivets with a small hammer, or it can sometimes be secured into place by squeezing with a pair of pliers.

Tuning

For the most part, all that is necessary to tune the organ is to return reeds to the same shape they were in when they left the factory. This means that all dirt and residue must be removed from the reed to insure proper distribution of mass along its tongue. The greater the mass at the point of the reed, the slower will be its vibration, and therefore the lower its pitch. Similarly, the less the mass at the butt of the reed near the rivets, the slower will be its vibration

Air-tightness of the bellows can be checked by putting masking tape over the holes and then pumping the exhauster by hand to evacuate the reservoir. It should take 15 to 30 seconds for the reservoir to refill with air if there are no punctures. The light area on the board around the holes is where an old gasket has been sanded away to preapre for placing another gasket between the bellows and the keyboard.

and the lower its tone. Therefore, to flatten the tone of the reed, material should be scraped, filed or sanded from the end of the tongue near the rivet. In order to sharpen the tone, material should be scraped, sanded or filed from near its point.

Sometimes the voice of the reed is created by a certain curvature near the point. This curvature should not be altered or the voice of the reed will be impaired.

It should be apparent that tuning a reed organ is considerably more complex than tuning a piano. The reed must be removed and altered and reinserted into the organ each time before the note can be retested for proper pitch. However, with appropriate care, there should be no need to tune a reed organ with any frequency. The reeds, unlike the strings of a piano, are not subject to stretching and contracting through simple changes in temperature. Therefore, the modern air-conditioned, dust-free environment should provide all that is necessary to keep a reed organ in tune for extended periods of time.

Dental Work

The "whites" or white keys of an organ can be made from either cellulose (an early form of plastic) or ivory. It should be easy to determine which material was used, because ivory has a tendency to discolor with age and is easily recognized by the very thin stripes or striations that appear on it. Animal tusks tend to grow much like trees with annual rings. When sliced, the growth rings in the ivory appear as alternating white and yellow stripes. Keys left in sun-light for extended periods of time tend to bleach and the striations are not as recognizable as they otherwise would be in aged ivory.

Celluloid material, on the other hand, is very uniform in color, and with a little experience is not easily confused with ivory.

Damaged keys can be repaired by removing the entire key surface and replacing it with material purchased from an organ or piano supply company. Occasionally, chips can be repaired by purchasing a kit from one of these companies that includes a brush and liquid material to be built up until the chip is no longer visible. These types of liquid repair are more successful on a celluloid surface than with the nonhomogeneous but more charismatic coloring of ivory.

Be Sensible

Other organ problems or maladies may be discovered upon examining a newly-acquired instrument. In general, common sense will usually find a solution to the problem. Examine the instrument thoroughly, move a stop in and out, press a key up and down, or have someone else aid you in this while you observe the action from behind. Take a few screws out and remove a few parts and put them back, so that you can slowly become familiar with the organ and its operation. Do not attempt to take every piece apart just to find out that you have a few extra pieces to the organ when it is reassembled.

The organ has many parts and its restoration is time consuming, but its operating principles are simple. If you don't think the solution to the problem is easy, examine it awhile longer to see if maybe you have overlooked something. For instance, problems with pedal straps do not require removing the entire inside of the organ. The straps were most likely fixed after the bellows were in place, and therefore should be able to be adjusted without removing the bellows. Most often, part of the front case of the organ below the keyboard can be removed. Reach your hand inside over a depressed pedal to find a clasp or catch that can be turned to free the panel that reveals the exhausters and straps to which they are attached.

Since no two models of reed organs are exactly like, it is impossible to anticipate all of the subtleties with which you must cope for proper restoration. But anyone with patience and reasonable intelligence can solve the most difficult of problems. The experience and knowledge gained from reading this chapter is also, therefore, easily transferable to the repair and restoration of other wind-operated reed instruments, including melodeons. Remember that a melodeon is simply the forerunner of the popular reed organ without multiple pedals or even stops.

One last thing to remember is that dummy stops were sometimes used to sell an organ, but with no useful purpose in playing the instrument. Don't be a dummy and spend many precious hours trying to figure out that these stops did nothing.

An organ that has been completely restored inside and out.

CHAPTER XVII

PANE (GLASS)

What is glass? Is it a bird? Is it a plane? No. It is a super-cooled liquid. Contrary to popular belief, glass is not technically a solid, even though it looks, smells and feels like a solid. Most transparent items, including ice, are formed by the symmetrical arrangement of molecules into a crystalline pattern that allows light to pass through it. Glass, on the other hand, has symmetrical molecules arranged arbitrarily in a way that allows light to pass through it. Glass is truly a liquid at very high temperatures—some-where around 1,000 degrees centigrade. As the glass cools, it becomes viscous, and therefore apparently more solid even though this is not really the case. At room temperature, glass is so viscous that it becomes brittle, and its resulting fragility is evidenced by the need to write this chapter.

For the most part, glass is composed of three major ingredients, and more in some cases. A glass-forming oxide, such as silica (sand), with one or more metallic oxides, such as sodium or calcium oxides, are melted together at extremely high temperatures and then cooled slowly.

The manufacture of artifacts made from glass is an art as well as a science. But in my high school days many years ago, I took a course on scientific glass-blowing in order to accomplish two things. One was to learn and appreciate the complexities involved in the fabrication of those complicated flasks and corkscrews that we see in the science-fiction movies. The other was to save money on equipment that I needed to fabricate my own science-fiction monsters.

When glass is being worked under extreme heat, it first turns red and then white—necessitating the use of special eyeglasses to filter out most of the intense radiation and allow the worker to see what is happening to the glass rather than be blinded by the bright light. When working with molten glass, one quickly learns to appreciate that glass is truly a liquid, and one also learns to develop an extra sense for gravity since that molten liquid always seems to be attracted toward the center of the earth.

The real challenge becomes apparent after all the complex portions of glass-blowing are completed—blowing bubbles, making joints, or altering the shape of an intial glass glob. Although the difficult attention-grabbing and talent-demanding portions of the work are over, the entire piece can be ruined if not cooled properly. Our technique was to leave the glass immersed in a cool orange flame (yes, flames can be cool) until carbon not burned in the flame was deposited on the glass. If the glass were still too hot, the carbon would be burned when it made contact with the glass. The glass was then put in a special annealing oven, which over a period of about 24 hours decreased the temperature from annealing to about room temperature. When the glass was to be moved, it was cleaned and observed through a polariscope which polarized the light passing through the glass and identified any unusual stresses or strains where fractures would be likely to develop because of improper annealing. Problems are more apparent as the thickness of the glass increases. If one side cools before the other side, it contracts more than the other side (heat causes expansion in most materials). One side contracting more rapidly than the other side causes a strain to develop someplace between and perhaps a fracture to occur.

It seems that the earliest records of glass date back to about 2600 B.C. The artifact was a green glass rod found at Eshnunna in Babylonia. Glass beads have been traced to the 6th dynasty in Egypt dating back to about 2500 B.C.

The science of manufacturing glass items has considerably advanced since that time. Glass sheets were formed originally by heating glass at the end of a blow pipe and allowing it to form into a large globule, cutting it off, and rotating it on a lathe while it was still warm so that it spread out with centrifugal force until it formed a disc. The disc could then be cut into whatever shape was desired for the sheet. Another method involved blowing a long cylinder of glass, sometimes 30 inches in diameter and 40 feet long. While the glass was warm, it was cut along its length and flattened to form a sheet.

The method known as Fourcault process drew glass from a pool of molten glass vertically into a ribbon which then formed a sheet. The Colburn process drew the glass in a ribbon vertically out of the pool, then over a nichrome roller and between two endless belts into an annealing furnace.

Eventually, plate glass was developed which was cast, rolled, ground and polished to a flat surface on each side, in contrast to the earlier blowing techniques. Modern glass has been polished to be flat on both sides and produces very little distortion when looking through the panes. On the other hand, glass in old mirrors and antique furniture or the glass panes in windows of older homes are examples of the earlier methods that did not provide completely uniform thickness across the surface. Distortions are obvious, and even small bubbles and voids can be found if you look carefully.

Needless to say, old glass missing from an old house or piece of furniture cannot be replaced with modern glass to give an identical appearance without salvaging some of that old glass from some other source.

Making The Incision

Glass cutting is both hard and easy at the same time. It is hard if you have never done it before, and it is easy with a little practice. To cut a sheet of glass, use a straight edge to mark the exact line that is to be cut. Clean the glass to remove all dirt and residue before starting to cut. Put a little kerosene or cutting fluid along the line that is to be scribed. Also put some of this fluid on the wheel of the glass cutter—unless, of course, you wish to use your diamond ring. Hold the glass cutter vertically and bring it with a uniform pressure into the edge of the glass. With this same pressure, pull the cutter toward you guided by the straight edge until the cutter has moved completely across the plate and off the edge nearest to you. It is important that you not go over the same area with the cutter again—one line is all that is necessary and any more than one line will be detrimental. The cutter has worked

Place the sheet of glass over a round object such as a pencil under one end of the scribed line.

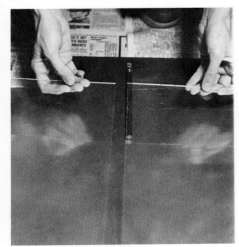

Uniform pressure applied by the thumbs pushing downward on either side of the pencil will break the glass cleanly along the length of the scribed line.

properly if you felt a uniform grinding action as it moved across the surface of the glass. It is important that the cut has been scribed through both edges of the glass plate.

Then put the plate over a finishing nail or a round pencil so that the length of the nail or pencil lies directly beneath the scribed line off one edge of the glass sheet. Place slight pressure on both sides of the scribed line with the thumbs a short distance away from it, and the plate should fracture along the scribed incision with little difficulty.

The glass along this cut will be sharp enough to cause blood to flow even with little pressure. Two or three passes with coarse emery cloth over the sharp corners and edges will shave off enough to make the glass safer to handle. Of course,

To cut glass along a straight line, use a straight edge to guide the glass cutter. A small amount of kerosene is placed along the length of the glass to be cut and also on the cutting wheel. The cutter is pulled with an even pressure so that a uniform grinding sound can be heard. The cutter must move across both edges of the sheet of glass and must not be run over the same area a second time—only one scribed line is necessary.

Sandpaper or other abrasive is gently used to dull the edge of the cut and make it less dangerous to handle.

The glass edge can also be sanded on a belt sander if you place a sheet of plywood underneath to support the glass except for the very edge. Be careful to always wear gloves when handling glass for protection from a severe cut.

all cut edges should be honed in this manner, both front and back.

Various techniques can be used for cutting into other than straight lines. Draw the outline of the shape you want to cut on a sheet of glass, and then little-by-little scribe straight lines tangent, or nearly so, to this shape. The glass is cut along each of these tangents until just a little glass remains that can then be ground off to the shape desired.

With a little experience, curved lines can be scribed and the glass broken close to the desired shape with the initial fracture. Templates made from a wooden board, or any other material for that matter, might be appropriate to help guide the cutter along a desired curve.

For cuts close to the edge of a piece of glass, the same procedure is followed, except the teeth of the glass cutter are used instead of the thumb to apply pressure next to the incision.

Grinding the glass to the desired shape with a belt sander or disc sander can be done with less trouble than you probably anticipate. However, always wear gloves when grinding glass and never hold a large sheet without some form of support. Any sudden movement may cause it to shatter, thereby ruining your work and perhaps your body. A wooden board placed an eighth to a quarter-inch back from the grinding edge will help support the glass and prevent its shattering without interfering with the grinding process.

Cut Glass

What we commonly call cut glass is the result of whatever forming or casting was completed on an object before using

abrasive wheels and polishing compounds. A carbide wheel or other kind of cutter is used to grind away certain portions of the glass, and then polishing compounds are subsequently used to return that portion of the glass to its original brilliance.

Etching

Certain pieces of furniture or windows of old homes have designs etched into glass. If an etched glass pane is broken, many people have despaired, thinking that there is no way to replace the original item. Actually, either of two techniques may be used with much success to return the article to its original appearance.

A smooth, satin translucent effect can be gotten on glass from sandblasting. Smoothness of the surface will depend upon the grain size in the sandblasting process. For simple designs with straight lines, it is simply a matter of masking the areas, on a precut pane of glass, that are to remain clear. Thick linen first-aid tape or plastic tape is suitable for this purpose. Regular masking tape would probably deteriorate under the sandblasting process and not give adequate protection to the area not to be sandblasted. The sandblasting can be done either by yourself, if you have appropriate equipment, or through some mill shop or even a body and fender shop for a minimal fee.

Provided that you do all the masking yourself ahead of time, the sandblasting operation should take no more than a minute or so.

Etching is another technique that can be used, and is probably the technique

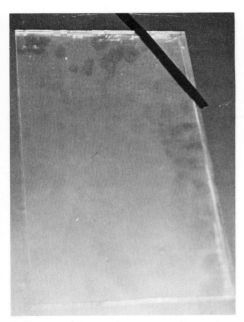

Before: Black plastic tape can be used to mask areas of glass and protect them from sand blasting.

After: The strips of tape are removed when the sand blasting is finished to reveal a beautifully textured pattern.

Before: This sheet of glass has been marked with a special wax marking pen.

An acid brush is used to apply ammonium bifluorite which will eat away the glass not covered by wax.

Water is used to wash away the chemical when the etching is complete, and turpentine is used to wash away the wax.

After: The design has been etched into the glass plate.

that was originally used to give the glass the appearance that you are trying to reproduce. Chemicals are used for etching. Hydrofluoric is used commonly for etching glass—however, it also etches clothes, furniture and people. It is a very dangerous substance that attacks almost everything except certain plastics, wax and lead. A very smooth etched finish on glass can be obtained by using a combination of sulfuric and hydrofluoric acid.

Other chemicals, however, are somewhat safer and easier to handle than those acids and still produce the desired effect. That is not to say that you can't mishandle these chemicals also, but rather that they can be used safely if appropriate precautions are followed. Potassium fluoride produces a rough translucent finish. Ammonium bifluoride produces a smoother finish. Ammonium bifluoride can be purchased commercially as a product known by the name "Etch-All". It comes in a small lead tube with a plastic cap. The chemical is in the form of a brown paste which, when placed on glass, eats away at the smooth surface. First, the glass must be made absolutely clean with all grease and grime removed by using a commercial glass cleaner. Any residues that remain will cause the chemical to act at a different rate on that area and thus cause nonuniformity in the translucence of the final product.

Of course, masking is necessary to protect the area not to be etched. This is done through the use of special metal stencils that can be purchased along with the Etch-All compound. See the appendix at the end of this chapter for the source for this material. The metal stencils have a heat-sensitive adhesive on their back. A stencil is cut to the shape desired, with all scraps saved for possible future use. Then by means of a light bulb or some other heat source, the stencil is heated and applied to the glass and burnished so that it makes complete contact and any chemical applied over it will not find its way underneath. The ammonium bifluoride compound is then wiped over the surface with an acid brush and allowed to do its job for about three minutes.

The full etching effect will not be observed at this time, because liquid fills the pores that have been created. If slight etching is desired, wash the ammonium bifluoride from the surface of the glass with warm water and remove the stencil. On the other hand, if a deeper etching is desired, wash the chemical away with cold water, apply a second coating of ammonium bifluoride and let it work for about three minutes. Then, wash the surface with hot water, remove the stencil and keep it ready for future use. Be careful not to wash the ammonium bifluoride into a kitchen or bathroom sink. The chemical is strong enough to etch its way through the glazing on porcelain, as well as into metal fixtures. Washing should be done in a plastic container and the resulting dirty solution should be disposed of properly.

Silver Linings

If you thought that the silver on a mirror was on the exterior surface, you are right, but you are wrong. The silver is on the exterior surface of the glass, but it is on the back surface. Silver deposited on glass to make a mirror is not very strong, and can be easily scratched or defaced. Some mirrors were made by putting silver on the front surface and then a coat of lacquer or varnish, but then the limiting factor and the quality of the mirror is determined by the thickness of the varnish applied and its discoloration. The quality of a back-silvered mirror is determined primarily by the quality of glass used to make it and the adequacy of the silvering job.

In general, most experts think that antique mirrors should not be resilvered. The judgment should be left with the owner, in any case, because I have seen some mirrors in such terrible shape from abuse that they are not suitable for display, let alone use. In attempting to refinish a mirror, be extremely careful in removing the glass from its frame. Many otherwise perfect mirrors have been ruined by carelessness in this phase of the operation. Any hard material scraped across the back of the mirror will most likely remove silver from it. If you are lucky, the protective coating applied over the silver will forestall silver removal by any of the minor abrasions that may result during disassembly. However, I have seen some mirrors with silver so soft that simply touching it with one's finger is enough to remove the silver coating.

The process of silvering a mirror is relatively simple, but it requires much practice and care to do a barely adequate job. Because of the cost and hazards of the chemicals used, it would probably be wiser to have the mirror resil-vered by a professional mirror maker. However, for the information of those interested, I will attempt to describe the procedure. Silver nitrate is the light-sensitive chemical used in photography. When mixed with water, silver nitrate forms nitric acid with a resulting precipitation of metallic silver. For silvering a mirror, silver nitrate is mixed with water in a ratio of 1 to 64 by weight. A few drops of pure ammonia are added to complete all of the necessary chemical preparation.

This solution will react with most materials except glass, and therefore the mixing must be done in a glass vessel with a glass stirring rod. An abrasive polish and ammonia must be used beforehand to insure that not a single trace of any contaminating material is present on the surface of the stirring rod, the mixing container, the glass tray into which the solution will be poured or the plate that is to be silvered. It is hard to emphasize enough the necessity of meticulously cleaning all of these surfaces. The first time I tried the silvering process, some 20 years ago, I cleaned and cleaned the glass surfaces until I thought they were adequate, but did not pay attention to removing 100 percent of the residue remaining after the detergent washing and polishing with distilled water and ammonia. The result was a tray with its sides nicely silvered and a murky non-homogeneous mess of a mirror.

The side to be silvered is placed face up in the glass tray and the silver nitrate solution poured in. The solution is allowed to continue its chemical deposition for about eight hours. Using rubber gloves, the mirror can be removed from the solution and held on edge until the chemicals have run off. After it has dried undisturbed for an hour or so, a spray of protective black lacquer can be put over the silvering to prevent loss of silver if the surface is touched.

Stained Glass

Stained glass is colored or painted upon with enamels and then fired in an oven so that the glass and the enamel become fused. It is not possible to use chemical strippers at this point to remove any of the staining, but since these stains were not inadvertent there should never be any desire to do so.

Leaded Glass

Leaded glass can be either leaded or coppered. That is, pieces of glass in different shapes and colors can be held together with strips of lead or strips of copper. On old church windows and house windows, lead strips called "cames" were produced in the shape of an "H". The edge of a piece of glass was slipped into the top of the "H" and an adjacent piece of glass slipped into the bottom of the "H" after they were cut to the appropriate shape. Pieces of lead from other sections of the window were then placed in their appropriate "jigsaw puzzle" places and soldered together around the pieces of glass. Lead cames can still be purchased in various sizes and thicknesses from American Handicrafts and other hobby shops. The came usually comes in a roll about three feet long, and is cut to

the appropriate thickness and shaped around the glass after it has been cut to size. A broken piece in a leaded glass window may necessitate removing a number of adjacent glass pieces, or at least severing or unsoldering adjacent sections of the came. The work should be done on a flat table and probably involves more patience than skill.

Lamps made to emulate stained glass windows, in general used copper strips instead of lead slugs. The thin copper sheet was flexible enough to be bent into a "U" shape around the edge of a piece of glass and then further bent to completely encircle it. Adjacent pieces were then soldered to form the design and shape. A mold or form was used to hold the pieces in their appropriate positions while being soldered to insure that all pieces were put at the appropriate angle during fabrication. To replace some of these parts, thin pieces of copper can be purchased from a plumbing supply house. If the copper is tempered and not very pliable, it can be heated and allowed to cool slowly in order to remove some of the temper. Some commercial firms also handle adhesive-backed copper strips for use in making lamp shades.

Broken Glass

Broken glass can never be mended if it is transparent to the point where a seam or crack will show. However, translucent or opaque glass can be put back together so that the broken seam is at least not apparent in most lighting. Clear epoxy glues are the best substances available to use for mending a broken glass artifact. The edges must be com-

This close-up shows the tiny crystals in an old mirror known as a "diamond dust" mirror.

pletely clean and free from any dirt or residue. The best time to fix a broken piece of glass is immediately after breaking it, before dust has had time to be electrostatically attracted to the broken edges. If any significant time has elapsed between the breaking and the reassembly procedure, acetone should be swabbed onto the edges to insure that all dirt has been removed. Place a minimal amount of epoxy on the glass edge with a toothpick, or your finger if you are willing to take a chance on cutting it. Pieces of the glass will not fit back together as they did initially, because any thickness of epoxy placed between them will keep them apart— even though the separation is only one-millionth of an inch. Because of this separation, it is most advisable to assemble the entire piece at one time, rather than put two pieces together and allow them to dry before putting the next piece into place. Any excess epoxy that contaminates the surface of the glass can be removed with a razor blade after the entire piece has been assembled and allowed to cure.

Small pieces of missing glass can be replaced by filling the void with epoxy. This technique leaves a lot to be desired when working on clear uncolored glass, because the repair will be immediately obvious to any observer. However, on colored glass, and especially on cameo glass where there are variations in coloration and transparency, the technique is most useful. Paints can be applied over the repaired area to make it blend closely with its surroundings. A kit with detailed instructions on how to make these types of repairs is available and can be found in the appendix at the end of this chapter.

GLASS APPENDIX

Master Mending Kit for China and Glass from:
    Atlas Minerals and Chemicals
    Incorporated
    Mertztown, Pennsylvania 19539
Sodium Bifluoride Glass Etching Compound from:
    Etch-All Incorporated
    Columbia, Missouri 65201

CHAPTER XVIII

YOU ONLY GET WHAT YOU PAY FOR (COINS)

DON'T DO ANYTHING!

Except

In general, coins should never be cleaned. Most cleaning processes reduce the grade and thus the value of the coin. Cleaning inevitably, number one, destroys the patina that took a hundred years to get there, or, number two, abrades the surface and removes detail that would have been there had the coin been left dirty. However, there are some circumstances when coin cleaning may be appropriate. If you are not well-schooled in the value of coins, checking with an authoritative coin dealer before proceeding may be advisable.

For the most part, coins that have been circulated and are not in very good condition probably require the most cleaning. It is also the least harmful to attempt cleaning these coins because they do not have a mirror-like finish to

preserve. Copper coins left in a moist environment will develop a green encrustation called verdigris. Nickel coins contain a significant fraction of copper and can develop a black encrustation. Coins in this condition can be cleaned by using a soft cloth moistened with lighter fluid or another organic solvent. Never use any type of acid. Acid will pit the surface of the coin and remove metal that can never be replaced and thus destroy detail and finish.

When I was a child, I used to shine pennies by scrubbing them with Boraxo. Never use any abrasive paste or powder on coins—and that includes toothpaste. Copper coins that are in virtually an uncirculated condition with a brown patina should not be touched—and that means literally. In addition to not cleaning them, they should not be held in your hands to collect oils from your fingers. Coins in extra fine condition, or bet-

The obverse of an 1856 large cent. It has never been cleaned or polished and it has a beautiful rich chocolate brown tone that should not be disturbed.

The reverse of the same coin.

This 1832 half-dollar shows some signs of wear, but does not require any cleaning or polishing.

Before: This recent quarter shows considerable tarnishing.

This picture shows how the curved plastic tweezers are made especially for gripping coins.

It is placed in special plastic coin tweezers and dipped into a solution of thiourea. It is then rinsed through a detergent solution and finally distilled water before it is dried.

After: No signs of tarnish remain on this coin, yet it has never been rubbed or polished.

240

ter, should be handled only under protective plastic or paper, or alternatively should be handled only while the handler is wearing protective gloves—preferably white cotton gloves. If the coin is inadvertently handled, it should be dipped in acetone or denatured alcohol and swirled for a few seconds, then removed and allowed to dry. Finger oil deposits may not be apparent at the time they are placed on a coin, but over the years the coin will discolor unevenly and reveal the fingerprints.

Silver and gold coins develop a rich appearance only if they have not been handled. Gold does not change very much with color over the years, but silver will take on a blackish tone as the surface tarnishes. Any handling of the silver surface will cause the tarnish to be deposited nonuniformly and it may result in contrasting silver and black spots on the coin. If it is desirable to clean the tarnish from a silver coin, it can be immersed in thiourea for a few seconds until the tarnish has disappeared; then immediately it should be removed and rinsed through a detergent solution and, finally, distilled water. It may then be dipped in alcohol to absorb the moisture and blown dry with a hair dryer or held near a light bulb until dry. Use plastic tweezers or rubber gloves for the thiourea dip. Never use metallic tweezers to dip a coin in this solution, because the other metal will react with the solution and may end up discoloring the coin more than the original tarnish.

If a coin has been glued to a background or taped to something, discoloration will appear even if the coin is in good condition and it may be desirable to remove the defacing chemical. It is also possible that a coin has been painted, either with regular paint or nail polish, to preserve it. Although the nail polish may preserve the original luster, it does not allow the coin to take on the desired patina. Paint remover, alcohol or other organic solvent should be used to dissolve the glue. After cleaning, wipe the coin with a soft cloth and protect it appropriately for the future.

Coins in bulk can be stored in plastic or glass tubes to prevent them from unduly interacting with environmental pollutants. If they are to be displayed or handled individually, clear plastic envelopes and protective mountings can be purchased from a coin supply house.

One last note: before attempting to clean any expensive or rare copper coin, first experiment by using COMMON CENTS.

CHAPTER XIX

BEING FIRED ISN'T WHAT IT'S CROCKED UP TO BE (CERAMICS)

Ceramics are clays baked in an oven at very high temperatures that causes the clays to fuse and create a hard, non-water-soluble agglomeration. Some clays are opaque after firing, while others are translucent. Up until about the 18th century, the Chinese were the sole holders of the secrets of making translucent ceramics. By the 19th century, however, the British were probably the most profuse manufacturers of china. Bisque, parian, porcelain and earthenware are all examples of ceramics. Dolls, plates, statues, vases and even clock faces have been made from ceramics.

Dealing with broken ceramics is very similar to dealing with broken glass. They are handled in about the same way and similar techniques are used to repair them. However, there is greater flexibility in working with items made from fired clay in that, for the most part, cracks and chips can be hidden to a much greater degree. The transparency of most glasses makes it impossible to hide the interface between two pieces caused by a fracture. However, the translucent nature or even, in some cases, the opaque nature of ceramic items makes it possible to complete a repair and obscure that interface from observation.

Cracks

The basic technique to make all ceramic and clay repairs is the use of epoxy. When a crack appears, a small void has been created between two pieces that otherwise would be intimate molecular contact. The void must be filled with some material, and epoxy is the most suitable because of its strength and workability. Various epoxies have different properties, and color is not the least of those that we should be concerned about. Clear epoxies, as opposed to amber epoxies, afford the greatest potential for use in most restoration operations. A clear epoxy can be made more translucent than transparent by the addition of kaolin (a clay available at drugstores) or some other whitening material, including plaster of paris or even talcum powder. Enamels can also be used to tint epoxies to whatever color is desired. In general, repairs made on broken pieces of wood require clamping to hold the pieces in very close contact while whatever adhesive is used cures. This is not the case with ceramics because of the inflexible nature of baked clay. Clamping with extreme pressure would result in additional fractures in the object. Gravity is used as the pressure-producing restraint, and the weight of the individual pieces that require repair should be enough to produce the desired pressure.

Of course, simple cracks that do not penetrate all the way through an artifact should not be clamped when repaired, because the uncured epoxy put in the void is still plastic, and when deformed would allow undesirable stresses to be exerted on the unbroken portion of the artifact. A kit called the "Master Mending Kit", described earlier in the chapter on glass repairs, contains all the materials necessary for most ceramic repairs. Most other epoxies, not in kit form, are suitable provided some experimentation is used to insure miscibility of colors, if necessary, with the epoxy.

Epoxy with the desired translucent property and color is placed into the crack with a spatula or palate knife. A slight excess is allowed to remain over the void until after it is cured. It can then be scraped away with a razor blade. Occasionally, a very fine abrasive needs to be used to polish the compound, and sometimes the item needs to be reglazed as described below.

Bad Breaks

When pieces of china or other ceramics are broken, they should be repaired immediately before dust has a chance to settle on the broken surfaces. Attempting to place the pieces back in their original configuration will be impossible if the edges have become dirty and they must be cleaned. But if the repair takes place immediately, no time has been allowed for dust to settle in various places to prevent the pieces from fitting exactly together. Even a particle as small as a millionth of an inch can prevent the perfect fit. If the edges have already become soiled, they must be cleaned by carefully soaking the edges in some form of solvent, depending upon the nature of the soil. Old breaks that have been rebroken usually have considerable contamination from old glue, and this old glue must be dissolved and removed. Very little abrasion or friction of any sort should be applied to the broken edges. Tiny fragments of clay can become dislodged and these voids will need to be filled to make a good fit.

Every attempt should be made to glue the item back together with all the pieces at one time, if possible. The epoxy ad-

hesive placed along the edges for regluing will take up some very small but still finite volume. This makes it very difficult to put together one or two pieces at a time hoping that the entire object can be reconstructed. The adhesive will take up slightly additional space and will change the dimensions of those pieces so that it may not be possible to fit all of them back together again. The only way to insure that the object can be reconstructed is to place all of the pieces together at one time. Sometimes because of the shape of the object, this will be impossible and one, or at best, several pieces need to be placed in position and allowed to cure before proceeding.

A bowl or tub filled with sand can be used as a base to hold the ceramic item in a position so that gravity will hold the broken pieces in contact. Modeling clay or putty may also be used for light items. Care should be taken not to scrape the ceramic item against the sand, because it may act like an abrasive and scratch the glaze. But care can be taken to gently place the object in the "sandbox" and move sand up against the object's sides so that it is securely in place without undue movement. Broken pieces can be held in place with masking tape while the epoxy is curing. The easiest way to apply the epoxy would be with a brush along the edges of the fractured clay. However, abrasion from the brush can cause particles to become dislodged. Therefore, either a very small brush with a very light touch needs to be used or the end of a toothpick with small droplets of epoxy would be used to place

To facilitate gluing ceramics, they can be placed in a small tub filled with sand and held in almost any position desired.

244

Before: This is a broken section from a piece of a china dresser set. Voids have been left where fragments of the ceramic could not be located for regluing.

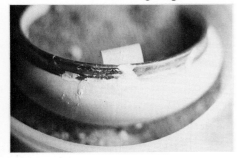

Masking tape has been placed on the inside of the bowl and epoxy used to fill the voids down to the masking tape.

After: Excess epoxy is trimmed away after curing, the surface sanded if necessary, and a finishing color or glaze applied. In this case, the rim of the bowl is being prepared for gold leafing.

a thin bead in the center of the edge along the fracture. When two pieces are placed together, this bead will flatten out and reach both surfaces. Too much epoxy will cause oozing at the surface, which will require that the excess material be removed. Not enough epoxy will allow voids to appear at the surface and make the break conspicuous. In that case, the void additionally will have to be filled. In general, a slight amount of extra epoxy will not hurt and simply will require that it be scraped from the surface after curing in the manner described above.

Missing Pieces

Sometimes pieces are missing and require replacement. They can be fashioned with either homemade or commercially available epoxy putties. For an opaque item, commercially available putties are usually suitable, because a paint can be placed over them that allow the repaired areas to blend in with their surroundings. On the other hand, a translucent ceramic will probably require that a transparent epoxy be mixed with some other agent to give it the properties it needs to make a nearly invisible repair. To a great extent, mixing unfired clays or other minerals with clear epoxy will make a putty that is workable like clay but more opaque than desired—unless the piece being made is extremely thin. Ground white translucent plastic can be mixed with the epoxy, however, to form a very nice translucent putty. Simply sand white translucent plexiglass with abrasive paper for the dust you need to mix with the epoxy glue.

The putty can then be shaped to form

the ear of a cup, knob or other missing piece. Voids or holes left in china can be filled with this material. A piece of masking tape can be put on one side of the void, and the putty is put into place from the opposite side.

Coloring

Coloring epoxy is a skill not unlike that of mixing oil paints. For the most part, it is a trial-and-error process in which only experience can decrease the amount of time necessary to make a skillful match. Depending on the base of the epoxy, enamels and lacquers can be used in very minute quantities to give some of the desirable hues. Opaque and transparent colors used for casting polyester resins are available in hobby shops and also can be used. Care must be taken to insure that the base in which the pigments are dissolved is compatible with the epoxy resin. Therefore, a small trial amount should be mixed and placed aside to cure before actually working on the object requiring repair.

When translucent repairs are made, any epoxy buildup over the edge of the object will show the repair. Under microscopic examination, the edge of the repair will appear as a step that casts a shadow by available light. The only way to make this repair less conspicuous is to minimize the edge of this microscopic step so that the shadow is no longer there. Air brush a thin layer of pigment over the repaired area "feathering" off toward the object. In this way, the material used to make the repair tapers from nearly nothing to some greater thickness. This greater thickness may only be 1/1,000 of an inch, but human eyes are capable of detecting the shadows from light passing over even such a microscopic dimension.

Glazing

Parian is a ceramic with a dull finish. It is not glazed and has the appearance of unpolished marble. On the other hand, china is normally fired to form a very thin layer of glass on the surface that produces its own characteristic shine. After making a repair and subsequent sanding with an abrasive or scraping with a sharp edge, the natural glaze of an epoxy will be worn away. In these cases, it is possible to brush on a very thin layer of epoxy, thinned with denatured alcohol, to fill in the microscopic pores caused by the abrasive and produce a shine upon curing. In some cases, the only way to give the item a uniform synthetic glaze is to spray or air brush it with clear lacquer. This glaze will have a suitable appearance, but certainly is not as durable as glass. It is appropriate for cosmetic purposes only. The item cannot be washed in hot water or scraped with any hard object. Eventually, the lacquer will either discolor or crack. It will then have to be "refinished". An item with a lacquer glaze is acceptable only because most items requiring cosmetic treatment are not designed for utilitarian purposes. They are usually intended for display, rather than for everyday use.

This china cover was broken in half on an almost straight line extending from arrow to arrow. The glue seam is virtually invisible.

246

CHAPTER XX

FILLING IN THE GAPS (STENCILING)

During the first part of the 19th century, stenciling was used extensively in both Britain and New England. During Victorian times, stenciling was an art employed profusely to decorate plaster wall areas below the ceiling molding. Although stenciling was not used very widely on Victorian furniture, examples are found from time to time. Folk stencils were used to decorate enameled bedroom furniture. In addition, stencils were used to apply gold and silver decorations over black enameled areas on certain pieces of Renaissance Revival and Eastlake furniture.

During the refinishing process, it is very likely that a stencil design would be removed. Therefore, it is in the best interests of the conservator to avoid stripping the finish from these areas of the furniture, if at all possible. In some instances, however, pieces may be missing or damaged so that the stencil design must be reproduced.

Becoming A Copycat

Some stencils with Florentine designs, as well as other patterns, can be purchased from wood finishing supply houses. But, of course, it is not likely that a stencil can be found that exactly duplicates the design which must be reproduced. The art of reproducing a stencil is time-consuming, requiring patience and a skilled hand. Tracing paper is placed over the available design that requires copying. A very sharp pencil should be used to trace the design. Stencils can be made out of either special stencil paper, which can be purchased from art supply stores, or in sheets of very thin brass. A sheet of carbon paper is placed with the carbon side down on top of the brass sheet which must be completely free of grease and fingerprints, or, alternatively, placed on top of the stencil paper. The tracing is placed over the carbon paper and very carefully the design is retraced so as to impregnate the soon-to-be stencil with the design. An Exacto knife is then used to cut the design from the new material. If necessary, the lines should be carefully redrawn on the stencil before cutting to insure their smoothness and completeness.

A Little Dab Will Do It

If it is necessary to completely rebuild an area where the stencil was, several coats of shellac are applied to the piece of wood intended to be decorated. Allow the shellac to dry and rub with steel wool between coats. Flat black oil-based paint is then applied over the shellac and allowed to dry. Another coat of shellac is then applied over the black painted area (other colors can be used for this base, but black was the color most often used). The shellac is buffed slightly with 0000 steel wool after it has dried, and any remaining dust is cleaned from the area.

A coat of spar vanish thinned with about 10 percent of turpentine is applied sparingly over the final shellacked surface. Spar varnish contains a great deal of linseed oil, and therefore dries very slowly. The spar varnish is allowed to become tacky over a period of three to four hours. The stencil is then applied to the tacky spar varnish and pressed firmly into place. It should stick of its own accord, but should be able to be

Before: Several coats of shellac are applied to the area to be stencilled.

Fine steel wool (0000) is rubbed lightly over the surface between dried coats of shellac, and again after the final coat.

Flat black oil-based paint is applied and allowed to dry.

Another coat of shellac is applied over the paint and buffed with steel wool after it has dried. The surface is cleaned of dust and spar varnish is applied sparingly.

After three or four hours, the stencil is applied over the tacky spar varnish. A roller may be used to insure that the stencil is flat.

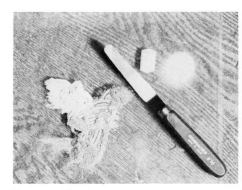

Fine metallic dusts are put on a glass plate and mixed to the desired color with a spatula.

A pounce bag or velvet wrapped around the finger is dipped into the powder and pushed through the stencil onto the tacky spar varnish.

A vacuum cleaner or damp cloth is used to wipe excess dust from the stencil.

After: The stencil is removed and the spar varnish is allowed to dry. A sprayed final finish can be applied if desired.

pulled free after the stenciling is completed. The stencil is made by applying metallic powders of various colors to the open varnished area within the stencil. These powders can be purchased from art supply houses. In general, they are made from aluminum, bronze and other alloys which allow them to be found in various shades ranging from silver through gold to having tinges of pink and even green.

The colors can be mixed like paints by placing a small amount of powder on a glass plate and then mixing with a toothpick or some other available stirring rod. A small piece of velvet is wrapped around some cotton to form a pounce bag to be dipped into the powder and then dabbed onto the spar varnish. Some stencilers prefer to wrap the cloth around one finger instead of around cotton to get a better feel for the stenciling being done. A firm pressure is applied to insure that the powder makes good contact with the tacky spar varnish.

When the stenciling has been completed, the residual powder remaining on the stencil should be vacuumed away, if possible. Otherwise, a damp cloth can be used to wipe the excess powder off the stencil. Great care should be taken not to allow the dust to settle on any of the spar varnished area that is not intended to be stenciled. When the stencil is pulled away, care should be taken to be sure that any small amounts of powder remaining at the interface of the stencil and the varnished area do not result in spreading the powder where it is not intended.

Normally, an additional coat of finish over the stencil is not required, but the stencil will look new compared to the rest of the furniture. To make the stencil appear older, first wait until it has completely dried and then brush a coat of spar varnish over the entire area. After it has dried, linseed oil is mixed with a little bit of pumice and rubbed with a lint free cloth over this area. The rubbing should be light so as not to penetrate the stencil.

A similar procedure is followed to re-stencil the glass on old clocks, except that the only base required is one coating of clear spar varnish over the glass three or four hours before the stenciling.

To gain some experience before working on an actual clock or furniture of significant value, the conservator should practice his stenciling technique on slices of scrap wood. Some experience usually needs to be gained with the technique so as not to contaminate areas where powder is not to be applied, as well as to determine when the spar varnish is of the appropriate tackiness to accept the powder.

INDEX